Introduction to
Numerical Simulation for
Trade Theory and Policy

Introduction to Numerical Simulation for Trade Theory and Policy

John Gilbert
Utah State University, USA

Edward Tower
Duke University, USA

 **World Scientific**

NEW JERSEY · LONDON · SINGAPORE · BEIJING · SHANGHAI · HONG KONG · TAIPEI · CHENNAI

Published by

World Scientific Publishing Co. Pte. Ltd.

5 Toh Tuck Link, Singapore 596224

USA office: 27 Warren Street, Suite 401-402, Hackensack, NJ 07601

UK office: 57 Shelton Street, Covent Garden, London WC2H 9HE

Library of Congress Cataloging-in-Publication Data
Gilbert, John, 1971–
 Introduction to numerical simulation for trade theory and policy / by John Gilbert and
Edward Tower.
  p. cm.
 ISBN 978-9814390811
 1. International trade--Mathematical models. 2. Commercial policy. I. Tower, Edward.
II. Title.
 HF1379.G55 2013
 382.01'51--dc23

                                      2012031332

British Library Cataloguing-in-Publication Data
A catalogue record for this book is available from the British Library.

In-house Editor: Alisha Nguyen

Printed in Singapore.

For Jeffrey Ken, Cameron Kay, Dan and Wells

Preface

Why build computable general equilibrium models? As Xunzi, the ancient Confucian philosopher, aptly observed, "I hear and I forget. I see and I remember. I do and I understand." In learning economics we build from hearing the intuitive story to mastering graphs. But in the process much of what we need to make the story logically correct is hidden. Students find that using algebra to build a model is tedious. But conjuring up the equations to tell a story and commanding the computer to solve them is fun. Tweaking a computable general equilibrium model is like working with a flight simulator. You get the feel for the economy. It is a form of doing that allows us to understand.

In this book we carry the reader from very simple models to more intricate ones that illustrate important, nuanced ideas in economics. Much of the book focuses on the important ideas in international economics, building on micro, macro and industrial organization. By focusing on core relationships in these areas students develop the skills to spin their own models, building on what they read in books and articles.

We find that learning by simulation is an effective way to teach the difference between Keynesian and neoclassical economics, tax incidence, the trade-offs between equity and efficiency in tax policy, how a negative income tax would work, and important ideas in international trade.

Students can start with the shining models of the profession: simple ones that illustrate the Hume specie flow mechanism, the Lerner symmetry theorem between import and export tariffs, Bhagwati's immizerizing growth, Stolper–Samuelson, Solow growth, the Metzler paradox, the equivalence or non-equivalence of tariffs and quotas under imperfect competition, the idea of first best through nth best policies, the importance of intervening as close to the distortion as possible, the superiority of the income tax to differential excise taxes, and the idea that for all important issues anything a tariff can do something else can do better.

Until simple general equilibrium models and computer modeling techniques were developed, along with the advent of widespread low-cost computing capacity, much of the skill of model-building consisted of couching the problem at hand in a tractable way, as Corden (1997) and Johnson (1960) did in some of their work. Computer modeling has freed us from such stringent restraints. From the roots of these simple models, students can expand their mastery of richer formulations, or at least understand what goes on in the models others have built.

Once the policy maker recognizes that import tariffs harm exports much of the intellectual battle against protectionism is won. Or when they realize that flexible exchange rates can substitute for protectionism to generate employment when nominal wages are downward inflexible, the same is true.

Tower's PhD advisee, Andy Stoeckel — who co-founded the Centre for International Economics, in Canberra, Australia — likes to say that Thomas Carlyle got it wrong when he said: "Teach a parrot the terms supply and demand and you've got an economist." Rather "That parrot needs to say opportunity cost" and the CGE model is well equipped to show the costs of ill-formed policy and the gain from better ideas. Andy also likes to say "it is not the answer you provide but the question you ask that is important," because what is important is to get policy makers to think about how well-developed markets fix things. Building these models is great for understanding what markets can do.

How can this book be used?   We like to ask our students on the first day of class, "Does an increase in government expenditure raise employment?" Students answer yes or no. Over the following weeks we invite them to work with models that answer: it all depends on how the labor market is closed (a flexible wage, a fixed nominal wage, or a fixed real wage), and whether the capital stock depends on its rate of return, so government spending shrinks the capital stock and the demand for labor. We like to ask whether cutting an import tariff increases the trade deficit. We invite students to answer with an analysis of whether the exchange rate is fixed or flexible. We work with them to build simple linearized (small change) models, which can be solved using matrix algebra in Microsoft Excel, that nicely illustrate the roles of exogenous and endogenous variables. Once students have mastered these models they move on to consider large change models and the issues of optimal interventions, which GAMS solves. Once students are comfortable with these core ideas in very simple models, they learn to build more sophisticated models and then solve variants of the models built in this book, either as exercises or as variants of their own devising.

These students have shown CGE modeling is an effective way to master and refine big ideas of international economics. For example, a tertiary burden of making a transfer occurs due to the distorting taxes necessary to finance it. There are some intellectual tools that arise from this kind of model building too. When you don't understand something you simplify until you understand it. You see that the elements of simple theoretical general equilibrium models play a role even when the model is more complex.

The book is organized as a series of short chapters. Each chapter ends with a completely programmed model. These are linked to downloadable versions, available online. The earlier chapters are building blocks for the later ones. Following a brief introduction to finding your way around GAMS, the book covers the following topics:

- Theory of consumption, production, and trade: Short- and long-run production, transition, higher dimensions, intermediate inputs, autarky, small and large country, non-traded goods, two country trading, higher dimensions and trade, reciprocal dumping, monopolistic competition.
- Commercial policy and distortions: tariffs and quotas, domestic taxes and subsidies, factor market distortions.
- Extensions: multiple households, Armington preferences, joint production, social accounting matrices, closure, a single country competitive CGE.
- Appendices on GAMS programming tips and tricks, sensitivity analysis, and debugging.

We welcome your corrections and suggestions for the next printing or edition of this book. Please email us at jgilbert@usu.edu and tower@econ.duke.edu.

J. Gilbert and E. Tower

Acknowledgments

We would like to thank students at the University of Auckland (New Zealand), Duke University, Utah State University, Chulalongkorn University (Thailand) and the University of Zagreb (Croatia) for helping to shape the book.

The book was improved by comments on it from Justina Adamanti, Ben Barber, Tevy Chawwa, Zhuo Chen, Jeff Faris, Ning Fu, Xiangu Gong, Vorapoj Hongpinyo, Yan Huang, Naoya Kato, Dax Kelso, Arthur Kim, Mengchen Ling, Daijing Lv, Kumi Morioka, Aditya Rachmanto, José Sierra Castillo, Will Snyderwine, Alecia Waite, Xiangyu Wang, Silu Xie, and Jing Zhao.

Gilbert would like to thank Mia Mikic, Ravi Ratnayake and Edward Tower for getting him interested in international trade theory and policy, and for introducing him to computable general equilibrium analysis, and Robert Scollay for helping him to learn how to ask interesting policy questions. He would also like to acknowledge the Jon M. Huntsman School of Business at Utah State University for providing summer funding to complete the manuscript.

Tower is grateful for the start on CGE modeling he got from Wassily Leontief, Allison Morgan, Karen Polenski, and David Simpson. Garry Pursell, Sherman Robinson and Andrew Stoeckel helped him hone his modeling skills. Charlie Becker, Teerana Bhongmakapat, Alistair MacCormick, and Mia Mikic arranged for him to teach CGE modeling to a variety of students throughout the world. Ed Flitton, Armando Lago, Jerome L. Stein and Tom Willett fanned his early enthusiasm for economics and sustained it. Tower recalls Leontief's kid-like joy when the LMPST team produced its first calculations of the economic effects of disarmament: a joy that is replicated as Tower's students discover that their models work as they are supposed to.

Tower introduced Gilbert to CGE modeling when he was a graduate student at Auckland, with lectures on the principles of CGE modeling that used a few toy models to illustrate what can be done with the tool. Since then, Gilbert has developed a sophisticated mastery of international trade and the intricacies of GAMS programming. His work binds the two together, and he wrote the vast majority of the book. Following his career and working with him on this project brings Tower great joy. Discovering things with him and his other students makes Tower appreciate the Talmud's statement: "I learned from all my teachers, but mostly from my students."

Contents

Theory of Consumption, Production and Trade   15

List of Figures

List of Tables

Chapter 1

Introduction

The traditional approach to learning the theory of international trade uses a variety of geometric devices to examine comparative statics. In advanced classes, this is usually supplemented by algebraic derivation of key results. A complementary technique that is less widely used is simulation with numerical models.

Using numerical simulation techniques can be beneficial in a number of ways. Working with numerical examples is often a useful aid to understanding abstract material, and is a hands-on activity where the user is free to experiment with the underlying data, parameters and model structure. It thereby helps to develop economic intuition, a feel for how key parameters affect results, and insights into the effect of model structures on outcomes. Numerical programming also encourages us to think about the models of international trade theory in terms of complete systems, and it can allow us to see more advanced results as being extensions of a common trade theoretic framework, a point that can sometimes be lost in trade theory's myriad of algebra and geometry.

Perhaps even more importantly, numerical programming is a skill that forms an increasingly crucial part of the international economist's toolbox. In addition to helping us to gain a better understanding of existing theory, the techniques of numerical simulation can be used as an aid to the development and testing of new economic ideas. Moreover, large scale numerical simulation models, in particular computable general equilibrium or CGE models, have become an integral part of modern trade policy analysis. These models have found widespread use in the assessment of a diverse range of real world trade policy problems and beyond. Well-known CGE models include the Michigan Model of World Production and Trade (Deardorff and Stern, 1986 and 1990), the ORANI model of the Australian

1

economy (Dixon *et al.*, 1982), GTAP (Hertel, 1997), and the World Bank's LINKAGE model (van der Mensbrugghe, 2005).

Unfortunately, computable general equilibrium modeling is sometimes regarded as a difficult area of study for the beginner to enter. It requires a diverse set of skills, including a solid foundation in trade theory, programming capability, and the ability to work with sets of complex data. Many computable general equilibrium models are large and complicated. Moreover, their structure and inner workings can sometimes be opaque, leaving them open to the "black box" criticism.

We argue, however, that learning numerical simulation methods and CGE modeling techniques is not as difficult as it may appear to the uninitiated. While CGE models are indeed often large and complex, their component parts are relatively straightforward, and are not so difficult to learn when approached systematically.

The aim of this volume then, is to help readers to develop the skills necessary to design, implement, and use numerical simulation models useful for trade and trade policy analysis. We start with simple "toy" models that are familiar from the pure theory of international trade, and gradually add complexity until we have systems that are representative of the current "standard" CGE models. The volume grew out of a series of GAMS programs developed by Tower for teaching trade theory at the University of Auckland, and extended by Gilbert for classes taught at Utah State University. The programs have also been used at Duke University and Chulalongkorn University.

The volume has several unique features. First, the model development emphasizes the underlying optimization problems which define the various economic models and their component parts. We have tried to be very consistent in the way that the models are presented. Readers coming to the volume with a limited background in trade theory or computable general equilibrium will still find the approach accessible.

Second, we emphasize using "toy" models to develop programming skill and economic intuition. Readers coming to the volume with a strong background in trade theory will find the models and their properties to be very familiar, and can concentrate on learning how to translate the models into a numerical simulation form. Readers with less background in trade theory will develop skill in programming numerical models at the same time as learning more about the structure and behavior of the basic models of international trade.

We have tried to provide a very clear link between the simulation models and the pure theory of international trade. Indeed, the majority of the topics covered in a typical advanced course in international trade theory are covered here, and the volume also provides a guide to important results in the trade theory literature, and references for further reading. While the volume is not intended to be a textbook on international trade theory, but rather to complement existing treatments, the model and topic development does follow typical textbook approaches such as Bhagwati *et al.* (1998). By integrating a treatment of trade theory with a treatment of computational models, we hope to provide a set of knowledge and skills that will ultimately make the reader a better numerical modeler.

Third, the volume features a gradual development of the models, introducing new features in small, easily digestible parts. Many of the more difficult models can be thought of as constructions of much simpler building blocks. Hence, the approach is to develop the building blocks sequentially, gradually putting them together in more complex and interesting ways. In doing so, the volume facilitates a stronger understanding of how each of these parts work, and avoids overwhelming the reader by presenting a complex CGE system in full at the outset.

Finally, we make all of the codes and models that are developed in the volume fully available to the reader. The programs described in each chapter can be downloaded through the RePEc database at http://econpapers.repec.org/software/uthsfware/, or through any of the other RePEc services. A search for "GAMS Models for Trade Theory" will bring up the site. The reader is free to use the provided models as a base, and to modify them to suit their own purposes.

All of the programs that we present in the volume are built with the General Algebraic Modeling System (GAMS). This is a high-level programming environment that is particularly well suited to building large-scale numerical simulation models. GAMS is in widespread use, and learning how to program in GAMS is a useful skill in its own right.

We assume no prior knowledge about GAMS or programming in this volume, although some familiarity with programming languages in general is probably useful. The volume is not intended to be a stand-alone guide to GAMS programming, a purpose for which the GAMS User's Guide is more than satisfactory, but we provide considerable detail on the mechanics of programming in GAMS, as well as advice for dealing with the inevitable problems that arise when building numerical models.

Of course, GAMS is not the only environment suitable for constructing the types of models that we discuss in this volume. Computable general equilibrium models are also commonly built in other languages, including GEMPACK and Matlab. It is even possible to construct quite sophisticated models in common programs like Excel (see Gilbert and Oladi, 2011, for example). The basic principles of model building that we set out in this volume are applicable to readers working in those environments also, although the mechanics will of course differ.

As the title suggests, the volume is introductory in nature. We have tried to make the material and approach amenable to researchers looking for a good way to get started in numerical modeling/CGE, and to make the volume accessible for advanced undergraduate or beginning graduate students. Hence, the volume's background requirements are relatively modest. Familiarity with the tools of microeconomics at the intermediate level is a prerequisite, as is basic algebra and calculus, although we have tried to be no more formal than is necessary. Varian (1992) or (2009), or Perloff (2011) provide sufficient background for the former. Dixit (1990) emphasizes the constrained optimization approach that we adopt here, and is another useful reference. For mathematics, Chiang and Wainwright (2005) covers all the necessary material.

1.1 CGE Models

So what exactly is a CGE model and why is it useful to learn how to build one? Computable general equilibrium models are a particular type of numerical simulation model based on general equilibrium theory. In essence, this just means that a (symbolic) model from economic theory is built using specific functional forms instead of abstract ones, implemented as a computer program and fitted to real world data. The model is then perturbed, or shocked, in a way that represents a policy or structural change, and the numerical results are evaluated to provide insights into the possible economic implications of the shock. Whereas general equilibrium theory is often concerned with issues such as the existence and uniqueness of equilibrium, the basic objective of CGE modeling is to turn the abstract models of general equilibrium theory into a practical tool for policy analysis.

A number of features distinguish CGE models from other quantitative methods used in international economics, such as partial equilibrium modeling or gravity models. They are multi-sectoral, and in many cases multiregional, and the behavior of economic agents is modeled explicitly through utility and profit maximizing assumptions. In addition, economywide constraints are rigorously enforced within the models. In other words, the markets in a computable general equilibrium model are all linked together. Distortions in an economic system will often have repercussions far beyond the sector in which they occur, and by linking markets, CGE techniques are effective at capturing the relevant feedback and flow-through effects.

Computable general equilibrium models have a number of advantages as a tool of policy analysis. First, they are theoretically consistent, with a solid foundation in microeconomic theory. Moreover, the theoretical choices that must be made in any modeling exercise are tackled front-on and are made explicit when programming a CGE model (although, regrettably, not always when reporting the results).

Second, CGE models are able to incorporate many unique features of an economic system. While the basic structure of most CGE models is recognizably Walrasian, many other types of economic features can and have been incorporated into CGE models, including imperfect competition and numerous other distortions. Hence, CGE models can adapt well to the analysis of a wide range of problems and economic circumstances.

Finally, CGE models can be used to predict values for many economic variables in an economic system. Unlike gravity models, for example, which are designed to help us understand and predict trade flows, the CGE approach models a complete economic system. Hence, we can use CGE models to evaluate the potential effect of a policy change on production, employment, trade, government revenue, and so on, or on all of these economic variables and more. The models also highlight the linkages between those economic variables.

On the other hand, CGE models have a number of limitations too.[1] The data requirements of CGE models are substantial (although they might be considered modest relative to the number of economic variables being considered). There is often uncertainty over parameters, specification, and experimental design. Because they cover all sectors in an economy, a CGE model may miss key features of critical sectors. It can also sometimes be difficult to know what is driving the results of CGE simulations. Finally, the human capital investment required for building/using these models can be high.

---

[1]The following points follow Mikic and Gilbert (2009), who present a slightly more detailed discussion.

There is no doubt that CGE analysis is not suitable for all types of problems. As a broad guide, CGE will be an appropriate methodological choice if (1) the policy question of interest involves large changes that are well outside of historical experiences; (2) there is the potential for significant general equilibrium effects; and (3) the policy question requires information on the economic system and not broad economic aggregates.

The first requirement is obvious enough, and it suggests the need to use simulation techniques of some kind. The second is less obvious. What do we mean by "significant general equilibrium effects"? Basically, we mean that the policy question of interest involves multiple sectors. For example, a typical free trade agreement involves at least two countries simultaneously liberalizing many different sectors of the economy. This suggests that we need general equilibrium rather than partial equilibrium techniques to capture the full effect of the shock. Alternatively, the policy question may involve only one sector directly, but that sector is large enough to have an impact on the overall economy. For example, for many least developed economies the textile industry is so large relative to the overall economy that general equilibrium may be justified even if the policy scenario involves only that sector.

The last condition simply recognizes that a trade-off must be made for the sectoral detail that a CGE model provides. Hence, for example, if trade flows are the only variable of interest, extrapolation from a gravity model may be preferred to CGE analysis. If, however, we need to know how sectoral employment patterns will change when a trade policy is implemented, computable general equilibrium makes more sense.

We argue that to a large degree the weaknesses of CGE models are often more weaknesses of CGE modeling practice than limitations of the models themselves. Uncertainty over parameters and specification can be addressed by careful model construction and through the use of sensitivity analysis, and advances are being made in parameter estimation techniques (see Jansson and Heckelei, 2010, for example). Moreover, we hope that readers who work through this volume, will find the experience dramatically diminishes the problems of building CGE models and knowing what is driving their simulation results.

1.2 Volume Organization

As noted above, the main objective of this volume is to illustrate how numerical simulation methods can be used to construct an array of useful models of international trade theory and the theory of commercial policy, and to help readers develop the skills necessary to build models for themselves. GAMS is used as the programming platform.

Because we assume many readers will be unfamiliar with GAMS, we begin the volume with a quick primer on obtaining, installing and using GAMS to solve simple problems. More details are provided in subsequent chapters, and Appendix B sets out some advanced topics in GAMS programming, including sensitivity analysis, data interface and reporting options, and debugging.

The remainder of the volume is divided into three parts. In the first we cover modeling the theory of consumption, production and trade. In the second we move on to modeling the theory of commercial policy and other distortions. The final part of the volume deals with extensions to the basic models of trade theory that are commonly incorporated into modern computable general equilibrium models.

In Part 1 of the volume, we begin with the familiar problems of utility maximization and cost minimization, then move on to models of short and long-run production, and extensions including higher dimensions and intermediate goods. Next, we bring the demand and supply components together in a series of models dealing with autarky, small and large open economies, a complete global economy, and extensions including non-traded goods. Finally, we consider the international trade implications of imperfectly competitive markets.

Part 2 consists of three chapters. The first deals with the implications of trade interventions (tariffs, export subsidies, quotas, and so on) in various contexts (small and large economy, and a two country world). The second deals with domestic taxes and subsidies to production, consumption and factor use. The third deals with modeling the implications of various distortions to factor markets, including wage differentials, minimum wages, and imperfect factor mobility.

The final part of the volume contains chapters dealing with incorporating multiple households and other sources of demand into the models, dealing with intra-industry trade using Armington preferences, and dealing with joint production. We also have chapters on organizing the data for a CGE model, and on choosing a closure rule. The last major chapter brings the material together in a description of what might be called the "standard" CGE model. We finish up with some notes on where the reader can go to learn more.

In each of the model-oriented chapters in the volume, we begin with an underlying optimization problem or problems, show how we can solve the problem generally, and then how we can form a version of the model using specific functional forms. Next we outline the process of translating the model to GAMS. The GAMS programs are presented in full in the early chapters. As we progress, only incremental changes are discussed in most cases. The models outlined in each chapter are all available for download in full.

Each chapter concludes with a series of exercises. Many of the exercises can be completed by perturbing the model developed in the chapter by altering data or parameters. The objective is help develop an intuition for the model's behavior. Other exercises involve extending the models in various ways, relaxing restrictions, changing functional forms, integrating new elements or elements from previous chapters, and so on. The aim here is to help develop independent programming skill. Most chapters conclude with a set of recommended readings on the topics covered.

The developmental sequence is important, and later chapters refer back frequently to structures covered and results obtained in earlier chapters. Hence, we suggest working through the chapters of the volume in the order in which they are presented.

Chapter 2

Getting Started With GAMS

Throughout this volume we will be developing a series of simulation models using GAMS. In this chapter we provide some basic notes to get you started with the GAMS system. We will introduce more complex features as we proceed. Appendix B provides further details on selected GAMS features.

2.1 What Is GAMS?

GAMS is an acronym that stands for the General Algebraic Modeling System. It is a high level programming language designed for building and solving mathematical models numerically. GAMS provides a framework for model development that is independent of the platform on which the model is to be run, and distinct from the mathematical algorithms that are used to solve the model.[1] This means that models built in GAMS can be run on different machines, and solved using different techniques, without any adjustment to the model itself. GAMS can solve a wide variety of problems, and is capable of handling very large mathematical systems. The environment is in very widespread use in both the academic and business worlds, and is the most widely used development platform for computable general equilibrium models.

2.2 Getting and Installing GAMS

GAMS Corporation provides a student/demonstration version of GAMS free of charge. This version of the software is limited in the dimensions of the

---

[1]GAMS is actually a front-end for numerous different commercial algorithms, all of which are packaged with the GAMS system and may be licensed independently.

models that can be built. However all of the models developed in this book are small enough to be solved using the student version of the software. The latest version can be downloaded from `http://www.gams.com/download/`. Various flavors are available. For most users the 32 bit Windows version will be appropriate. If you are using a 64 bit version of Windows you can download the 64 bit Windows version. Versions are also available for users of Linux (32 or 64 bit) and Mac OS X.

To install any Windows version of the software, right click the link on the GAMS site and choose the `Save Link As` option from the context menu. Then save the installation file in an appropriate location on your local computer (the file is approximately 60mb). Once the file has downloaded, double click on it to start the installation process. The installer will prompt you for a directory in which to install the GAMS system (the default should be fine). It should also prompt you for a start menu location, and again the default should be fine. A prompt will appear asking if you wish to copy a license file. You can click no (without the license file GAMS will run in student/demonstration mode). Once it has installed, GAMS will ask if you want to launch the IDE, or integrated development environment. This is the main GAMS interface. Click `yes` and GAMS should appear.

Your first task is to set the default solver. For the exercises in this book, we will be using the nonlinear programming (NLP) solvers. Under the `File` menu select `Options`, then choose the `Solvers` tab. Under the NLP column scroll down until you see `CONOPT`, then click in the box. An `X` will appear indicating that `CONOPT` has been selected as the default solver for NLP problems. You can then click `OK` to close the options box.

Further details on the installation process are available for various platforms at the GAMS website (`http://www.gams.com/docs/document.htm`). At the same location you can also find the detailed GAMS User's Guide, a GAMS Tutorial, and other useful documentation in electronic form.

2.3   A Quick GAMS Primer

A GAMS program is a text file that describes the model structure in terms of its component variables, parameters and relationships. The text file is usually given the suffix `gms`. To run the program, the text file is submitted to the GAMS system. GAMS then checks for syntax errors, and then translates the model into a form usable by the solution algorithm. This process is invisible to the user. The solution algorithm attempts to solve the model, and then reports back to GAMS the result. A list file (with the suffix 1st) is produced that contains information on the solution. Figure 2.1 illustrates the process. If something went wrong in the process, the list file will contain information on where the problem lies.

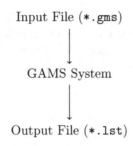

Input File (*.gms)

GAMS System

Output File (*.1st)

Fig. 2.1   GAMS Input/Output.

To illustrate, we'll use GAMS to solve a simple algebraic problem. Suppose that we want to know the simultaneous solution to $y = 10 + 2x$ and $y = 100 - x$ (before we start, verify the solution for yourself).

First we open GAMS and choose New from the File menu. GAMS will create a new program (called by default untitled_1.gms) for us to use. Now type in the following lines of code:

```
VARIABLES
Y, X;
EQUATIONS
EQ1, EQ2;
EQ1..Y=E=10+2*X;
EQ2..Y=E=100-X;
MODEL EXAMPLE /ALL/;
SOLVE EXAMPLE USING LP MAXIMIZING Y;
```

The first two lines tell GAMS the names of the two variables in the model (Y and X). The next two lines tell GAMS the names of the two equations (EQ1 and EQ2). These names are arbitrary. The next two lines define the equations. The expression =E= just means equals. Finally, the last two lines tell GAMS that the model consists of both equations, and asks GAMS to look for a solution. We will discuss the details of GAMS syntax much more in later chapters.

To run the model, choose **Run** from the **File** menu. A new window (called the log window) will appear indicating that GAMS is processing the program. If all goes well you will see the message:

*** Status: Normal Completion

At this point you can close the log window. GAMS will have automatically opened a list file. The list file contains the solution and other useful information on the model. We consider some of the most important elements in turn (this is a partial list).

2.3.1   *Echo Prints*

In this section of the list file GAMS will echo (repeat) your input to the list. It should look like this:

```
1 VARIABLES
2 Y, X;
3 EQUATIONS
4 EQ1, EQ2;
5 EQ1..Y=E=10+2*X;
6 EQ2..Y=E=100-X;
7 MODEL EXAMPLE /ALL/;
8 SOLVE EXAMPLE USING LP MAXIMIZING Y;
```

Notice how each input line is given a number by GAMS (this will include blank lines). GAMS will reference these line numbers if it finds an error in the model.[2]

2.3.2   *Equation Listing*

In this section of the list file GAMS shows a specific instance of the model when the current values for the variables are substituted into the general algebraic form of the model. The section looks like:

```
EQ1..  Y - 2*X =E= 10 ; (LHS = 0, INFES = 10 ****)
EQ2..  Y + X =E= 100 ; (LHS = 0, INFES = 100 ****)
```

Unless we tell it otherwise, GAMS will start with zero values (usually we will want to give GAMS better values to start with). The **INFES** tells us that these values do not satisfy the equations. For nonlinear models, this

---

[2]For more on GAMS errors, see Appendix B.

section will contain the total differential evaluated at the current values of the variables.

2.3.3 *Model Statistics*

This section of the list reports some statistics on the size of the model. It should look something like:

```
MODEL STATISTICS

BLOCKS OF EQUATIONS 2    SINGLE EQUATIONS 2
BLOCKS OF VARIABLES 2    SINGLE VARIABLES 2
NON ZERO ELEMENTS    4
```

For this model, we have two equations and two variables. Because our model is defined using scalars, the number of blocks of equations and blocks of variables is the same as the number of single equations and single variables. We will see later that one of the most powerful aspects of GAMS is the ability to define many equations with a single equation block, and many variables with a single indexed assignment.

2.3.4 *Status Reports*

After attempting to solve the model, GAMS will report back on the status of the solve. The relevant section of the list file looks like:

```
S O L V E    S U M M A R Y

MODEL     EXAMPLE     OBJECTIVE Y
TYPE      LP          DIRECTION MAXIMIZE
SOLVER    CPLEX       FROM LINE 13

**** SOLVER STATUS     1 Normal Completion
**** MODEL STATUS      1 Optimal
**** OBJECTIVE VALUE   70.0000
```

The most important parts of this section of the listing are the SOLVER STATUS and the MODEL STATUS lines. A value of 1 for SOLVER STATUS indicates a normal completion. Otherwise an error will be reported here (this is the same as we saw in the log). A MODEL STATUS of 1 indicates that an optimal solution has been found. For most of the problems we will be dealing with, which are nonlinear, we will be looking for a MODEL STATUS of 2, or locally optimal.

2.3.5   *Solution Reports*

If a solution has been determined by GAMS, we will want to know what that solution looks like. The answer can be found in the solution reports. The format of this section of the list is:

	LOWER	LEVEL	UPPER	MARGINAL
---- VAR Y	-INF	70.000	+INF	.
---- VAR X	-INF	30.000	+INF	.

We are interested in the LEVEL of each variable. You will recognize the numbers as the solution values that you obtained by manual evaluation. Later on we will deal with more convenient ways of accessing the results.

2.4   Exercises

(1) See if you can construct and solve a few other simple linear algebraic problems using GAMS.
(2) What happens if you try and solve $y = 10 + 2x$ and $y = 10 + 2x$. How about $y = 10 + 2x$ and $y = 12 + 2x$? What does GAMS report in both cases?

2.5   Further Reading

Further details on GAMS can be found in the GAMS User's Guide. Zenios (1996) is another useful reference on the capabilities of GAMS. The GAMS User's Guide contains a tutorial (Chapter 2) that is a useful starting point for basic programming in GAMS. Bruce McCarl also has an online reference to GAMS that has very useful programming advice.

PART 1

Theory of Consumption, Production and Trade

Chapter 3

Utility Maximization

In this chapter we set out a familiar problem from microeconomic theory, the consumer choice problem characterized as maximization of utility subject to a budget constraint. We then show how, by choosing specific functional forms and data, this problem can be implemented as a numerical simulation model in GAMS. This simple problem is well-understood, but working through it in detail will allow us to develop all of the basic techniques for building a numerical simulation model in GAMS. The solution to the problem will also form the demand block of our later trade models.

3.1 Formal Problem

Consider a consumer that has preferences satisfying the axioms of consumer choice, and where their preferences can be summarized by the utility function $U = U(c_1, c_2)$, where c_i is consumption of the ith good. The usual properties apply to the utility function (i.e., continuity, monotonicity, and quasi-concavity). The consumer choice problem can be viewed as choosing c_1 and c_2 such that the consumer maximizes $U = U(c_1, c_2)$ subject to the budget constraint $Y = p_1 c_1 + p_2 c_2$, where Y is money income. We assume an internal solution for simplicity.[1] We can solve the consumer's constrained maximization problem by forming the Lagrangian:[2]

$$\mathscr{L} = U(c_1, c_2) + \lambda[Y - p_1 c_1 - p_2 c_2] \qquad (3.1)$$

---

[1]This will be the case if the consumer's preferences exhibit non-satiation in both goods and overall.

[2]For brevity, we omit the max or min statement throughout the text, as it is always obvious from context.

where λ is the multiplier (in this case representing the marginal utility of income). Taking the partial derivatives of the Lagrangian with respect to consumption and λ gives us the first order conditions for a maximum:

$$\partial \mathscr{L}/\partial c_1 = \partial U/\partial c_1 - \lambda p_1 = 0 \tag{3.2}$$

$$\partial \mathscr{L}/\partial c_2 = \partial U/\partial c_2 - \lambda p_2 = 0 \tag{3.3}$$

$$\partial \mathscr{L}/\partial \lambda = Y - p_1 c_1 - p_2 c_2 = 0. \tag{3.4}$$

The solution to the maximization problem is the simultaneous solution to these three equations for c_1, c_2 and λ, expressed in terms of p_1, p_2 and Y. Equation (3.4) is the original budget constraint. Equations (3.2) and (3.3) state that, at the optimal choice, the marginal utility per dollar spent on each good must equal the marginal utility of income, or alternatively, that the money value of the utility generated by the last unit of each good purchased must equal its price.[3] Using conditions (3.2) and (3.3) we can eliminate λ:

$$\frac{\partial U/\partial c_1}{\partial U/\partial c_2} = \frac{p_1}{p_2}. \tag{3.5}$$

This is the equation for the income consumption path, it reflects tangency of the indifference curve with the budget constraint at any optimal choice. Solving (3.4) and (3.5) for the optimal consumption bundles yields the Marshallian demand functions. Substituting these back into the utility function yields the indirect utility function, which expresses utility directly in terms of prices and income.

The typical geometry of the problem is presented in Figure 3.1. The optimal solution is at (c_1^*, c_2^*), on the highest attainable indifference curve, labeled U^*, which is tangent to the budget constraint.

3.2   Example

Now suppose that the utility function takes the Cobb–Douglas form $U = \alpha c_1^\beta c_2^{1-\beta}$, where $0 < \beta < 1$. We can solve the consumer's problem for this special case by forming the Lagrangian:

$$\mathscr{L} = \alpha c_1^\beta c_2^{1-\beta} + \lambda[Y - p_1 c_1 - p_2 c_2]. \tag{3.6}$$

---

[3]The shadow price of a constraint is the incremental change in the objective which an incremental relaxation of the constraint makes possible. Thus, it is the incremental change in the objective per unit change in the constraint, while allowing the choice variables to continually adjust to their optimum levels. In this case the shadow price of income in utility numéraire, i.e., measured in units of utility, is the marginal utility of income. The logic of the Lagrangian and the interpretation of the Lagrangian multiplier as a shadow price are discussed further in Appendix A.

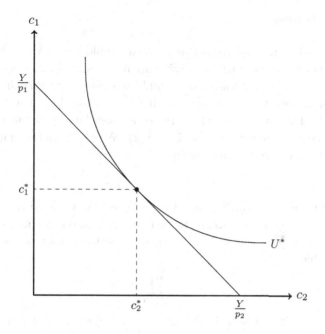

Fig. 3.1   Utility Maximization.

Taking the partial derivatives of the Lagrangian with respect to consumption and λ gives us the first-order conditions:

$$\partial \mathscr{L}/\partial c_1 = \alpha \beta c_1^{\beta-1} c_2^{1-\beta} - \lambda p_1 = 0 \tag{3.7}$$

$$\partial \mathscr{L}/\partial c_2 = \alpha c_1^{\beta}(1-\beta)c_2^{-\beta} - \lambda p_2 = 0 \tag{3.8}$$

$$\partial \mathscr{L}/\partial \lambda = Y - p_1 c_1 - p_2 c_2 = 0. \tag{3.9}$$

Using (3.7) and (3.8) we eliminate λ:

$$p_1 c_1 = \frac{\beta}{1-\beta} p_2 c_2. \tag{3.10}$$

and from (3.9) we have:

$$p_2 c_2 = Y - p_1 c_1. \tag{3.11}$$

Solving (3.10) and (3.11) yields the Marshallian demands:

$$c_1 = \beta Y/p_1 \tag{3.12}$$

$$c_2 = (1-\beta)Y/p_2. \tag{3.13}$$

With these, we can solve for the utility level if desired, by forming the indirect utility function.

3.3   Set Notation

Our next task is to implement this familiar problem in GAMS. As a first step, we will rewrite the problem using set notation. GAMS is a set based language, a feature that allows us to build models of arbitrary dimensions easily. Of course, GAMS can work with scalars too, but that is usually more work. The underlying set for the consumer choice problem is the set of goods the consumer can choose, $I = \{1, 2\}$. We can write the Marshallian demands that we have derived compactly as:

$$c_i = \beta_i Y / p_i \qquad \forall i \in I.$$

This is equivalent to (3.12) and (3.13). Note that we have treated each exponent as a separate share, so to be equivalent to our original representation we need $\sum_{\forall i \in I} \beta_i = 1$. The utility function can be rewritten in a similar fashion:

$$U = \alpha \prod_{\forall i \in I} c_i^{\beta_i}.$$

This way of writing the model is much more compact. It is also easier to expand. For example, if we want to handle more goods, we simply add more elements to I. This is the form of the model that we will use in our GAMS program.

3.4   GAMS Implementation

Now let us consider exactly how the problem can be expressed in the GAMS language. As noted above, because GAMS allows for set based notation, we save a lot of time by working in terms of sets rather than scalars. Our first task is then to create a set which will index the goods:

```
SET I Goods /1,2/;
```

The keyword `SET` (not case sensitive) is followed by an arbitrary name for the set, `I`, an optional description, then the elements of the set enclosed in forward slashes and separated by commas. The names used for set elements are also arbitrary. The command is completed with a semicolon.

Next, we need to define labels for all of the parameters and exogenous variables in the model. We are also going to define labels for the initial values of our endogenous variables:

```
PARAMETERS
ALPHA       Shift parameter in utility
BETA(I)     Share parameters in utility
Y           Income
P(I)        Prices
U0          Initial utility level
C0(I)       Initial consumption levels;
```

The keyword here is **PARAMETERS**, which in GAMS means anything with a fixed value. It is followed by a list of parameter names, along with an optional description. At the end of the list we have a semicolon to tell GAMS that the **PARAMETERS** command is finished. Notice how we have used the dimensions of the set I in the definition of **BETA**, P and C0. This tells GAMS that we want two values of **BETA**, one for each element of I. Set I must be defined before it is used in this way. With the labels created, we can assign some suitable values to the parameters:

```
P(I)=1;
Y=100;
C0(I)=50;
U0=Y;
BETA(I)=P(I)*C0(I)/Y;
ALPHA=U0/PROD(I, C0(I)**BETA(I));
```

PROD is the product operator, * is used for multiplication and ** for bringing a term to a power. The format for the PROD command is PROD followed by an opening bracket, the index over which the product is to be calculated, a comma, and then the expression, followed by a closing bracket. Each assignment is a separate statement, and so is followed by a semicolon.

When we make an assignment to an indexed parameter, all occurrences are given the same assigned value. Hence, the first line normalizes all prices to unity. If we want to assign different values to different occurrences, we can specify exactly which one we want. For example, P('1')=1 would set only the price of good 1 to unity. Notice how we have set values for the terms sequentially. Since the price of each good is set at one, if we choose Y=100, we must choose values for consumption that sum to 100, or the budget constraint would be violated. Notice also that we can (and should) use previously defined values to make subsequent assignments. The value for utility is arbitrary because utility is ordinal not cardinal. We have set it for convenience at the same value as Y (i.e., 100). Similarly, the demand functions have been used to determine consistent values for BETA, and the utility function has been used for ALPHA. This process of solving for the parameters from the initial equilibrium values that we choose is called *calibration*. Mathematically, it may seem strange to solve the model first to determine the parameters, given that GAMS is capable of determining the solution for any given parameters. But, in real modeling work we usually have a particular economic system that we want to replicate, so we know the solution. It is the parameters that we usually do not know. Of course, we could have solved for the values of BETA and ALPHA by hand and entered them as numbers, but it is easier to let GAMS do that work, especially if we later decide to change the underlying data.

Our next task is to assign names for the variables:

```
VARIABLES
U          Utility level
C(I)       Consumption levels;
```

This is very similar to the PARAMETERS statement: the keyword VARIABLES is followed by a list of variable names, indexed as appropriate, and their descriptions. Since the values of the variables are determined by the model solution, we cannot assign values to them as such. But, we can give GAMS starting values for the variables. We use the initial values we calculated:

```
U.L=U0;
C.L(I)=C0(I);
```

The format is variable name followed by .L (for level) then by the value either as a number or as a previously defined parameter value.[4] These are the values from which GAMS will begin to search for a solution. If we have calibrated correctly, it will not have to search very far. We can also assign logical bounds on the values the variables can take:

```
C.LO(I)=0;
```

The format is similar to setting levels, the variable name followed by .LO (for lower bound). The format for setting an upper bound is the same, using .UP. The suffix .FX can be used to fix the value of a variable (equivalent to

---

[4]It is good practice to always define initial values for variables. A set of initial values close to the solution helps the algorithms that are searching for a solution to find it quickly. Also, by default, if an initial value is not assigned, GAMS will assume an initial value of zero. If any operations in the model are not defined for a value of zero (e.g., there is a division by zero) the model will fail.

setting both the upper and lower bound to the same value). The statement tells GAMS that consumption cannot be less than zero, which restricts the space in which GAMS will search for a solution.[5] It is good practice to use economic logic to impose bounds whenever possible. Notice that we do not impose a bound on U. We will use this as the objective, so it must be able to take any value.

We enter names for equations in the model in the same way that we enter names for parameters and variables, and they can be descriptive terms:

```
EQUATIONS
UTILITY    Utility function
DEMAND(I) Demand functions;
```

The keyword is EQUATIONS, followed by a list of names, which are also indexed, with optional descriptions. A semicolon finishes the statement. Next we define the structure of the equations in terms of the variables and parameters:

```
UTILITY..U=E=ALPHA*PROD(I, C(I)**BETA(I));
DEMAND(I)..C(I)=E=BETA(I)*Y/P(I);
```

These are the GAMS equivalents of the equations we derived in the preceding section. Each equation name is followed by .. and then the expression. The term =E= indicates that the expression is an equality.

The last stage is to tell GAMS which of our equations constitute the model, in this case all of them, and then run a test solution:

```
MODEL UMAX /ALL/;
SOLVE UMAX USING NLP MAXIMIZING U;
```

The first statement says that the model that we will call UMAX consists of all the equations (i.e., it is equivalent to MODEL UMAX /UTILITY, DEMAND/). Listing equations separately may be useful if, for example, you have a number of different specifications with the same basic structure. The format is keyword MODEL followed by an arbitrary name, then the model equations inside forward slashes, separated by commas (or the keyword ALL). The second line says SOLVE the model using nonlinear programming (NLP) to maximize the value of utility U. The objective must be a scalar, and must

---

[5]Since it is often the case that the relevant lower bound is zero, GAMS offers a short-cut. By declaring a variable with the statement POSITIVE VARIABLE rather than simply VARIABLE, GAMS will automatically assign the lower bound.

be unconstrained. In this case, our model is square (has the same number of equations as variables), so the choice of the objective is arbitrary.

A complete version of the model is presented in Table 3.1, which is available for download through RePEc. The model can be run by submitting the text file containing all the commands to the GAMS compiler. Lines beginning with a * are explanatory, and are ignored by GAMS. The results of the model should replicate the original equilibrium that we specified.

We have now built our first simple numerical simulation model. Once we are satisfied that the model is correctly replicating the solution, we can examine the effects of changes in the economic situation by altering the values of parameters and/or exogenous variables and executing another SOLVE command. For example, adding the lines:

```
Y=Y*1.1;
SOLVE UMAX USING NLP MAXIMIZING U;
```

immediately after the first SOLVE statement and running the model again would show us the initial equilibrium and the effect of a 10 percent increase in income. Inserting many different Y values, each paired with a SOLVE statement, allows us to build a complete picture of how the utility measure and consumption depend on income.[6] By altering the values of other underlying parameters or exogenous variables and observing how the solution responds, we can develop an understanding of the behavior of a consumer with these preferences, under the utility maximization hypothesis.

3.5   Exercises

(1) (a) What happens if you increase the price of good 1 by 10 percent? (b) What if you increase the price of both goods by 10 percent? (c) What if income increases by 10 percent? What do you conclude about the consumer's perceptions of the goods as described by the utility function? (d) What if all prices and income rise by 10 percent? Think carefully about the results. Do they match with your intuition? Checking GAMS results against what your knowledge of the theory tells you should be the result is a good way to debug your program.

---

[6] As we shall see in Chapter 8, GAMS has some tricks for achieving this very efficiently using looping. There are also mechanisms for outputing the results directly to Excel, which is very useful for graphing, etc. Further details can be found in Appendix B.

Table 3.1   GAMS Program for Utility Maximization.

```
* Define the indexes for the problem
SET I Goods /1,2/ ;

* Create names for parameters
PARAMETERS
ALPHA                                 Shift parameter in utility
BETA(I)                               Share parameters in utility
Y                                     Income
P(I)                                  Prices of goods
UO                                    Initial utility level
CO(I)                                 Initial consumption levels;

* Assign values to the parameters
P(I)=1;
Y=100;
CO(I)=50;
UO=Y;
BETA(I)=P(I)*CO(I)/Y;
ALPHA=UO/PROD(I, CO(I)**BETA(I));

* Create names for variables
VARIABLES
U                                     Utility level
C(I)                                  Consumption levels;

* Assign initial values to variables, and set lower bounds
U.L=UO;
C.L(I)=CO(I);
C.LO(I)=0;

* Create names for equations
EQUATIONS
UTILITY                               Utility function
DEMAND(I)                             Demand functions;

* Assign the expressions to the equation names
UTILITY..U=E=ALPHA*PROD(I, C(I)**BETA(I));
DEMAND(I)..C(I)=E=BETA(I)*Y/P(I);

* Define the equations that make the model, and solve
MODEL UMAX /ALL/;
SOLVE UMAX USING NLP MAXIMIZING U;
```

---

(2) Does changing the value of ALPHA change the solution? Why or why not? How about if you replace the utility function with the following: $U = \ln \alpha + \beta \ln c_1 + (1 - \beta) \ln c_2$?

(3) Rather than solving the utility maximization problem, try building a GAMS model of the corresponding expenditure minimization problem: minimize $E = p_1 c_1 + p_2 c_2$ subject to a target level of utility $\bar{U} = U(c_1, c_2)$. The solution to this problem yields the Hicksian demand functions $c_1(p_1, p_2, \bar{U})$ and $c_2(p_1, p_2, \bar{U})$, and the expenditure function $E(p_1, p_2, \bar{U})$, which describes the minimum outlay to achieve the target level of utility. If you solve this problem with the target level of utility set at the level obtained from the utility maximization problem, what do you notice?

(4) To describe changes in utility as economic circumstances change, it is common to use a money-metric measure. Standard measures are the equivalent variation (EV), defined as $E(p_1^0, p_2^0, U^1) - E(p_1^0, p_2^0, U^0)$ and the compensating variation (CV), defined as $E(p_1^1, p_2^1, U^1) - E(p_1^1, p_2^1, U^0)$, where a superscript 0 represents the initial value, a superscript 1 represents a value post change, and $E(.)$ is the expenditure function. See if you can add calculations of EV and CV to your model after the SOLVE statement. (Hints: You can access the post-solution value of a variable by using the variable name followed by .L. From Section 3.2, we can substitute the Marshallian demands into the utility function to get the indirect utility function. Rearranging the indirect utility function to put income/expenditure on the left gives us the expenditure function).

(5) The Cobb–Douglas utility function is easy to work with, but quite restrictive. More flexible functional forms include the constant elasticity of substitution utility function (CES), the Stone–Geary utility function, and the transcendental logarithmic utility function (or translog). The CES function takes the form $U = \alpha[\beta c_1^\rho + (1 - \beta)c_2^\rho]^{\frac{1}{\rho}}$, where ρ is a free (unconstrained) parameter that relates to the elasticity of substitution in consumption (the elasticity of substitution equals $1/(1 - \rho)$, see if you can prove it). The function converges to the Cobb–Douglas case as $\rho \to 0$, is linear when $\rho = 1$ and approaches the Leontief (min) function as $\rho \to -\infty$. The Stone–Geary utility function has the form $U = \alpha(c_1 - \gamma_1)^\beta(c_2 - \gamma_2)^{1-\beta}$. The γ parameters are free, and can be thought of as "subsistence" levels of consumption. For a given level of the marginal utility of income, the γ parameters can be calibrated to known/estimated values for the

income elasticities of demand. The translog function has the form
$U = \ln \alpha + \beta_1 \ln c_1 + \beta_2 \ln c_2 + \beta_{11}(\ln c_1)^2 + \beta_{22}(\ln c_2)^2 + \beta_{12}(\ln c_1 \ln c_2)$.
The β parameters are all free, and this form is easily amenable to
econometric estimation. The function does not satisfy convexity globally, however. See if you can construct working simulation models using
these alternative functional forms.

3.6 Further Reading

Most of the material discussed in this chapter is covered in intermediate
microeconomics texts such as Perloff (2011) or Varian (2009). For a somewhat more in-depth, but still easily accessible, discussion, see Varian (1992).
Varian (1992) also covers money metric utility functions as described in exercise 4, and details working with utility functions of various forms, including Cobb–Douglas and CES. For an excellent introduction to optimization
in economics, focusing on the Lagrangian technique and its extensions, see
Dixit (1990).

Chapter 4

Cost Minimization

In this chapter we turn to the optimization problem of the firm, which is mathematically very similar to the consumer choice problem. For a given level of output, the firm seeks to minimize its expenditure on inputs, subject to the constraints of its technology. This is a familiar problem from microeconomics, but a solid understanding of how to implement it as a numerical simulation model in GAMS will help to develop basic skill in GAMS programming, and give us the principal building block for modeling the production side of an economic system in subsequent chapters. We also introduce and work with the constant elasticity of substitution production function in this chapter. This functional form is widely used in numerical models in a variety of different contexts.

4.1 Formal Problem

Suppose that the firm uses inputs of labor (L) and capital (K), for which it must pay market prices w and r. Its technology is described by the production function $q = q(K, L)$. This function represents the relationship between inputs and the maximum output that can be produced, and is assumed to be continuous and to exhibit diminishing returns to each factor. If the firm seeks to minimize its expenditure for a given level of output, $\bar{q}$, we can form the Lagrangian for its constrained optimization problem as follows (again assuming an internal solution for simplicity):

$$\mathscr{L} = rK + wL + \lambda[\bar{q} - q(K, L)]. \tag{4.1}$$

In this case λ is the shadow value of output (the marginal cost), which in the competitive equilibrium context is the output price. It represents how much the objective, cost, rises per unit increase in the exogenously determined output constraint, $\bar{q}$. Differentiating the Lagrangian with respect to the input choices and the multiplier yields the first-order conditions for a minimum:

$$\partial\mathscr{L}/\partial K = r - \lambda\partial q/\partial K = 0 \tag{4.2}$$

$$\partial\mathscr{L}/\partial L = w - \lambda\partial q/\partial L = 0 \tag{4.3}$$

$$\partial\mathscr{L}/\partial\lambda = \bar{q} - q(K, L) = 0. \tag{4.4}$$

The first two conditions state that the factor price is equal to the value of the marginal product. The third condition repeats the constraint, meaning that an optimal choice must achieve the output objective. The solution to the minimization problem is the simultaneous solution to these three equations for K, L and λ, expressed in terms of w, r and $\bar{q}$. We proceed by using (4.2) and (4.3) to eliminate λ:

$$\frac{\partial q/\partial L}{\partial q/\partial K} = \frac{w}{r}. \tag{4.5}$$

This expression describes the expansion path. It reflects tangency of the isoquants with the isocosts at constant factor prices. Its interpretation is that, at an optimum, the firm is indifferent between spending its last dollar on capital or labor. Solving (4.4) and (4.5) yields the factor demands. With these in hand, we can solve for the expenditure level, if desired, by substituting the factor demands back into the objective function to obtain the cost function. This function describes the minimum cost of production as a function of the factor prices and the level of output.

The geometry of the problem is shown in Figure 4.1. The isoquant labeled $\bar{q}$ denotes the inputs that can produce the target level of output. The optimal solution is (K^*, L^*) on the lowest possible isocost, where the total cost is C^*.

4.2 Example

Suppose the firm's technology can be described by the constant elasticity of substitution (CES) production function $q = \gamma[\delta K^\rho + (1 - \delta)L^\rho]^{1/\rho}$, where $\rho \leq 1$ and $\rho \neq 0$. As we shall see, this functional form is very widely used in simulation models in a variety of contexts, so it is well worth careful study. Note that as $\rho \to 0$ the function replicates Cobb–Douglas, while $\rho = 1$ implies a linear production function (i.e., the inputs are perfect substitutes). As $\rho \to -\infty$ the function is Leontief (i.e., the inputs are perfect complements). We can form the Lagrangian for the firm's constrained

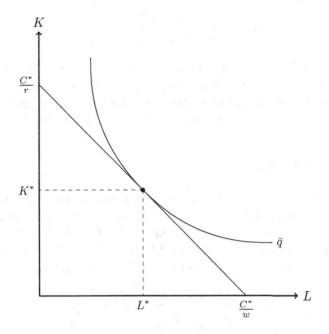

Fig. 4.1   Cost Minimization.

optimization problem as follows:

$$\mathscr{L} = rK + wL + \lambda[\bar{q} - \gamma[\delta K^\rho + (1 - \delta)L^\rho]^{1/\rho}]. \tag{4.6}$$

Differentiating with respect to K, L and λ yields the first-order conditions for a minimum:

$$\partial\mathscr{L}/\partial K = r - \lambda q[\delta K^\rho + (1 - \delta)L^\rho]^{-1}\delta K^{\rho-1} = 0 \tag{4.7}$$

$$\partial\mathscr{L}/\partial L = w - \lambda q[\delta K^\rho + (1 - \delta)L^\rho]^{-1}(1 - \delta)L^{\rho-1} = 0 \tag{4.8}$$

$$\partial\mathscr{L}/\partial\lambda = \bar{q} - \gamma[\delta K^\rho + (1 - \delta)L^\rho]^{1/\rho} = 0. \tag{4.9}$$

Using (4.7) and (4.8) we eliminate λ:

$$K = \left[\frac{1 - \delta}{\delta}\frac{r}{w}\right]^{\frac{1}{\rho-1}} L. \tag{4.10}$$

This is the expansion path. From (4.9) we have:

$$\delta K^\rho + (1 - \delta)L^\rho = [\bar{q}/\gamma]^\rho. \tag{4.11}$$

Solving (4.10) and (4.11) yields the factor demands:

$$K = \frac{\bar{q}\delta^\sigma r^{-\sigma}}{\gamma\left[(\delta r^{-\rho})^\sigma + ((1 - \delta)w^{-\rho})^\sigma\right]^{\frac{1}{\rho}}} \tag{4.12}$$

$$L = \frac{\bar{q}(1-\delta)^{\sigma} w^{-\sigma}}{\gamma \left[(\delta r^{-\rho})^{\sigma} + ((1-\delta)w^{-\rho})^{\sigma}\right]^{\frac{1}{\rho}}} \tag{4.13}$$

where $\sigma = 1/(1 - \rho)$ (it is the elasticity of substitution, the ratio of the proportional change in the factor proportions to the proportional change in the relative factor prices, a measure of the curvature of the isoquant). With these expressions in hand, we can solve for the cost function, if desired.

4.3 Set Notation

As in the preceding chapter, our next task is to transform the model into a form more amenable to programming in a general form within GAMS by using index notation. Let the set of factors be $\mathbf{J} = \{K, L\}$. We can then let the factor demands be represented by F_j, and the factor prices by r_j. Using this notation, we can write the factor demands compactly as:

$$F_j = \frac{\bar{q}\delta_j^{\sigma} r_j^{-\sigma}}{\gamma \left[\sum_{\forall k \in \mathbf{J}} \left(\delta_k r_k^{-\rho}\right)^{\sigma}\right]^{\frac{1}{\rho}}} \qquad \forall j \in \mathbf{J}$$

which is equivalent to (4.12) and (4.13). Note how the summation term is defined over k rather than j. The reason is that the expression is defining a factor demand equation for each of the elements in $\mathbf{J}$, so we can't have a statement that allows j to represent both a single element and multiple elements at the same time. Expenditure can be rewritten:

$$E = \sum_{\forall j \in \mathbf{J}} r_j F_j.$$

This is the form of the model that we will use in our GAMS program.

4.4 GAMS Implementation

The implementation of this problem is very similar to the utility maximization problem presented in Chapter 3, and is presented in full in Table 4.1. We begin by defining a set J containing the factors of production. The keyword ALIAS allows us to define another set called JJ that has exactly the same elements.[1]

---

[1]The ALIAS is necessary because the factor demand equations will require us to both index and sum over the set J. The discussion in Appendix B provides further details.

Table 4.1   GAMS Program for Cost Minimization.

```
SET J Factors /K,L/ ;
ALIAS (J, JJ);

PARAMETERS
GAMMA                       Shift parameter in production
DELTA(J)                    Share parameters in production
RHO                         Elasticity parameter in production
Q                           Output level
R(J)                        Factor prices
EO                          Initial expenditure
FO(J)                       Initial factor use levels;

R(J)=1;
Q=100;
FO(J)=50;
EO=SUM(J, R(J)*FO(J));
RHO=0.1;
DELTA(J)=(R(J)/FO(J)**(RHO-1))/(SUM(JJ, R(JJ)/FO(JJ)**(RHO-1)));
GAMMA=Q/(SUM(J, DELTA(J)*FO(J)**RHO))**(1/RHO);

VARIABLES
E                           Expenditure level
F(J)                        Factor use levels;

E.L=EO;
F.L(J)=FO(J);
F.LO(J)=0;

EQUATIONS
EXPENDITURE                 Expenditure function
FDEMAND(J)                  Factor demand functions;

EXPENDITURE..E=E=SUM(J, R(J)*F(J));
FDEMAND(J)..F(J)=E=(Q/GAMMA)*DELTA(J)**(1/(1-RHO))*R(J)**(-1/(1-RHO))
  /SUM(JJ, (DELTA(JJ)*R(JJ)**(-RHO))**(1/(1-RHO)))**(1/RHO);

MODEL PRODUCTION /ALL/;
SOLVE PRODUCTION USING NLP MINIMIZING E;
```

Next we define and assign values to the parameters, exogenous variables, and initial values of endogenous variables, using the calibration approach. We have set output at 100 units, the prices of each input at unity, and the factor demands for each input at 50 units. The initial value of expenditure is then defined as the sum of initial factor payments. The SUM command is the summation operator, and follows the same format as the PROD command. The parameter RHO is free and can be set at a value less than one (other than zero). The expression for DELTA is obtained by solving (4.10), and we can then use the production function to calibrate GAMMA. You should verify these aspects of the calibration for yourself. Note the use of the set JJ in the summation term in the denominator of the expression for DELTA. The reason is the same as that for using k rather than j in the preceding section.[2] We next assign variable names, and set the initial values and bounds, much the same way as in the consumer choice example. The expenditure level is left free as the objective for GAMS.

Next we set the equation names and assign the expressions, using the forms from the previous section. Note that the expression for the factor demands is quite long, and flows over into two lines. GAMS uses a semicolon to indicate the end of an expression, not a new line, so we are free to break lines wherever it is convenient.

Finally, we define the model and run a test solve to verify that it calibrates correctly. Once the calibration is confirmed, you can begin experimenting with the model by changing parameters and/or exogenous variables, re-solving the model, and observing how the solution changes from the initial point. Some suggestions can be found in the exercises below.

4.5   Exercises

(1) How does the firm's input choice change if the price of labor increases by 10 percent? What happens to the minimum expenditure level?
(2) How does the firm's input choice change if the prices of both labor and capital increase by 10 percent? What happens to the minimum expenditure level?
(3) Does this production function exhibit constant returns to scale? Can you devise an experiment to prove your assertion?
(4) What does an increase in the value of GAMMA signify?
(5) For a given factor price shock, how does changing the value of RHO change the outcome? What happens if you set RHO equal to zero?

---

[2]Try changing it to J and see the error message that GAMS returns.

(6) See if you can build a model of cost minimization using the Cobb–Douglas production function $q = \gamma K^\delta L^{1-\delta}$. Calibrate it to the same initial values as used in the example, and verify that as RHO is set close to zero, the effects of an economic shock in your model and the sample model become very close.

(7) As with consumer choice, we can also specify a dual problem for the firm. See if you can set up a model to describe input choices when a firm tries to maximize output subject to a fixed level of total expenditure. What happens if the expenditure level is set at the minimized expenditure obtained from the primal problem?

4.6   Further Reading

As with Chapter 3, much of this material is probably quite familiar. The material discussed in this chapter is covered in intermediate microeconomics texts such as Perloff (2011) or Varian (2009), or at a somewhat more advanced level in Varian (1992).

Chapter 5

Long-Run Production

Now that we have considered the basic problems of the consumer and the firm, we turn to a more complex problem — resource allocation across multiple industries. We will consider this issue in detail over the course of several interrelated chapters. To begin, suppose that we have two sectors that operate under perfect competition. Under this condition, the number of firms in the industry is irrelevant, since they are all price takers and have constant returns to scale, so we may proceed with two representative firms. The firms hire both labor and capital, which are available in fixed supply, from a common market. Both firms attempt to maximize their profit given their production technology, taking input and output prices as given. If capital and labor are both perfectly mobile across industries, we have the Heckscher–Ohlin–Samuelson (HOS) model of production, one of the most important models in standard trade theory.

5.1   Formal Problem

The problem can be posed in various ways. For now we will consider only the production side of the economy. Demand will be introduced later. Accordingly, consider the problem of maximizing the value of total output (GDP), at given prices, subject to the constraints imposed by resource limitations.[1] The Lagrangian for this problem is written:

$$\mathscr{L} = p_1 q_1(K_1, L_1) + p_2 q_2(K_2, L_2) + \lambda[\bar{K} - K_1 - K_2] + \mu[\bar{L} - L_1 - L_2] \quad (5.1)$$

---

[1]Although this sounds like a social planning problem and may in fact be viewed as such, it is not necessary to do so. When there are no factor market distortions, factor endowments are fixed, and competition prevails, the market maximizes the value of output at given output prices.

where $\bar{K}$ and $\bar{L}$ represent the given endowment of capital and labor, respectively. The production functions are assumed to exhibit the usual neoclassical properties, including constant returns to scale. The resource constraints state that the total resource use is equal to the fixed endowment, and imply mobility of factors across production activities.

Taking the derivatives of the Lagrangian with respect to the factor inputs and the multipliers we have the following first order conditions:

$$\partial \mathscr{L}/\partial K_1 = p_1 \partial q_1/\partial K_1 - \lambda = 0 \qquad (5.2)$$

$$\partial \mathscr{L}/\partial L_1 = p_1 \partial q_1/\partial L_1 - \mu = 0 \qquad (5.3)$$

$$\partial \mathscr{L}/\partial K_2 = p_2 \partial q_2/\partial K_2 - \lambda = 0 \qquad (5.4)$$

$$\partial \mathscr{L}/\partial L_2 = p_2 \partial q_2/\partial L_2 - \mu = 0 \qquad (5.5)$$

$$\partial \mathscr{L}/\partial \lambda = \bar{K} - K_1 - K_2 = 0 \qquad (5.6)$$

$$\partial \mathscr{L}/\partial \mu = \bar{L} - L_1 - L_2 = 0. \qquad (5.7)$$

We interpret the multipliers, λ and μ, as the shadow values of capital and labor, respectively. They represent how much the objective, output value, rises per unit increase in the exogenously determined resource supplies. Thus they are shadow prices in market value numéraire, or more simply, market prices. In the competitive equilibrium context, they are the factor prices, r and w. Equations (5.2) and (5.3) are therefore the same conditions that we saw in the previous chapter as (4.2) and (4.3), and they have the same interpretation. They state that the wage (rent) must equal the value of the marginal product of labor (capital).[2] Equations (5.4) and (5.5), which apply to the second industry, are similar. Equations (5.6) and (5.7) are the resource constraints. Solving these six equations simultaneously yields the factor prices (multipliers) and the optimal allocation of inputs, which can in turn be converted to an output measure using the production functions.[3] Rearranging (5.2)–(5.5) we have:

$$\frac{\partial q_1/\partial L_1}{\partial q_1/\partial K_1} = \frac{\partial q_2/\partial L_2}{\partial q_2/\partial K_2} = \frac{w}{r} \qquad (5.8)$$

---

[2]To see this, recall that in (4.2) and (4.3), the multiplier, λ can be interpreted as the price p.

[3]As usual, we have assumed an interior solution. In this particular problem an interior solution occurs provided that the ratio of the endowment of capital to labor lies between the ratios of capital to labor used by each industry (the factor intensity ratios) at the optimum. If this is not the case, only one good will be produced. The solution is unique provided that the factor intensities do not reverse. In other words, the isoquants for a common monetary value of output of each good should cross only once. The latter condition is violated if, for example, we use CES production functions with different elasticities in each sector.

which states that the isoquants of both industries are tangent at an optimum. This expression defines the efficiency locus, the collection of Pareto efficient input allocations across industries.

The standard geometry is the Edgeworth production box given in Figure 5.1. The dimensions of the box denote the endowments of capital and labor. An optimal solution lies along the efficiency locus connecting the two origins. The efficiency locus itself is the locus of tangencies of the isoquants for each good. All points on the locus are efficient: the optimal solution depends on the relative prices of the goods. Given these, the optimal solutions for the quantities are (K_1^*, L_1^*), (K_2^*, L_2^*), and (q_1^*, q_2^*). As drawn, industry 1 is capital intensive. The slope of the line tangent to both isoquants at the optimal output levels is the relative price of labor.

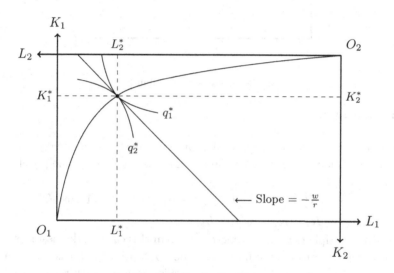

Fig. 5.1 Production Box.

Now, using (5.2) and (5.4), or (5.3) and (5.5), and recognizing that $\partial K_1 = -\partial K_2$ and $\partial L_1 = -\partial L_2$ from (5.6) and (5.7), respectively, we have:

$$\frac{\partial q_1}{\partial q_2} = -\frac{p_2}{p_1} \tag{5.9}$$

which states that, to maximize the value of income at given prices, the marginal rate of transformation (the slope of the production possibilities frontier) must equal (negative) the price ratio, as illustrated in Figure 5.2 below.[4]

---

[4]The production possibility frontier is obtained directly by maximizing the output of good 1 subject to a fixed level of output of good 2, and the resource constraints.

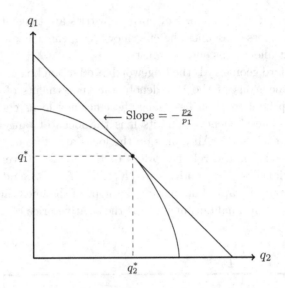

Fig. 5.2   Production Possibilities.

5.2   Example

Suppose that the technology of both representative firms can be represented by CES functions as used in Chapter 4. The Lagrangian for the problem is then:

$$\mathscr{L} = p_1\gamma_1[\delta_1 K_1^{\rho_1} + (1 - \delta_1)L_1^{\rho_1}]^{1/\rho_1} + p_2\gamma_2[\delta_2 K_2^{\rho_2} + (1 - \delta_2)L_2^{\rho_2}]^{1/\rho_2}$$
$$+ r[\bar{K} - K_1 - K_2] + w[\bar{L} - L_1 - L_2]. \tag{5.10}$$

Since the multipliers represent factor prices in this case (under assumptions of perfect competition), we have used the appropriate symbols (i.e., r and w) rather than the usual Greek letters. Differentiating with respect to K_1, L_1, K_2, L_2, r and w yields the first order conditions:

$$p_1q_1[\delta_1 K_1^{\rho_1} + (1 - \delta_1)L_1^{\rho_1}]^{-1}\delta_1 K_1^{\rho_1-1} - r = 0 \tag{5.11}$$

$$p_1q_1[\delta_1 K_1^{\rho_1} + (1 - \delta_1)L_1^{\rho_1}]^{-1}(1 - \delta_1)L_1^{\rho_1-1} - w = 0 \tag{5.12}$$

$$p_2q_2[\delta_2 K_2^{\rho_2} + (1 - \delta_2)L_2^{\rho_2}]^{-1}\delta_2 K_2^{\rho_2-1} - r = 0 \tag{5.13}$$

$$p_2q_2[\delta_2 K_2^{\rho_2} + (1 - \delta_2)L_2^{\rho_2}]^{-1}(1 - \delta_2)L_2^{\rho_2-1} - w = 0 \tag{5.14}$$

$$\bar{K} - K_1 - K_2 = 0 \tag{5.15}$$

$$\bar{L} - L_1 - L_2 = 0. \tag{5.16}$$

Rather than manipulate these expressions further as we did in Chapter 4, we will use them directly in our GAMS representation.

5.3 Set Notation

As usual, it is convenient to express the problem in terms of the underlying sets rather than scalars. Let the set of factors be $\mathbf{J} = \{K, L\}$ and the set of industries be $\mathbf{I} = \{1, 2\}$. Then the endowments can be expressed as $\bar{F}_j$, and the demand for factor j in industry i becomes F_{ji}. Using this notation, we can then rewrite (5.11)–(5.14) in the following compact way:

$$r_j = p_i q_i \left[\sum_{\forall k \in \mathbf{J}} \delta_{ki} F_{ki}^{\rho_i} \right]^{-1} \delta_{ji} F_{ji}^{\rho_i - 1} \qquad \forall j \in \mathbf{J}, \forall i \in \mathbf{I}.$$

The power of using this method of expression becomes very clear with this example, where we can use a single statement to define four first order conditions. The resource constraints become:

$$\bar{F}_j = \sum_{\forall i \in \mathbf{I}} F_{ji} \qquad \forall j \in \mathbf{J}.$$

Finally, the production functions (if desired) can be rewritten:

$$q_i = \gamma_i \left[\sum_{\forall j \in \mathbf{J}} \delta_{ji} F_{ji}^{\rho_i} \right]^{\frac{1}{\rho_i}} \qquad \forall i \in \mathbf{I}.$$

This is the form of the model that we will use in our GAMS program.

5.4 GAMS Implementation

The GAMS implementation is presented in Table 5.1, and follows a similar pattern to previous examples. In fact, much of the code (including the calibration) is common with Chapter 4. We begin by defining the sets of goods and factors, aliasing the factor set as in the previous example. Next we set the names of parameters and exogenous variables, including the initial values of the endogenous variables. Factor demands are now indexed by both industry and factor as appropriate, as are the parameters of the production functions.

Table 5.1   GAMS Program for Long-Run Production.

```
SET I Goods /1,2/;
SET J Factors /K,L/;
ALIAS (J, JJ);

PARAMETERS
GAMMA(I)                        Shift parameters in production
DELTA(J,I)                      Share parameters in production
RHO(I)                          Elasticity parameters in production
P(I)                            Output prices
FBAR(J)                         Endowments
QO(I)                           Initial output levels
RO(J)                           Initial factor prices
FO(J,I)                         Initial factor use levels
GDPO                            Initial gross domestic product;

P(I)=1;
RO(J)=1;
QO(I)=100;
FO('L','1')=20;
FO('L','2')=80;
FO('K',I)=(QO(I)*P(I)-FO('L',I)*RO('L'))/RO('K');
FBAR(J)=SUM(I, FO(J,I));
GDPO=SUM(I, P(I)*QO(I));
RHO(I)=0.1;
DELTA(J,I)=(RO(J)/FO(J,I)**(RHO(I)-1))/(SUM(JJ, RO(JJ)
  /FO(JJ,I)**(RHO(I)-1)));
GAMMA(I)=QO(I)/((SUM(J, DELTA(J,I)*FO(J,I)**RHO(I)))**(1/RHO(I)));

VARIABLES
Q(I)                            Output levels
R(J)                            Factor prices
F(J,I)                          Factor use levels
GDP                             Gross domestic product;
```

---

continued on next page

Next we assign the parameter values. Note that we have used product exhaustion to define the initial values of capital in each sector, have used the resource constraints to define the total factor endowments, and the value of output to define GDP.[5] Note also that the calibration of the DELTA and GAMMA parameters is exactly the same as in the cost minimization example.

---

[5] Product exhaustion means that factor payments in accordance with marginal productivity to each factor exactly exhaust the total product. In other words, total payments to capital and labor must equal the total value of output.

continued from previous page

```
Q.L(I)=Q0(I);
R.L(J)=R0(J);
F.L(J,I)=F0(J,I);
GDP.L=GDP0;
Q.LO(I)=0;
R.LO(J)=0;
F.LO(J,I)=0;

EQUATIONS
PRODUCTION(I)          Production functions
RESOURCE(J)            Resource constraints
FDEMAND(J,I)           Factor demand functions
INCOME                 Gross domestic product;

PRODUCTION(I)..Q(I)=E=GAMMA(I)*SUM(J, DELTA(J,I)*F(J,I)**RHO(I))**(1/RHO(I));
RESOURCE(J)..FBAR(J)=E=SUM(I, F(J,I));
FDEMAND(J,I)..R(J)=E=P(I)*Q(I)*SUM(JJ, DELTA(JJ,I)*F(JJ,I)**RHO(I))**(-1)*
  DELTA(J,I)*F(J,I)**(RHO(I)-1);
INCOME..GDP=E=SUM(I, P(I)*Q(I));

MODEL HOS /ALL/;
SOLVE HOS USING NLP MAXIMIZING GDP;
```

Next we define the variables, which are also indexed over industries/factors as appropriate, and assign initial levels and bounds. GDP remains unbounded for use as the objective. We define equations and assign the expressions derived in Section 5.3 to them, and finally set up and solve the model with MODEL and SOLVE statements. Running a test solve verifies that the model calibrates correctly. Again, once the calibration is confirmed, you can begin experimenting with the model by changing parameters and/or exogenous variables, re-solving the model, and observing how the solution changed from the initial point.

This model differs from the preceding two examples in that it is a complete general equilibrium representation of the production side of an economic system, albeit a simple one. The HOS model of production is a workhorse of standard trade theory, and understanding it well takes us a long way toward understanding the more complex models of modern CGE analysis.

5.5   Exercises

(1) What happens to factor prices when you increase the price of good 1 by 10 percent? What if you increase the price of good 2 by 10 percent?

(2) What happens to production and factor prices if you increase both prices by 10 percent? What does this result tell you about the nature of prices in a general equilibrium model like this?

(3) If you increase the endowment of capital by 10 percent, what happens to the pattern of production? What if you increase the endowment of labor by 10 percent? Do factor prices change in either scenario? Why or why not?

(4) In this model, GDP has been defined as the sum of the values of output. Could we define it in another, equivalent way?

(5) In this model we can implement factor neutral technology shocks by changing the GAMMA parameters. Can you reprogram the model to accommodate factor-specific technology shocks in each industry?

(6) Can you replicate this model with Cobb–Douglas technology rather than CES?

5.6   Further Reading

A good treatment of the HOS model and its characteristics is Bhagwati *et al.* (1998). After working through their exposition, you may find it rewarding to revisit the classic articles by Stolper and Samuelson (1941) and Rybczynski (1955).

Chapter 6

Short-Run Production

The short run is usually defined as the period of time over which at least one input into the production process cannot be varied. We can modify our model of the production side of the economy to allow capital to be fixed, while labor continues to be mobile across activities. This generates the specific factors model of production.

6.1 Formal Problem

The problem is not very different from that examined in the previous chapter. Consider maximizing the value of total output (GDP), for given prices, subject to the constraints imposed by resource limitations and mobility restrictions. The Lagrangian for the problem is:

$$\mathscr{L} = p_1 q_1(K_1, L_1) + p_2 q_2(K_2, L_2) + \lambda_1[\bar{K}_1 - K_1] + \lambda_2[\bar{K}_2 - K_2]$$
$$+ \mu[\bar{L} - L_1 - L_2] \tag{6.1}$$

where $\bar{K}_j$ represents the stock of capital available to each industry, and $\bar{L}$ represents the given endowment of labor. Once again, the production functions are assumed to exhibit the usual neoclassical properties, including constant returns to scale. Taking the derivatives of the Lagrangian with respect to the factor inputs and the multipliers we have:

$$\partial \mathscr{L}/\partial K_1 = p_1 \partial q_1/\partial K_1 - \lambda_1 = 0 \tag{6.2}$$

$$\partial \mathscr{L}/\partial L_1 = p_1 \partial q_1/\partial L_1 - \mu = 0 \tag{6.3}$$

$$\partial \mathscr{L}/\partial K_2 = p_2 \partial q_2/\partial K_2 - \lambda_2 = 0 \tag{6.4}$$

$$\partial \mathscr{L}/\partial L_2 = p_2 \partial q_2/\partial L_2 - \mu = 0 \tag{6.5}$$

$$\partial \mathscr{L}/\partial \lambda_1 = \bar{K}_1 - K_1 = 0 \tag{6.6}$$

$$\partial \mathscr{L}/\partial \lambda_2 = \bar{K}_2 - K_2 = 0 \tag{6.7}$$

$$\partial \mathscr{L}/\partial \mu = \bar{L} - L_1 - L_2 = 0. \tag{6.8}$$

We interpret the multipliers λ_j and μ as the shadow values of capital and labor, respectively. In the competitive equilibrium context, these are the factor prices, r_j and w, as before. Now, however, capital will earn a different return depending on the industry in which it is employed.[1] Solving these seven equations simultaneously yields the factor prices (multipliers) and the optimal allocation of inputs, which can in turn be converted to an output measure using the production functions.

The system is easier to work with than it might first appear. Equations (6.6) and (6.7) determine the inputs of capital to each sector immediately. Then, using (6.3), (6.5) and (6.8) we can formulate the production possibilities. Given prices, we can determine the optimal output level, and then (6.2) and (6.4) can be used to determine the returns to capital. In terms of the optimality conditions that must hold at a solution, using (6.3) and (6.5) we can see that the value of the marginal product of labor must be equalized across sectors. Further rearrangement yields the familiar:

$$\frac{\partial q_1}{\partial q_2} = -\frac{p_2}{p_1} \tag{6.9}$$

which states that the marginal rate of transformation must equal (negative) the price ratio. Using (6.2)–(6.5) we obtain the usual isoquant/isocost tangency condition, but the slope of the isocost is different in each industry since relative factor prices differ.

Two geometric approaches are commonly used for illustrating the first order conditions. The first concentrates attention on the market for labor, the second on the market for goods. In Figure 6.1, the length of the horizontal axis represents the labor constraint (6.8). The vertical axes measure the wage, which under perfect competition is the shadow price of labor (μ). Equations (6.6) and (6.7) determine the capital allocation directly, and can be substituted into (6.1) through (6.5). Equations (6.3) and (6.5) describe the value of the marginal product of labor (VMPL), and are solved simultaneously for the optimal labor price. Hence, the optimal solution depicted directly in the figure is L_1^* and w^* ($= \mu^*$).

An alternative geometry, which emphasizes the tangency condition (6.9), is shown in Figure 6.2. The diagram is divided into four quadrants. In quadrants 2 and 4 we have the total product curves, derived directly

---

[1] In fact, the model can be interpreted as a three factor model, with each type of capital interpreted as a unique input, e.g., land and machines.

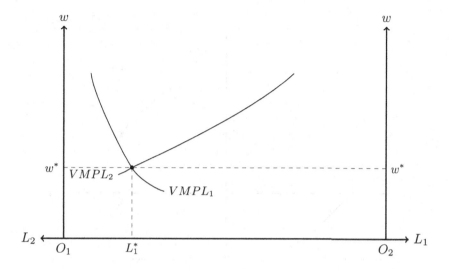

Fig. 6.1   Short-Run Labor Market.

from the production functions for a given capital allocation. In quadrant 3 we have the labor resource constraint. Tracing every possible labor allocation through the total product curves yields the production possibilities in quadrant 1. An isovalue line shows the collections of output that add up to a given GDP. Its slope is $-p_2/p_1$. The one shown in Figure 6.2 is for maximum GDP, given resources and technology. The optimal solution is (q_1^*, q_2^*), determined by the tangency of the PPF with the isovalue line at slope (minus) the price ratio. The corresponding input solution is (L_1^*, L_2^*). The slopes of the total product curves at L_1^* and L_2^* are the equilibrium marginal products of labor in each sector, i.e., the wages, measured in the product produced.

6.2   GAMS Implementation

There is little difference in the structure of this model and that of Chapter 5, so we move directly to the GAMS implementation. Rather than building an entirely new model, we proceed by modifying the model from the previous chapter.

In principle there are several ways that we could modify the program to handle specific factors. One way would be to define two different types of factors, mobile and specific. It turns out, however, that in many

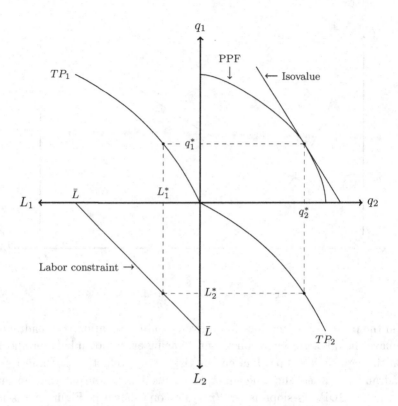

Fig. 6.2   Quadrant Production Possibilities.

circumstances there is a more efficient way to proceed. We are going to use a method that exploits one of the advanced features of GAMS, exception handling. As noted above, since in the short-run capital used in sector 1 cannot move to sector 2, and vice-versa, we can think of each as being an entirely distinct factor of production. Hence, we can define our set of factors as $\mathbf{J} = \{K, L, N\}$, where N is the new factor of production. This is accomplished easily in GAMS just by extending the dimension of the set:

`SET J Factors /K,L,N/;`

All of the parameters of the model remain the same, and we keep the equilibrium outputs and prices at the same levels as before. However, we change the calibration of the capital input to:

```
FO('K','1')=(QO('1')*P('1')-FO('L','1')*RO('L'))/RO('K');
FO('N','2')=(QO('2')*P('2')-FO('L','2')*RO('L'))/RO('N');
```

Note the use of 'K' in the first line and 'N' in the second. We are letting N play the role of capital in industry 2. Now, since GAMS treats any unassigned parameter as having a value of zero, and since we have not assigned a value for K in industry 2 nor N in industry 1, this implies that the use of K in industry 2 is zero, and the use of N in industry 1 is zero, (i.e., K is specific to industry 1 and N is specific to industry 2). Next we make a small adjustment to the calibration of DELTA and GAMMA:

```
DELTA(J,I)$FO(J,I)=(RO(J)/FO(J,I)**(RHO(I)-1))
    /(SUM(JJ$FO(JJ,I),RO(JJ)/FO(JJ,I)**(RHO(I)-1)));
```

The change is the introduction of dollar ($) controls, which are how GAMS creates exceptions. On the left hand side, DELTA(J,I)$FO(J,I) has the meaning: assign a value to DELTA(J,I) only if the corresponding value of FO(J,I) is *not* equal to zero. Alternatively, we can write the condition in full as DELTA(J,I)$(FO(J, I) NE 0), which has the same effect (NE is the GAMS format for $\neq$), and illustrates how exception handling may be used more generally. The effect of the $ control here is to ensure that GAMS will not attempt to assign a share parameter for K in industry 2 or N in industry 1.

The $ control on the right hand side of the expression is similar, it says to sum across only those elements of the set JJ for which FO(JJ,I) is not equal to zero, thereby dropping out factors that are not used in production. The calibration of GAMMA, below, has a similar $ expression, serving the same purpose, on the right:[2]

```
GAMMA(I)=QO(I)/(SUM(J$FO(J,I),
    DELTA(J,I)*FO(J,I)**RHO(I)))**(1/RHO(I));
```

The rest of the program is identical to the HOS model developed in chapter 5 except for the expressions for outputs and factor demands, into which we introduce exception handling in a very similar manner to that used in the calibration:

---

[2]Because the corresponding DELTA values will be zero, in this case the $ control on the right is not necessary, but is good practice. If, for example, the production functions were Cobb–Douglas rather than CES, then exception handling on the right would be mandatory, because the presence of any zero in the product would imply zero production. Of course, the CES approximation to Cobb–Douglas, with RHO close to but not equal to zero, does not suffer from this problem. In the Cobb–Douglas case the command would need to be GAMMA(I)=QO(I)/(PROD(J$FO(J,I), FO(J,I)**DELTA(J,I))), where the DELTA terms are the exponents of the factors in the Cobb–Douglas function.

```
PRODUCTION(I)..Q(I)=E=GAMMA(I)*SUM(J$FO(J,I), DELTA(J,I)*
   F(J,I)**RHO(I))**(1/RHO(I));
FDEMAND(J,I)$FO(J,I)..R(J)=E=P(I)*Q(I)*SUM(JJ$FO(JJ,I),
   DELTA(JJ,I)*F(JJ,I)**RHO(I))**(-1)*DELTA(J,I)*F(J,I)
   **(RHO(I)-1);
```

On the production function, we again control the index of summation on the right hand side. For the factor demands, we have a $ control option that states that a demand function exists for factor j in industry i only if FO(J,I) NE 0. While in the context of the assignment of a value to the parameter the exception prevents an assignment from being made, in the context of an equation, the exception prevents GAMS from generating the equation. Hence, in this model GAMS does not generate a demand for K in sector 2, or a demand for N in sector 1, which is exactly what we want. This kind of exception handling is a very useful technique.

All that remains is to verify the calibration of the model by running an initial SOLVE without any additional shocks, and then to explore the properties of the model by shocking the economic system in various ways. As with the HOS model of production covered in Chapter 5, the specific factors model is one of the workhorse models of standard trade theory, and understanding how to build it and how it behaves is very useful in terms of building and interpreting more complex models. In Chapter 8 we will return to the specific factors model and its relationship with the HOS model.

6.3   Exercises

(1) What happens to factor prices when you increase the price of good 1 by 10 percent? What about if you increase the price of good 2 by 10 percent? How does the pattern differ from the HOS model examined in Chapter 5? What are the implications for political economy?

(2) When you increase the price of good 1 by 10 percent, does labor benefit in real terms? What factors determine your answer?

(3) If you increase the endowment of a specific factor, what happens to the production pattern? What if you increase the endowment of labor?

(4) If you increase the endowments in the specific factors model, do factor prices change? How are the results different from the HOS model examined in Chapter 5?

(5) What happens to factor prices and outputs if all product prices rise by 10 percent?

(6) What happens to factor prices and outputs if all endowments rise by 10 percent? You should be able to intuit the answers to (5) and (6). As we have noted, checking the answers from GAMS against your intuition is a good way to debug your GAMS model when theory is clear about what must happen.

6.4 Further Reading

As with the HOS model, you might start with the exposition of the specific factors model in Bhagwati *et al.* (1998). The classic reference for the specific factors model is Jones (1971).

Table 6.1   GAMS Program for Short-Run Production.

```
SET I Goods /1,2/;
SET J Factors /K,L,N/;
ALIAS (J, JJ);

PARAMETERS
GAMMA(I)                        Shift parameters in production
DELTA(J,I)                      Share parameters in production
RHO(I)                          Elasticity parameters in production
P(I)                            Output prices
FBAR(J)                         Endowments
QO(I)                           Initial output levels
RO(J)                           Initial factor prices
FO(J,I)                         Initial factor use levels
GDPO                            Initial gross domestic product;

P(I)=1;
RO(J)=1;
QO(I)=100;
FO('L','1')=20;
FO('L','2')=80;
FO('K','1')=(QO('1')*P('1')-FO('L','1')*RO('L'))/RO('K');
FO('N','2')=(QO('2')*P('2')-FO('L','2')*RO('L'))/RO('N');
FBAR(J)=SUM(I, FO(J,I));
GDPO=SUM(I, P(I)*QO(I));
RHO(I)=0.1;
DELTA(J,I)$FO(J,I)=(RO(J)/FO(J,I)**(RHO(I)-1))/(SUM(JJ$FO(JJ,I), RO(JJ)
  /FO(JJ,I)**(RHO(I)-1)));
GAMMA(I)=QO(I)/(SUM(J$FO(J,I), DELTA(J,I)*FO(J,I)**RHO(I)))**(1/RHO(I));

VARIABLES
Q(I)                            Output levels
R(J)                            Factor prices
F(J,I)                          Factor use levels
GDP                             Gross domestic product;
```

continued on next page

continued from previous page

```
Q.L(I)=Q0(I);
R.L(J)=R0(J);
F.L(J,I)=F0(J,I);
GDP.L=GDP0;
Q.LO(I)=0;
R.LO(J)=0;
F.LO(J,I)=0;

EQUATIONS
PRODUCTION(I)              Production functions
RESOURCE(J)               Resource constraints
FDEMAND(J,I)              Factor demand functions
INCOME                   Gross domestic product;

PRODUCTION(I)..Q(I)=E=GAMMA(I)*SUM(J$F0(J,I), DELTA(J,I)*F(J,I)**
  RHO(I))**(1/RHO(I));
RESOURCE(J)..FBAR(J)=E=SUM(I, F(J,I));
FDEMAND(J,I)$F0(J,I)..R(J)=E=P(I)*Q(I)*SUM(JJ$F0(JJ,I), DELTA(JJ,I)*
  F(JJ,I)**RHO(I))**(-1)*DELTA(J,I)*F(J,I)**(RHO(I)-1);
INCOME..GDP=E=SUM(I, P(I)*Q(I));

MODEL SF /ALL/;
SOLVE SF USING NLP MAXIMIZING GDP;
```

Chapter 7

Dual Approach

The models presented in the preceding two chapters were described using what is called the "primal" approach. That is, the decision variables were quantities, while the multipliers represented shadow prices, which are equivalent to market prices under perfect competition. In many optimization contexts we can formulate the primal problem in terms of an equivalent "dual" problem. In the context of the HOS or specific factors models, this means we solve for the prices directly rather than the quantities. This has a number of advantages in some contexts, and is widely used. In this chapter we reformulate the HOS model of production in dual form, and implement it as a GAMS program.

7.1 Formal Problem

Let us consider again the first-order conditions for the firm's cost minimization problem from chapter 5:

$$r - \lambda \partial q / \partial K = 0 \qquad (7.1)$$

$$w - \lambda \partial q / \partial L = 0 \qquad (7.2)$$

$$\bar{q} - q(K, L) = 0. \qquad (7.3)$$

We can solve these equations for the optimal purchases of capital and labor as a function of the factor prices and the desired level of output. That is $K^* = K(w, r, \bar{q})$ and $L^* = L(w, r, \bar{q})$. These are the factor demands. Now, cost is defined as $C = wL + rK$ for any input choice, so evaluated at the optimal input choices we have $C(w, r, \bar{q}) = wL(w, r, \bar{q}) + rK(w, r, \bar{q})$. The expression $C(w, r, \bar{q})$ is called the cost function. It tells us the minimal expenditure necessary to obtain a target level of output, given the factor prices. The cost function has some very desirable properties. Most notably, taking the derivative of the cost function with respect to a factor price yields the optimal factor demand for that factor, by Shepherd's lemma (an application of the envelope theorem).[1] Hence:

$$\partial C / \partial w = L^* \tag{7.4}$$

$$\partial C / \partial r = K^* \tag{7.5}$$

where both L^* and K^* are, of course, functions of factor prices and the level of output. Moreover, if the production function q exhibits constant returns to scale, the optimal input choices for given factor prices must have the same factor proportions for any output level. That is, at any given factor prices the firm will always choose the same ratio of capital to labor for any output level. Hence, we can define the unit cost function as $c(w, r) = w a_L(w, r) + r a_K(w, r)$, where the a_j are the optimal inputs *per unit* of output (and we have dropped the * notation for convenience). Shepherd's lemma applies here too, so we can have:

$$\partial c / \partial w = a_L \tag{7.6}$$

$$\partial c / \partial r = a_K \tag{7.7}$$

where both a_L and a_K are functions of factor prices. Now consider the first order conditions for the HOS production problem of Chapter 5, reproduced below with the multipliers denoted for convenience by the appropriate competitive prices:

$$p_1 \partial q_1 / \partial K_1 - r = 0 \tag{7.8}$$

$$p_1 \partial q_1 / \partial L_1 - w = 0 \tag{7.9}$$

$$p_2 \partial q_2 / \partial K_2 - r = 0 \tag{7.10}$$

$$p_2 \partial q_2 / \partial L_2 - w = 0 \tag{7.11}$$

$$\bar{K} - K_1 - K_2 = 0 \tag{7.12}$$

$$\bar{L} - L_1 - L_2 = 0. \tag{7.13}$$

In addition, the optimal levels for the quantities can be obtained directly from the production functions used in the cost minimization problem:

$$q_1 = q_1(K_1, L_1) \tag{7.14}$$

$$q_2 = q_2(K_2, L_2). \tag{7.15}$$

---

[1]To see this, differentiate C with respect to w to obtain $\partial C / \partial w = L + w(\partial L / \partial w) + r(\partial K / \partial w)$. The last two terms drop out. To see this, set the last two terms equal to zero, then rearranging we have $\partial K / \partial L = -w/r$. This is the familiar tangency condition between an isocost and an isoquant. We used this condition to derive the optimal input choices, so it must hold true at an optimum.

Taken as whole, we have a system of eight simultaneous equations in eight unknowns. Given prices and endowments, we can solve the system (noting that we will get the same solution for any equivalent set of relative prices). This is the primal form of the HOS model of production as used in Chapter 5.

In Chapter 5 we looked at the geometry of the problem using the production box and production possibilities diagrams. Another approach is the unit value isoquant diagram shown in Figure 7.1. Under constant returns to scale, all units are produced in the same way. Consider the isoquants associated with producing $1 worth of each good. These are labeled q_1 and q_2, respectively. Since each firm is profit maximizing, each isoquant must be tangent to an isocost. Moreover, since profit is zero and the firms pay the same prices for factors of production, both q_1 and q_2 must be tangent to the same isocost, that representing $1 worth of expenditure. With positive quantities of both goods produced at equilibrium, the intercepts of the isocost measure the inverses of the equilibrium factor prices. The slopes of the rays from the origin through each point of tangency represent the factor intensities.[2]

Using the unit cost functions, we can rewrite the system of equations in the following alternative way:

$$c_1(w, r) = p_1 \tag{7.16}$$

$$c_2(w, r) = p_2 \tag{7.17}$$

$$a_{K1}(w, r)q_1 + a_{K2}(w, r)q_2 = \bar{K} \tag{7.18}$$

$$a_{L1}(w, r)q_1 + a_{L2}(w, r)q_2 = \bar{L}. \tag{7.19}$$

This is the dual representation of the model. It is very widely used because it emphasizes the dependence of the factor prices only on the goods prices (in the 2 × 2 model), and in many cases allows a more compact representation of the economic system. The first two equations state that, under perfect competition, the minimized cost of producing a single unit of each good must equal the price (i.e., profit is zero). Embedded within equation (7.16) are equations (7.8), (7.9) and (7.14) from the primal representation. Similarly, embedded within equation (7.17) are equations (7.10), (7.11) and (7.15). The next two equations are the resource constraints, which simply replicate (7.12) and (7.13), since multiplying a unit factor demand by the number of units produced generates the total factor demand. The dual representation is four equations in four unknowns. Again, given a set of

---

[2]The quantities at the tangencies in the diagram are the optimal demands per unit of value.

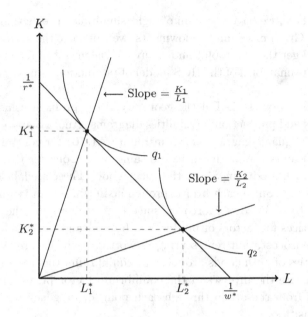

Fig. 7.1   Unit Value Isoquants.

relative prices and endowments we can determine the solution. Moreover, note how the dual approach blocks the model very conveniently. Given prices, we can solve the first two equations for factor prices. We can then determine all the a_{ji} using Shepherd's lemma. Finally, having solved for the optimal unit factor demands, we can solve the factor constraints for outputs.

A geometric device that is commonly used to illustrate the solution to the dual problem is the isoprice diagram shown in Figure 7.2. The isoprice curves labeled p_1 and p_2 represent the factor price combinations that are consistent with the given prices, and are derived directly from equations (7.16) and (7.17). The simultaneous solution to these equations yields the factor prices directly, w^* and r^*.

Unlike the Edgeworth production box construction, or the closely related unit isoquant diagram described above, which depict the input choice directly and the factor prices indirectly, the isoprice diagram depicts factor prices directly and factor intensities indirectly, as the tangent lines to the isoprice curves where they intersect. Figure 7.2 is drawn with p_1 steeper than p_2. This reflects the assumption that sector 1 is capital intensive relative to sector 2. In the extreme case where sector 1 uses no labor, wage does not affect cost in sector 1 and p_1 is vertical.

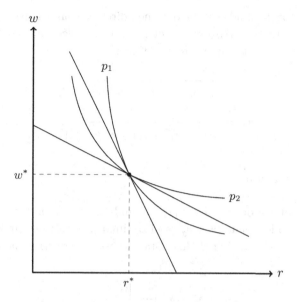

Fig. 7.2   Isoprice Diagram.

7.2   Example

Consider again the CES production function $q = \gamma[\delta K^\rho + (1-\delta)L^\rho]^{1/\rho}$. We have already seen in Chapter 4 (equations 4.12 and 4.13) that the solutions for the optimal factor demands can be written:

$$K = \frac{\bar{q}\delta^\sigma r^{-\sigma}}{\gamma\left[(\delta r^{-\rho})^\sigma + ((1-\delta)w^{-\rho})^\sigma\right]^{\frac{1}{\rho}}} \qquad (7.20)$$

$$L = \frac{\bar{q}(1-\delta)^\sigma w^{-\sigma}}{\gamma\left[(\delta r^{-\rho})^\sigma + ((1-\delta)w^{-\rho})^\sigma\right]^{\frac{1}{\rho}}}. \qquad (7.21)$$

Multiplying (7.20) and (7.21) by factor prices and summing gives us the cost function, which can be written:

$$C = \bar{q}\gamma^{-1}\left[\delta^\sigma r^{1-\sigma} + (1-\delta)^\sigma w^{1-\sigma}\right]^{\frac{\rho-1}{\rho}} \qquad (7.22)$$

and the unit cost function is:

$$c = \gamma^{-1}\left[\delta^\sigma r^{1-\sigma} + (1-\delta)^\sigma w^{1-\sigma}\right]^{\frac{\rho-1}{\rho}}. \qquad (7.23)$$

The unit factor demands can be obtained directly from the factor demands by dividing through by $\bar{q}$ or by using Shepherd's lemma and taking the partial derivative of the unit cost functions:[3]

$$a_K = \frac{\delta^\sigma r^{-\sigma}}{\gamma \left[(\delta r^{-\rho})^\sigma + ((1-\delta)w^{-\rho})^\sigma \right]^{\frac{1}{\rho}}} \tag{7.24}$$

$$a_L = \frac{(1-\delta)^\sigma w^{-\sigma}}{\gamma \left[(\delta r^{-\rho})^\sigma + ((1-\delta)w^{-\rho})^\sigma \right]^{\frac{1}{\rho}}}. \tag{7.25}$$

7.3   Set Notation

Let the set of factors be $\mathbf{J} = \{K, L\}$ and the set of industries be $\mathbf{I} = \{1, 2\}$. The endowments are $\bar{F}_j$, and optimal per unit demand for factor j in industry i is a_{ji}. Using this notation, we can rewrite the zero profit conditions as:

$$p_i = \gamma_i^{-1} \left[\sum_{\forall j \in \mathbf{J}} \delta_{ji}^{\sigma_i} r_j^{1-\sigma_i} \right]^{\frac{\rho_i - 1}{\rho_i}} \qquad \forall i \in \mathbf{I}.$$

The resource constraints become:

$$\bar{F}_j = \sum_{\forall i \in \mathbf{I}} a_{ji} q_i \qquad \forall j \in \mathbf{J}.$$

Finally, the optimal unit factor demands are:

$$a_{ji} = \frac{\delta_{ji}^{\sigma_i} r_j^{-\sigma_i}}{\gamma_i \left[\sum_{\forall k \in \mathbf{J}} \left(\delta_{ki} r_k^{-\rho_i} \right)^{\sigma_i} \right]^{\frac{1}{\rho_i}}} \qquad \forall j \in \mathbf{J}, \forall i \in \mathbf{I}.$$

We are now ready to write up and solve the model in GAMS.

7.4   GAMS Implementation

The GAMS implementation of this model is presented in Table 7.1. Much of the material can be duplicated from Chapter 5. Since we intend to replicate the same equilibrium, and since the basic program structure should be getting familiar, we focus on the new elements.

The only changes to the parameter section are that we have defined the elasticity of substitution (ESUB) for convenience, and replaced the initial factor demands F0(J,I), which appear in the primal version, with

---

[3]As an exercise you can verify for yourself that you get the same answer either way.

Table 7.1   GAMS Program for Dual General Equilibrium Problem.

```
SET I Goods /1,2/;
SET J Factors /K,L/;
ALIAS (J, JJ);

PARAMETERS
GAMMA(I)                        Shift parameters in production
DELTA(J,I)                      Share parameters in production
RHO(I)                          Elasticity parameters in production
ESUB(I)                         Elasticities of substitution
P(I)                            Output prices
FBAR(J)                         Endowments
QO(I)                           Initial output levels
RO(J)                           Initial factor prices
AO(J,I)                         Initial per unit factor use levels
GDPO                            Initial gross domestic product;

P(I)=1;
RO(J)=1;
QO(I)=100;
AO('L','1')=0.2;
AO('L','2')=0.8;
AO('K',I)=(P(I)-AO('L',I)*RO('L'))/RO('K');
FBAR(J)=SUM(I, AO(J,I)*QO(I));
GDPO=SUM(I, P(I)*QO(I));
RHO(I)=0.1;
ESUB(I)=1/(1-RHO(I));
DELTA(J,I)=(RO(J)/AO(J,I)**(RHO(I)-1))/(SUM(JJ, RO(JJ)
  /AO(JJ,I)**(RHO(I)-1)));
GAMMA(I)=QO(I)/(SUM(J, DELTA(J,I)*(AO(J,I)*QO(I))**RHO(I)))**(1/RHO(I));

VARIABLES
Q(I)                            Output levels
R(J)                            Factor prices
A(J,I)                          Per unit factor use levels
GDP                             Gross domestic product;
```

---

continued on next page

the initial unit factor demands AO(J,I), which appear in the dual version. We then adjust the calibration section accordingly (i.e., AO(J,I)*QO(I) replaces FO(J,I) wherever it occurs). In the variable definitions, assignments, and bounds we do the same thing, replacing F(J,I) with the unit factor demands A(J,I).

continued from previous page

```
Q.L(I)=Q0(I);
R.L(J)=R0(J);
A.L(J,I)=A0(J,I);
GDP.L=GDP0;
Q.LO(I)=0;
R.LO(J)=0;
A.LO(J,I)=0;

EQUATIONS
ZERO(I)                 Zero profit functions
RESOURCE(J)             Resource constraints
UFDEMAND(J,I)           Unit factor demand functions
INCOME                  Gross domestic product;

ZERO(I)..P(I)=E=GAMMA(I)**(-1)*SUM(J, DELTA(J,I)**ESUB(I)*R(J)**
   (1-ESUB(I)))**((RHO(I)-1)/(RHO(I)));
RESOURCE(J)..FBAR(J)=E=SUM(I, A(J,I)*Q(I));
UFDEMAND(J,I)..A(J,I)=E=DELTA(J,I)**(1/(1-RHO(I)))*R(J)**(-1/(1-RHO(I)))/
   (GAMMA(I)*SUM(JJ, (DELTA(JJ,I)*R(JJ)**(-RHO(I)))**(1/(1-RHO(I))))**
   (1/RHO(I)));
INCOME..GDP=E=SUM(I, P(I)*Q(I));

MODEL HOSD /ALL/;
SOLVE HOSD USING NLP MAXIMIZING GDP;
```

The major changes come in the equations block. We drop the production functions, and replace them with the zero profit conditions (ZERO) from the previous section. We then adjust the resource constraints, replacing F(J,I) with A(J,I)*Q(I). Finally, the factor demand equations are replaced by the unit factor demands (UFDEMAND) from the previous section. The model is then defined and solved to check the benchmark equilibrium, which should be identical to that used in Chapter 5. You might want to try replicating the simulations you conducted with the model in chapter 5 with this model to verify that we are indeed representing the same economic system.

7.5 Exercises

(1) See if you can build a version of the model using Cobb–Douglas technology. You will have to begin by working out the form of the unit cost functions.

(2) By Euler's theorem, we can write the unit cost function (7.23) as $c = a_K r + a_L w$. Rewrite the GAMS code to take advantage of this expression. (You will be able to simplify the zero profit functions.)

(3) Try and construct a GAMS program that implements the specific factors model of Chapter 6 using the dual approach. The easiest way will be to directly implement the same kind of $ controls that we used in Chapter 6 into this model. Once you have it working, verify that the solutions are the same as those that you obtained in the exercises in the previous chapter.

7.6   Further Reading

An excellent example of the dual approach in action is the very influential paper by Jones (1965). The geometry of the dual version of the HOS model is covered in Mussa (1979). More advanced treatments of duality as it applies to international trade (with extensive discussion of cost functions and beyond) are Dixit and Norman (1980) and Woodland (1982).

Chapter 8

Transition

We have seen in Chapter 6 that we can think of the specific factors model as a model of a "short-run" economy, while the HOS model presented in Chapters 5 and 7 can be thought of as a representation of a long-run economy. In this chapter we consider the relationship between the two models, and in doing so introduce the concept of "looping" in GAMS programs.

8.1 Formal Problem

One way to think about the close relationship between the two models is to compare the underlying optimization problems. Consider the problem posed in Chapter 5, maximization of the value of output subject to the resource constraints and technology. Suppose we were to solve the problem for the optimal factor allocations. Now, suppose we added additional constraints such that the allocation of capital was fixed. The maximization problem would be equivalent to that examined in Chapter 6. But, if the technology and resources were the same and we fixed the capital allocation at the level determined by the solution to the long-run problem, the solution to the short-run problem would have to be the same. It wouldn't matter that capital was fixed since it would be at the optimal level anyway. In other words, every long-run equilibrium is, by definition, also a short-run equilibrium, although the converse is not true.

Another way of exploring the relationship between the models is to consider the incentives of capital in the short run. We have seen that changes in endowments or prices will generally have a differential impact on the prices of capital in the short run. For example, if the price of good 1 increases, the return to capital in sector 1 must rise, along with the wage, while the return to capital in sector 2 must fall. In the short run this can represent an equilibrium. But in the long run, if capital can earn a higher return in sector 1 than in sector 2, we would expect capital to shift from sector 2 to sector 1. We might hypothesize a series of transitional short-run equilibria in which small amounts of capital shift from one sector to the other. The process stabilizes when the incentive to shift capital disappears (i.e., when the returns to capital equalize across sectors).

Figure 8.1 illustrates the idea using the geometric approach of Neary (1978). In the top half we replicate Figure 6.1, while in the bottom half we replicate Figure 5.1. The economy is in both a short and long-run equilibrium at w^*, L_1^*, K_1^*, and so on, with the specific factors at the level generated by the solution to the long-run problem. With an increase in the price of good 1, the VMPL curve for good 1 shifts upward. There is an increase in the wage and the return to capital in sector 1, and a decline in the return to the capital in sector 2. In the short run, capital is fixed, and we move off the efficiency locus to L_1'. Now, as argued above, capital shifts to sector 1. The VMPL for good 2 will shift down as it loses capital, and the VMPL for good 1 will rise. At the same time, labor is released. Since good 2 is labor-intensive (as drawn) the VMPL for good 2 shifts further to the right than the VMPL for good 1 does. As the process continues, the economy moves along the dotted transition path to the final solution at w'', L_1'' and K_2'', back on the efficiency locus and again at long-run equilibrium. At this point, the wage has fallen and the return to capital has risen (to see this consider the factor intensities in each industry at the new solution).

Other scenarios can be analyzed similarly, and we can use the "looping" features of GAMS to explore the possibilities efficiently.

8.2   GAMS Implementation

To set up a program to examine the transition dynamics of the specific factors model we will use the base model we developed in Chapter 6, and append some new code (in Table 8.1) to the end of the file. The first line of the new code simply introduces a shock to the model. We increase the price of good 1 by 5 percent, and then solve the model. This will generate a new *short-run* solution. It is important to note that whenever we solve the model, by default GAMS will retain the solutions to the model in the levels for the variables. Hence, for example, we may start by defining a level for the return to labor using statement like R.L('L')=R0, where R0=1. If we subsequently shock and solve the model for a new equilibrium, R.L('L')

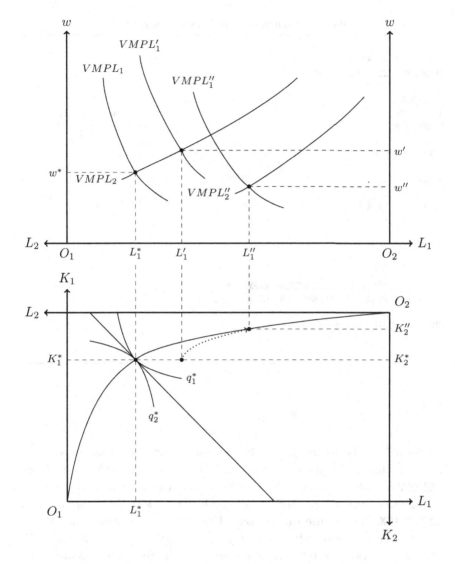

Fig. 8.1 Transition From the Short to Long-Run Equilibrium.

will contain the new value from the solution, and we can use it in subsequent calculations if we wish, just as if it were any other value.

Our hypothesis is that capital will move across sectors until the returns are equalized. Of course, we could check this manually, shifting the capital stock a little at a time and re-solving the model until we observe

Table 8.1   Modifications for Transition Simulation.

```
P('1')=P('1')*1.05;
SOLVE SF USING NLP MAXIMIZING GDP;

PARAMETERS
TOLERANCE                                   Control on the accuracy
DIRECTION                                   Direction of capital flow;

TOLERANCE=0.01;

WHILE(ABS(R.L('N')-R.L('K')) > TOLERANCE,

IF (R.L('N')>R.L('K')),
DIRECTION = -1;
ELSE
DIRECTION = 1;
);

FBAR('N')=FBAR('N')-(DIRECTION*TOLERANCE);
FBAR('K')=FBAR('K')+(DIRECTION*TOLERANCE);

SOLVE SF USING NLP MAXIMIZING GDP;
);
```

equalization. Fortunately, GAMS can make our lives a lot easier. To see how this works, let us define two new parameters. One we will call **TOLERANCE**, which we use to determine when our transition process is close enough to complete that we can stop running the model. The other is called **DIRECTION**. We will use this to control the direction in which capital will move (from the lower return industry to the higher return industry). We choose a tolerance of 0.01. In other words, if the return to capital across the two sectors is within 0.01, we regard them as equalized. We can make the tolerance as small as we like, at the cost of taking a longer time to solve the problem.

The next part of the program is new. We have introduced a loop, which will enable us to solve the model many times automatically. GAMS has several different ways of accomplishing this. We have used the **WHILE** command, which loops over the **SOLVE** command until a condition is met.

For a set number of solutions the FOR and LOOP commands can be used in a similar manner.[1] Let us look at the statement in detail:

```
WHILE(ABS(R.L('N')-R.L('K')) > TOLERANCE,
  :
);
```

The syntax begins with the keyword WHILE and then an open bracket (. Next we have a condition, followed by a comma, then a series of commands for GAMS to repeat. Any commands can be within the loop except definitions. The construct is completed with the closing bracket, and a semicolon. In words, the statement tells GAMS to keep on repeating the actions specified within the loop (between the comma and the closing bracket) until the condition is satisfied. In this case, our condition is capital-market clearing. The return to capital in both sectors should be the same (within tolerance). ABS is the GAMS function for absolute value.

Now let us consider the commands that we have placed within the loop, since these introduce some new GAMS features too. The first set of commands illustrates the use of an IF...THEN...ELSE command, which is used for logical branching.

```
IF (R.L('N')>R.L('K'),
DIRECTION = -1;
ELSE
DIRECTION = 1;
);
```

The syntax is similar to the WHILE command. We begin with the keyword IF followed by an open bracket, then a logical condition, then a comma. If the condition is satisfied, the next line is executed. The optional ELSE tells GAMS what to do if the condition is not satisfied (the default is nothing). A closing bracket and semicolon complete the statement. In words, the code says that if the return to capital is greater in sector 2 than in sector 1,

---

[1] The FOR command is used to loop over a defined range, in equal steps, so it is useful in such contexts as evaluating model sensitivity to parameters. The LOOP command is used to loop over the elements of a set. For example, the FOR command could be used to calculate the equilibrium for a range of labor endowments. The LOOP command could be used to make a change for each factor separately, e.g., increase the endowment of capital, then labor. Both have a very similar syntax to the WHILE statement. For further details, see exercises 4 and 5 at the end of the chapter.

set the direction of movement of capital to out of sector 1. If it is less than sector 1, set the direction of movement of capital to into sector 1.

The next set of instructions in Table 8.1 is straightforward. They shift a small amount of capital (equal to the value of the TOLERANCE parameter) into/out of sector 2, and a corresponding small amount of capital out of/into sector 1, then solve for the new equilibrium. The whole process repeats until the capital market clearing condition is satisfied.

When you run the model, you will find that GAMS will solve the model repeatedly. The list file should show the results of each SOLVE statement, in the order in which it was completed. If you scroll to the bottom of the list file you will find the final solution (after the transition process). To consider the transition process for any other change in the economy, you can alter the shock introduced in the first line of the code in Table 8.1.

8.3   Exercises

(1) Using the HOS model from chapter 5, run a scenario where the price of good 1 increases by 5 percent. Observe the equilibrium carefully. Now run the same scenario using the specific factors model from chapter 6. How do the solutions differ? What are the changes in rental rates in the two models?

(2) Now consider the same scenario in the specific factors model with the transition module added. Run the model and compare the final solution to your results from the HOS model. What does the outcome tell you?

(3) Consider the same process for an increase in the amount of labor in the economic system, and an increase in the amount of capital (be careful, the endowment in the HOS model refers to all the capital in the system, which is the sum of the capital used in the two sectors in the specific factors model). What happens? What are your conclusions on the relationship between the HOS model and the specific factors model under this type of transition dynamics?

(4) In this chapter we introduced the WHILE command, which can be used to repeat a series of GAMS statements until a condition is met. A similar command is FOR. Try adding the following line of code to the end of the model from Chapter 6: FOR(H = 100 TO 150 BY 10, FBAR('L')=H; SOLVE SF USING NLP MAXIMIZING GDP;);. This will solve the model repeatedly for values of the labor stock between 100 and 150, in increments of ten. Try the same technique for solving for equilibria with a range of capital, or prices, technology, etc.

(5) Another program control device is the `LOOP` command, which repeats a series of GAMS statements for each element of a set.
Try adding the following code to the end of the model from
chapter 6: `LOOP(I, GAMMA(I)=GAMMA(I)*1.1; SOLVE SF USING NLP
MAXIMIZING GDP;);`. This will show the effect of an improvement in
technology first in sector 1, then in both sector 1 and sector 2. Now
that you have seen how this works, try using a `LOOP` to sequentially
change prices, or endowments.

8.4 Further Reading

The relationship between the short and long-run equilibria is examined by
Mayer (1974), and in Neary (1978), which focuses more on factor markets.
A recent paper by Gilbert and Oladi (2008) shows how the geometry developed by Neary is related to the geometry used by Mayer, in addition to
linking the geometry of the production possibilities in the long and short
run.

Chapter 9

Higher Dimensions

The HOS production model has two goods and two factors of production. Hence, it is often called the 2×2 model of trade theory. The specific factors model is sometimes called the 2×3 model. Both are special cases of a more general class of problems that are typically called "higher dimensional" models, which we consider in further detail in this chapter.

The 2×2 model is rather unique in terms of the strength of its predictions. These are inevitably weakened in the context of higher dimensions. Nonetheless, we can continue to maintain much of the flavor of the results from our earlier analysis, under certain conditions. As we shall see, the effort that we put into programming earlier models using a set-oriented approach pays great dividends when increasing the dimensionality of the models.

9.1 Formal Problem

The maximization problem remains essentially the same as that used in Chapters 5 and 6; we simply express it with more generality. Consider an economy in which n goods are (potentially) produced under competition at some given set of goods prices, using m factors of production competitively supplied in fixed quantities. We continue to assume that the production functions exhibit the usual properties, including constant returns to scale. Let the set of all goods be $\mathbf{I}$ with elements indexed by i, and the set of all factors be $\mathbf{J}$ with elements indexed by j. The Lagrangian for the GDP maximization problem can then be written:

$$\mathscr{L} = \sum_{\forall i \in \mathbf{I}} p_i q_i(\mathbf{V_i}) + \sum_{\forall j \in \mathbf{J}} \lambda_j \left[V_j - \sum_{\forall i \in \mathbf{I}} v_{ji} \right] \tag{9.1}$$

where $\mathbf{V_i}$ is the vector of inputs v_{ji} to sector i, and V_j is the endowment of factor j.[1] Not all factors are necessarily inputs in any given sector, but at least one input in each sector i must be non-zero if $q_i > 0$. The multipliers λ_j again represent the shadow values of the factors of production, and will be interpreted as factor prices under competition. Differentiating the Lagrangian with respect to each v_{ji} and the multipliers yields the first-order conditions:

$$p_i \frac{\partial q_i}{\partial v_{ji}} - \lambda_j \leq 0 \quad \text{with equality if} \quad v_{ji} > 0 \qquad \forall i \in \mathbf{I}, \forall j \in \mathbf{J} \qquad (9.2)$$

$$V_j - \sum_{\forall i \in \mathbf{I}} v_{ji} = 0 \qquad \forall j \in \mathbf{J}. \qquad (9.3)$$

The solution to this set of conditions is the optimal factor demands for each industry, and the factor prices (multipliers). Notice that we have explicitly used the inequality form of the first order conditions. The reason is twofold. First, some factors may not be used by some industries, in which case the value of the marginal product of the factor in that industry must be less than (or at most equal to) its price. Second, for arbitrarily given goods prices, in general the number of products produced in equilibrium must be less than or equal to the number of factors (see Samuelson, 1953). Hence, for example, although we may specify an equilibrium in which three goods are produced with two (mobile) factors, it is rather special, and a small movement in goods prices will lead to one good ceasing to be produced. For cases where the number of factors is equal to the number of goods, the factor prices are independent of factor endowments, as in the HOS model. For cases where the number of factors is greater than the number of goods, the factor prices will depend on factor endowments, as in the specific factors model.[2]

---

[1] We follow Dixit and Norman (1980) in using V's instead of F's to represent factors.

[2] The nature of the problem is perhaps most easily seen using the dual. Let the number of factors be m and the number of goods n. Now let $\mathbf{A}$ be an $n \times m$ matrix of the optimal unit factor demands, $\mathbf{R}$ be an m-dimensional vector of factor prices, $\mathbf{P}$ be an n-dimensional vector of goods prices, $\mathbf{Q}$ be an n-dimensional vector of outputs, and $\mathbf{V}$ be an m-dimensional vector of endowments. The first order conditions can then be written compactly as $\mathbf{AR} = \mathbf{P}$ and $\mathbf{A^T Q} = \mathbf{V}$. Since $\mathbf{A}$ is a function of $\mathbf{R}$, this represents a set of $n + m$ equations to determine $n + m$ variables, the factor prices and the outputs. Notice that we have n equations in the factor prices, and m equations in outputs. If it so happens that $m = n$, as in the HOS model, the first equations will neatly form an independent block, i.e., we can solve for factor prices independent of endowments. If, however, $m > n$, the zero profit conditions alone cannot determine the factor prices, and the resource constraints are needed too (as in the specific factors model). The case where $n > m$ is more problematic. It appears on the surface that we have enough equations to

9.2 GAMS Implementation

Because of the set based structure of GAMS, implementing higher dimensional models is quite straightforward in principle. We can take the model of Chapter 6, and simply extend the dimensions of the underlying sets, and provide an appropriate set of initial data.[3]

The program we use is presented in Table 9.1, and follows a similar structure to previous examples. We concentrate our discussion on the new features. The first change we make is to the dimensions of the sets. For a 3×3 model the set of goods becomes $i = \{1, 2, 3\}$, and the set of factors $j = \{K, L, N\}$. Next we introduce a new GAMS programming idea, the use of subsets. The following line contains the relevant code:

```
SET H(J) /K,L/;
```

If the set J has already been defined, this expression tells GAMS to create another set H that is a subset of J containing the elements K and L (which must be elements of J). We could, of course, simply create another set labeled H without telling GAMS that it is a subset of J by using the command SET H /K,L/;, but declaring as a subset has a couple of advantages. First, GAMS will check that the elements of H correspond to elements of J, thus helping to catch errors. Second, we can now use H anywhere we would otherwise have used J, but apply the operation only to the subset. The benefit of this will become clear soon.

The next section declares the parameter names, and is the same as in Chapter 6. For assigning values to the parameters, we again use a calibration approach, starting with assigning values to the factor demands, prices and output, and calculating the remaining values from the model relationships. When we have higher dimensions of data to input, the line-by-line

---

solve the system, but of the n zero profit conditions, only m can be independent. One way to think about this is that when there are two factors if two isoprice curves intersect at a particular point, thereby determining a pair of factor prices, the isoprice curves of all other goods must intersect the same point if the goods are all to be produced at equilibrium.

[3]We use the model of Chapter 6 rather than chapter 5 because the exception handling that we used to implement the specific factors model allows us to have a more general factor allocation pattern, including allowing some factors not to be employed in some sectors if we wish. As an exercise, you might want to verify that for the same sets and data, the two models are identical.

Table 9.1   GAMS Program for Higher Dimensions.

```
SET I Goods /1,2,3/;
SET J Factors /K,L,N/;
SET H(J) /K,L/;
ALIAS (J, JJ);

PARAMETERS
GAMMA(I)                      Shift parameters in production
DELTA(J,I)                    Share parameters in production
RHO(I)                        Elasticity parameters in production
P(I)                          Output prices
FBAR(J)                       Endowments
QO(I)                         Initial output levels
RO(J)                         Initial factor prices
GDPO                          Initial gross domestic product;

TABLE FO(J,I)                 Initial factor use levels
   1  2   3
L 20  80  10
K 80  20  15;

P(I)=1;
RO(J)=1;
QO(I)=150;
FO('N',I)=(QO(I)*P(I)-SUM(H, FO(H,I)*RO(H)))/RO('N');
FBAR(J)=SUM(I, FO(J,I));
GDPO=SUM(I, P(I)*QO(I));
RHO(I)=0.1;
DELTA(J,I)$FO(J,I)=(RO(J)/FO(J,I)**(RHO(I)-1))/(SUM(JJ$FO(JJ,I), RO(JJ)
   /FO(JJ,I)**(RHO(I)-1)));
GAMMA(I)=QO(I)/(SUM(J$FO(J,I), DELTA(J,I)*FO(J,I)**RHO(I)))**(1/RHO(I));
```

---

continued on next page

approach can become tedious. An alternative is to use the TABLE command. This defines and assigns data in one step, and allows a convenient tabular representation. We use the command to set the initial values of the factor demands:

```
TABLE FO(J,I) Initial factor use levels
            1   2    3
L          20  80   10
K          80  20   15;
```

continued from previous page

```
VARIABLES Q(I)      Output levels
R(J)                Factor prices
F(J,I)              Factor use levels
GDP                 Gross domestic product;

Q.L(I)=QO(I);
R.L(J)=RO(J);
F.L(J,I)=FO(J,I);
GDP.L=GDPO;
Q.LO(I)=0;
R.LO(J)=0;
F.LO(J,I)=0;

EQUATIONS
PRODUCTION(I)       Production functions
RESOURCE(J)         Resource constraints
FDEMAND(J,I)        Factor demand functions
INCOME              Gross domestic product;

PRODUCTION(I)..Q(I)=E=GAMMA(I)*SUM(J$FO(J,I), DELTA(J,I)*F(J,I)**RHO(I))**
  (1/RHO(I));
RESOURCE(J)..FBAR(J)=E=SUM(I, F(J,I));
FDEMAND(J,I)$FO(J,I)..R(J)=E=P(I)*Q(I)*SUM(JJ$FO(JJ,I), DELTA(JJ,I)*F(JJ,I)**
  RHO(I))**(-1)*DELTA(J,I)*F(J,I)**(RHO(I)-1);
INCOME..GDP=E=SUM(I, P(I)*Q(I));

MODEL HD /ALL/;
SOLVE HD USING NLP MAXIMIZING GDP;
```

The keyword is **TABLE**, followed by a two-dimensional parameter, and optional description. On the next line we have column labels for the elements of one dimension (here the goods), then rows for each element of the other dimension (here the factors). The data must be aligned in the correct column. Note that we do not provide values for N in the table. The reason is that we want to calibrate these to ensure that the model balances, as before. The relevant line in the calibration is:

```
FO('N',I)=(QO(I)*P(I)-SUM(H, FO(H,I)*RO(H)))/RO('N');
```

The expression is very similar to that used in Chapters 5 and 6. Here we also see the use of the subset H, which we use to define the index of summation in the numerator. The statement says that the factor use of N in each sector is equal to the value of output, less the sum of the cost of all other inputs, divided by the price of N.

The remainder of the program is the same as in Chapter 6. Once you have verified the initial equilibrium, try some of the exercises below to get a feel for the behavior of the model.

The program we have built in this chapter features three goods and three factors of production. As we noted in Section 9.1, when the number of goods exceeds the number of factors, small changes in the exogenous goods price vector will generally lead to production of some goods being unprofitable, and an equilibrium in which there are only as many goods as there are factors being produced. In other words, a corner solution. Try removing N from the set of factors and removing the line calibrating its value. You also need to change the initial inputs of K and L into good 3 to sum to 100 because of product exhaustion. If you run the model it will solve as before. But now try a scenario where the price of, say, good 1 increases by 10 percent. What happens? The model will fail to solve, with GAMS reporting it as infeasible.

The problem is that we have set the model up under the assumption that the solution is interior, but under the conditions we have posed it is in fact at a corner, and some of the conditions cannot hold. While a complete discussion of the intricacies of dealing with this type of problem is beyond the scope of this book, and most of the models we will deal with will be characterized by interior solutions, it is relatively easy to alter the program so that it will handle corner solutions gracefully. One way to do so is to ask GAMS to solve the nonlinear programming problem directly, specifying only the objective (as an equality) and the constraints (as inequalities), and allowing GAMS to determine the marginal conditions itself.

Hence, in this case, we delete the factor demand equations from the model, and replace the production function and resource constraints by their inequality versions. So the equation block becomes:

```
PRODUCTION(I)..Q(I)=L=GAMMA(I)*SUM(J$FO(J,I), DELTA(J,I)*
    F(J,I)**RHO(I))**(1/RHO(I));
RESOURCE(J)..SUM(I, F(J,I))=L=FBAR(J);
INCOME..GDP=E=SUM(I, P(I)*Q(I));
```

Note the use of =L= instead of =E= in the constraints. The term =L= means "less than or equal to," and =G= means "greater than or equal to." In the production function this means that the right hand side is the maximum quantity that can be produced given the technology. Similarly, in the resource constraint **FBAR** is the maximum amount that can be employed in production. Note also that we have switched **FBAR** to the right hand side. We could, of course, keep it on the left and replace the =L= with =G=, but this is somewhat cleaner (why?).

We retain the lower bounds set by the line **F.LO(J,I)=0**, etc., and in fact with the inequality version of the model the lower bounds are crucial. They are not only reducing the solution space over which GAMS will search, but they are in fact (potentially) determining the solution if the optimum is at a corner.

If you run the model, GAMS will solve for the factor demands, outputs and GDP as before. Moreover, if you impose a price shock, the model will continue to solve, and GAMS will find a corner solution (i.e., production of one good will cease). One difference is that because we do not have equations/variables for factor prices GAMS does not report them. Nonetheless, we can still obtain them easily since they will be the multipliers on the resource constraints. These are reported in the listing file as the "marginal" values of the resource equations. To find them, look for a section of the listing file like:

```
---- EQU RESOURCE Resource constraints
                 LOWER LEVEL UPPER MARGINAL
K                -INF  150.0 150.0 0.9418
L                -INF  150.0 150.0 1.2762
```

The numbers under the heading **MARGINAL** are the shadow values of the constraints, which in this context are the competitive factor prices. Note also that the marginal values on the production functions are the goods prices, as we would expect.

9.3 Exercises

(1) See if you can extend the program to a 4×4 model.
(2) In higher dimensional models, a good is called a "friend" of a factor if an increase in the price of the good alone causes an even larger proportional increase in the price of that factor so that the real return to that factor is necessarily increased. Using the 3×3 model, can you identify which goods are friends of which factors?
(3) Similarly, a good is an enemy of a factor if an increase in the price of

the good alone causes a fall in the price of that factor, so that the real return to that factor is necessarily decreased.[4] Using the 3 × 3 model, identify which goods are enemies of which factors.

(4) A factor is called a "friend" of a good if an increase in the endowment of the factor alone results in an even larger proportional increase in the production of the good, while it is an "enemy" if it causes a reduction. Using the 3 × 3 model, identify which factors are friends/enemies of which goods.

(5) Try setting up the model so that three goods are produced using just two factors. Can you generate an initial solution? What happens when you change prices a little bit in either direction? Does the intuition of the Stolper-Samuelson theorem continue to apply? In what sense?

(6) Can you implement a higher dimensional version of the model using the dual approach discussed in Chapter 7?

(7) Using the version of the model that allows for corner solutions, simulate a price rise that leaves only good 1 and 2 produced. How does the outcome compare to the same set of prices in a model in which only good 1 and 2 exist initially?

(8) When the price of a good rises with more goods than factors, is it possible that the good which has seen its price rise is the one that disappears? Why or why not?

(9) We have seen that in general the number of goods produced is no more than the number of factors. Under what circumstances would it be less? Can you construct a simulation to illustrate?

9.4   Further Reading

The classic treatment of the case of more goods than factors is Samuelson (1953). More on the basic theory of international trade with many goods and factors can be found in Ethier (1974), while the generalizations of the Stolper–Samuelson and Rybczynski theorems to higher dimensions are discussed in Jones and Scheinkman (1977).

---

[4]Deardorff's "Glossary of International Economics" (2010) provides useful definitions of terms such as these, which are used in international economics.

Chapter 10

Intermediate Inputs

Up until now we have assumed that production uses only primary factors of production (capital, labor and so on). Many production processes, however, make use of not only primary factors, but also goods produced by other industries, or intermediate inputs, such as steel, concrete, etc. In fact, a large fraction of both domestic transactions and international trade are in intermediate rather than final goods, so as we move toward building models that are more suitable for representing actual economies, it is important to introduce this feature. In this chapter we consider how our basic general equilibrium models of production can be modified to incorporate intermediates, and address some of the issues that arise with choice of functional form.

10.1 Formal Problem

The basics of the problem can be seen by reconsidering the cost minimization problem of Chapter 4, this time introducing a single intermediate input. Suppose we are interested in industry 1, which produces a good q_1 using capital and labor, along with intermediate good 2. The production function exhibits the standard properties. The Lagrangian for the industry's cost minimization problem is:

$$\mathscr{L} = rK_1 + wL_1 + p_2q_{21} + \lambda[\bar{q}_1 - q_1(K_1, L_1, q_{21})]. \qquad (10.1)$$

We use the notation q_{21} to denote purchases of good 2 by industry 1. In this case λ is again marginal cost. Differentiating the Lagrangian with respect to the input choices and the multiplier yields the first order conditions for a minimum:

$$\partial\mathscr{L}/\partial K_1 = r - \lambda\partial q_1/\partial K_1 = 0 \qquad (10.2)$$

$$\partial \mathscr{L} / \partial L_1 = w - \lambda \partial q_1 / \partial L_1 = 0 \tag{10.3}$$

$$\partial \mathscr{L} / \partial q_{21} = p_2 - \lambda \partial q_1 / \partial q_{21} = 0 \tag{10.4}$$

$$\partial \mathscr{L} / \partial \lambda = \bar{q}_1 - q_1(K_1, L_1, q_{21}) = 0. \tag{10.5}$$

The fourth condition repeats the constraint, meaning that an optimal choice must achieve the output objective. The first three conditions look familiar. They state that for each input to the production process, whether a primary factor or an intermediate input, the price paid is equal to the value of the marginal product (again assuming an interior solution for simplicity). Solving the four equations yields the optimal factor demands K_1^*, L_1^* and the optimal intermediate good demand q_{21}^*, all as functions of the desired output level and the prices of all inputs. Hence, as we can see, the introduction of intermediate inputs does not change the basic model of the firm in any fundamental way.

Now consider a model of a complete production economy with intermediates. For simplicity we take the case of only one factor of production (labor) and one intermediate good in each sector, but the extensions should be obvious. As in Chapters 5 and 6, the problem can be viewed as one of maximizing GDP subject to the constraints posed by technology and resources. The Lagrangian is:

$$\mathscr{L} = p_1[q_1(L_1, q_{21}) - q_{12}] + p_2[q_2(L_2, q_{12}) - q_{21}] + \lambda[\bar{L} - L_1 - L_2]. \tag{10.6}$$

Note that we are now maximizing the total value of *net* industrial outputs, i.e., value added, to avoid double-counting.[1] Taking the derivatives of the Lagrangian with respect to the inputs (both factors and intermediates) and the multipliers we have the following first order conditions:

$$\partial \mathscr{L} / \partial L_1 = p_1 \partial q_1 / \partial L_1 - \lambda \leq 0 \quad \text{with equality if} \quad L_1 > 0 \tag{10.7}$$

$$\partial \mathscr{L} / \partial L_2 = p_2 \partial q_2 / \partial L_2 - \lambda \leq 0 \quad \text{with equality if} \quad L_2 > 0 \tag{10.8}$$

$$\partial \mathscr{L} / \partial q_{21} = p_1 \partial q_1 / \partial q_{21} - p_2 \leq 0 \quad \text{with equality if} \quad q_{21} > 0 \tag{10.9}$$

$$\partial \mathscr{L} / \partial q_{12} = p_2 \partial q_2 / \partial q_{12} - p_1 \leq 0 \quad \text{with equality if} \quad q_{12} > 0 \tag{10.10}$$

$$\partial \mathscr{L} / \partial \lambda = \bar{L} - L_1 - L_2 = 0. \tag{10.11}$$

Note that we have used the inequality form of the first order conditions, as in Chapter 9. Samuelson (1951) has shown that the production possibilities frontier for this model is linear, so in general a corner solution is likely (we have more goods than factors). We interpret the multiplier, λ, as the

---

[1]Value added must be positive, implying that each industry's intermediate usage cannot exceed production.

shadow value of labor, i.e., the wage. The key point should be clear, however: introducing intermediate goods does not change the basic structure of the model of production.

10.2 Nested Functional Forms

In fact then, the main issue in implementing intermediate goods in numerical models of production and trade relates not to the basic economics of the problem, but rather to the choice of functional form for the production function.

Since we have argued that intermediate inputs are not fundamentally different from primary factors, one possibility would be to simply use Cobb–Douglas or CES, as we have been doing so far. While this is possible, and relatively simple, in most CGE models this approach is not adopted. The reason lies in the relatively restrictive assumptions of the CES form, of which Cobb–Douglas is a special case. In particular, this functional form assumes a common elasticity of substitution across inputs, implying that capital and labor are as substitutable with each other as, say, labor is with steel. This seems unlikely to be the case in practice. As a result it is common to use a 'nested' functional form.[2] Figure 10.1 illustrates the idea.

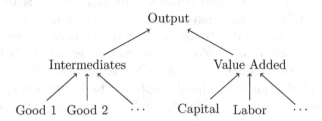

Fig. 10.1 Nested Production Structure.

We think of primary factors (capital, labor, etc.) as being combined into a composite that we call the value-added composite. Similarly, we think of the intermediate goods that the firm uses as being combined into a composite that we call the intermediates composite. For short we will

---

[2]As we shall see, this type of nested structure is also seen in the modeling of joint production and for incorporating love of variety into demand, so it is very useful to get a good feel for how it works.

refer to these two composites as intermediates and value added. Finally, intermediates and value added are combined to form output.

Most commonly, the intermediate branches are combined using a Leontief (min) function, while the primary factor branches are combined using a CES function of the type that we have been using. Value added and aggregate intermediates are then usually combined with another Leontief function. Because the Leontief function implies fixed proportions, this specification imposes the restriction that intermediate goods are not substitutable with each other, nor with value added overall.

Alternatively, we could use CES functions at each level, one for intermediates, one for value added, and one to combine the two. This would allow us to specify three different elasticities governing substitution possibilities. Obviously a single-level function is just a special case, where all of the elasticities take a common value. We call the case where each intermediate good is combined in fixed proportions to produce output the *fixed proportions* specification. We call the case where this does not hold the *variable proportions* specification.[3] In the following sections we look at these two specifications in more detail.

10.3   Fixed Proportions Case

Let's consider now a two good economy, with two primary factors. Each final good can be used as an intermediate good in each industry, including its own. Prices are fixed. We assume that the technology governing the relationship between value added and intermediate good usage is Leontief. Since the Leontief function is not differentiable, the marginal analysis that we have applied so far is not directly applicable to the use of intermediates in this case, although it remains applicable to the components of value added.[4]

The key to incorporating intermediate use of this form is to recognize that in each sector each intermediate good must be used in a fixed proportion to output, irrespective of relative prices, and similarly, that the use of the intermediate composite must be in fixed proportion to value added,

---

[3]By adding more levels to the nesting, it is even possible to allow for different substitution possibilities among different factors and/or intermediates. For example, steel might be substituted easily with aluminum in some applications, but not so easily with concrete.

[4]We may, however, approximate the Leontief case using continuous functions. See exercise 2 below.

again, independent of prices.

We consider only industry 1; the analysis of the other industry is the same. With fixed proportions and two intermediate inputs, the production function is $q_1 = \min(V_1, q_{11}, q_{21})$, where V_1 is the value added composite, q_{11} is the quantity of good 1 used as an intermediate in production, and q_{21} is the quantity of good 2 used in production.

Let the quantity of good 1 used in the production of each unit of good 1 be defined as a_{11}, so $a_{11} = q_{11}/q_1$. Similarly, let the quantity of good 2 used per unit of output of good 1 be a_{21}. These are the input-output coefficients, and we can think of them as unit intermediate demands. Unlike the unit factor demands we saw in Chapter 7, however, these are constants. Similarly, let the unit demand for the value added composite be $a_{V1} = V_1/q_1$. Again, this is a constant.

For convenience, let's normalize the initial prices of all goods, including the initial price of the value added composite, which we denote p_1^V, to unity.[5] With this normalization, $a_{V1} + a_{11} + a_{12} = 1$. It must be that each unit demand is less than one, since otherwise production could not be economically justified. Moreover, $a_{V1} = 1 - a_{11} - a_{12}$. To see this, note from product exhaustion that:

$$V_1 = q_1 - q_{11} - q_{21} \tag{10.12}$$

when all prices are normalized to one. We have $q_{11} = a_{11}q_1$ and $q_{21} = a_{21}q_1$, and substituting these into (10.12), we have:

$$V_1 = [1 - a_{11} - a_{21}]q_1. \tag{10.13}$$

Next, we define the value added composite in industry 1 using a CES function, using exactly the same form as the ordinary production function we have used in previous chapters:

$$V_1 = \gamma_1[\delta_1 K_1^{\rho_1} + (1 - \delta_1)L_1^{\rho_1}]^{1/\rho_1}. \tag{10.14}$$

Finally, combining (10.13) and (10.14), we have the production function:

$$q_1 = \gamma_1[\delta_1 K_1^{\rho_1} + (1 - \delta_1)L_1^{\rho_1}]^{1/\rho_1}(1 - a_{11} - a_{21})^{-1}. \tag{10.15}$$

Now that we have the production function, we need to derive the demands for intermediate inputs and factors of production. For intermediates, which do not depend on relative prices, we already have them: $q_{11} = a_{11}q_1$ and $q_{21} = a_{21}q_1$. For factors, the factor price must be equal to the value of the marginal product. The marginal products of each factor are obtained by

---

[5]In fact, we have been using this convenient normalization in all of our numerical examples.

taking the partial derivatives of the production function, as usual. However, we need to be careful about converting them to a value. For each unit of output, there must be a proportional purchase of each intermediate good, at market prices. The payment available to value added must therefore be net of the cost of intermediates (again, this is really just a matter of product exhaustion, the value of output must be fully absorbed by the payments to all inputs in the production process). Hence, we define net prices as:

$$p_1^N = p_1 - p_1 a_{11} - p_2 a_{21}. \tag{10.16}$$

This is what the firm has available with which to buy the value added composite, and is the price we need to use when calculating the value of marginal products. Hence, for capital the demand function is $r = p_1^N(\partial q_1/\partial K_1)$, which we rewrite using (10.15) as:

$$r = p_1^N q_1 [\delta_1 K_1^{\rho_1} + (1 - \delta_1) L_1^{\rho_1}]^{-1} \delta_1 K_1^{\rho_1 - 1}. \tag{10.17}$$

At an optimal choice, the net price must be equal to the cost of purchasing the amount of the value-added composite that is required to produce one unit of output. Since we have defined this amount as $1 - a_{11} - a_{21}$, it follows that the price of the value added composite must be $p_1^V = p_1^N/[1 - a_{11} - a_{21}]$. Consequently, $p_1^N q_1 = p_1^V V_1$, so alternatively we can derive (10.17) as $r = p_1^V(\partial V_1/\partial K_1)$, i.e. the payment to capital is equal to the price of the value added composite multiplied by the increment to the composite per increment in capital. The demand for labor follows similarly; we leave it to you as an exercise.

As in previous examples, before implementing the problem in GAMS it is convenient to express the problem in terms of the underlying sets rather than scalars. Let the set of factors be $\mathbf{J} = \{K, L\}$ and the set of industries be $\mathbf{I} = \{1, 2\}$. The demand for factor j in industry i is F_{ji}. The production function can then be written:

$$q_i = \frac{\gamma_i}{1 - \sum_{\forall h \in \mathbf{I}} a_{hi}} \left[\sum_{\forall j \in \mathbf{J}} \delta_{ji} F_{ji}^{\rho_i} \right]^{\frac{1}{\rho_i}} \qquad \forall i \in \mathbf{I}.$$

The net price equation is:

$$p_i^N = p_i - \sum_{\forall h \in \mathbf{I}} p_h a_{hi} \qquad \forall i \in \mathbf{I}$$

and the factor demand equations are:

$$r_j = p_i^N q_i \left[\sum_{\forall k \in \mathbf{J}} \delta_{ki} F_{ki}^{\rho_i} \right]^{-1} \delta_{ji} F_{ji}^{\rho_i - 1} \qquad \forall j \in \mathbf{J}, \forall i \in \mathbf{I}.$$

There is very little that is different here relative to the models of production that we have already developed without intermediates. We just need to define the intermediate usage in each industry and the per unit demands, adjust the production function to incorporate the intermediates, add a new equation to calculate net prices (along with the associated variable), adjust the factor demands to use the net price, and redefine GDP as the value of net rather than gross output.

The completed program, which is based on the model used in Chapter 6, is presented in Table 10.1. Comparing the code with the code used in Chapter 6, the first difference is the introduction of an **ALIAS** for the set of goods, since we will need to sum over goods in both the production and net price equations. Next, in the **PARAMETERS** section, we introduce new parameter names for initial net prices (**PNO**), the input-output coefficients (**A**) and the initial intermediate use (**INTO**). The latter is defined and assigned values using the **TABLE** command that we introduced in Chapter 9.

Next we calibrate the input-output coefficients and the initial net price, using the definitions above. We then use product exhaustion to determine the value of one input in each sector. Note that we need to adjust the calibration to incorporate payments to intermediates. There are two other changes in the calibration section of the model. First, we have defined **GDP** in terms of payments to primary factors (which in each sector must equal the price of value added multiplied by the value added composite). Second, we adjust the equation calibrating **GAMMA** to account for the new structure of the production function.

In the **VARIABLES** section we add a new variable **PN**, the net price. We then assign a level and lower bound as with all other variables. In the **EQUATIONS** section we add a new equation **NET_PRICE**, adjust the definition of production to incorporate intermediates, and the factor demands to use the net price. We now have a fully scalable model of production that incorporates intermediate goods.

10.4 Variable Proportions Case

The preceding example makes some quite strict technological assumptions, which are relaxed in the variable proportions case. Let's again start out with a two good economy, with two primary factors and prices given. Again, each final good can be used as an intermediate good in each industry, but now we allow for the possibility that value added might substitute for intermediates, and that intermediates might be substituted among each other. Suppose that production of good 1 is described by the function:

Table 10.1   GAMS Program for Intermediates (Fixed Proportions).

```
SET I Goods /1,2/;
SET J Factors /K,L,N/;
ALIAS (J, JJ);
ALIAS (I, II);

PARAMETERS
GAMMA(I)                      Shift parameters in production
DELTA(J,I)                    Share parameters in production
RHO(I)                        Elasticity parameters in production
P(I)                          Output prices
PNO(I)                        Initial net prices
FBAR(J)                       Endowments
QO(I)                         Initial output levels
RO(J)                         Initial factor prices
FO(J,I)                       Initial factor use levels
A(II,I)                       Input-output coefficients
GDPO                          Initial gross domestic product;

TABLE INTO(II,I)              Initial intermediate use levels
   1  2
1 40 10
2 10 40 ;

P(I)=1;
RO(J)=1;
QO(I)=150;
FO('L','1')=20;
FO('L','2')=80;

A(II,I)=INTO(II,I)/QO(I);
PNO(I)=P(I)-SUM(II, P(II)*A(II,I));
FO('K','1')=(QO('1')*P('1')-FO('L','1')*RO('L')-SUM(II,INTO(II,'1')*P(II)))
  /RO('K');
FO('N','2')=(QO('2')*P('2')-FO('L','2')*RO('L')-SUM(II,INTO(II,'2')*P(II)))
  /RO('N');
FBAR(J)=SUM(I, FO(J,I));
GDPO=SUM(J, RO(J)*FBAR(J));
RHO(I)=0.1;
DELTA(J,I)$FO(J,I)=(RO(J)/FO(J,I)**(RHO(I)-1))/(SUM(JJ$FO(JJ,I), RO(JJ)
  /FO(JJ,I)**(RHO(I)-1)));
GAMMA(I)=(QO(I)/(SUM(J$FO(J,I), DELTA(J,I)*FO(J,I)**RHO(I)))**(1/RHO(I)))*
  (1-SUM(II,A(II,I)));
```

---

continued on next page

continued from previous page

```
VARIABLES
Q(I)                    Output levels
R(J)                    Factor prices
F(J,I)                  Factor use levels
PN(I)                   Net prices
GDP                     Gross domestic product;


Q.L(I)=QO(I);
R.L(J)=RO(J);
F.L(J,I)=FO(J,I);
PN.L(I)=PNO(I);
GDP.L=GDPO;
Q.LO(I)=0;
R.LO(J)=0;
F.LO(J,I)=0;
PN.LO(I)=0;


EQUATIONS
PRODUCTION(I)           Production functions
RESOURCE(J)             Resource constraints
FDEMAND(J,I)            Factor demand functions
NET_PRICE(I)            Net price functions
INCOME                  Gross domestic product;

PRODUCTION(I)..Q(I)=E=(GAMMA(I)/(1-SUM(II,A(II,I))))*SUM(J$FO(J,I),
  DELTA(J,I)*F(J,I)**RHO(I))**(1/RHO(I));
RESOURCE(J)..FBAR(J)=E=SUM(I, F(J,I));
NET_PRICE(I)..PN(I)=E=P(I)-SUM(II, P(II)*A(II,I));
FDEMAND(J,I)$FO(J,I)..R(J)=E=PN(I)*Q(I)*SUM(JJ$FO(JJ,I),DELTA(JJ,I)*F(JJ,I)**
  RHO(I))**(-1)*DELTA(J,I)*F(J,I)**(RHO(I)-1);
INCOME..GDP=E=SUM(J, R(J)*FBAR(J));

MODEL SF /ALL/;
SOLVE SF USING NLP MAXIMIZING GDP;
```

$$q_1 = \gamma_1^q [\delta_1^q V_1^{\rho_1^q} + (1 - \delta_1^q) M_1^{\rho_1^q}]^{1/\rho_1^q} \tag{10.18}$$

where ρ^q is a parameter governing the overall level of substitutability between intermediate goods (M) and value added (V). Value added is in turn defined as:

$$V_1 = \gamma_1^V [\delta_1^V K_1^{\rho_1^V} + (1 - \delta_1^V) L_1^{\rho_1^V}]^{1/\rho_1^V} \tag{10.19}$$

where ρ^V governs substitutability between primary factors. Similarly, aggregate intermediate use is defined as:

$$M_1 = \gamma_1^M [\delta_1^M q_{11}^{\rho_1^M} + (1 - \delta_1^M) q_{21}^{\rho_1^M}]^{1/\rho_1^M} \tag{10.20}$$

where ρ^M governs substitutability across intermediates. Production is therefore a nested form, with each of the nests composed of the now familiar CES function.

As we have seen a number of times now, the demand for primary factors must equate the factor price with the value of the marginal product, and as we have seen above, nothing about adding intermediates changes this basic model feature. One way to obtain the marginal products would be to substitute V_1 and M_1 into q_1, and take the partial derivatives. However this would be very messy, and there is no need. We can simply apply the chain rule. The key point is that the change in output as capital changes, *ceteris paribus*, is given by the change in value added as capital changes multiplied by the change in output as value added changes. Hence, for capital the demand function is:

$$r = p_1 \frac{\partial q_1}{\partial V_1} \frac{\partial V_1}{\partial K_1} = p_1 q_1^{1-\rho_1^q} V_1^{\rho_1^q - \rho_1^V} (\gamma_1^q)^{\rho_1^q} (\gamma_1^V)^{\rho_1^V} \delta_1^q \delta_1^V K_1^{\rho_1^V - 1}. \tag{10.21}$$

While an apology is perhaps in order for the crime against notational simplicity, the demand function reduces to a much less complex form than might be apparent at first glance. The demand for capital in industry 2 is the same with the subscripts replaced, and the demands for labor are similar also. We leave them for you to evaluate as an exercise.

For intermediate goods, the value of the marginal product must equal the price paid. Applying the chain rule we can obtain firm 1's demand for good 2 as:

$$p_2 = p_1 \frac{\partial q_1}{\partial M_1} \frac{\partial M_1}{\partial q_{21}} = p_1 q_1^{1-\rho_1^q} M_1^{\rho_1^q - \rho_1^M} (\gamma_1^q)^{\rho_1^q} (\gamma_1^M)^{\rho_1^M} (1 - \delta_1^q)(1 - \delta_1^M) q_{21}^{\rho_1^M - 1}.$$
$$\tag{10.22}$$

The conditions for the other intermediate, and the corresponding conditions for the other industry, are much the same. Again, we leave them for you to derive as an exercise.

Before implementing in GAMS we can generalize the equations to allow for an arbitrary number of goods and factors. Given the CES structure this is not too different from what we have seen already (see if you can do it yourself). The complete model consists of a production, value added and intermediate function for each good, a resource constraint for each factor, a factor demand equation for each factor/good pair (if the factor enters value added), an intermediate demand for each good/good pair, and the objective function (GDP).

Partial GAMS code is presented in Table 10.2 (the full model, like all the models discussed in the volume, is available for download). The code for the model is based on the specific factors model of chapter 6, and many of the adjustments are similar to those we used in the fixed proportions case presented above, so here we present only the equation block. The new elements are that production is now broken into three equations (PRODUCTION, VALUE and INTERMED, corresponding to the q, V and M equations introduced above. We still have factor demand equations FDEMAND, but these now take the form indicated by (10.21), and we introduce intermediate demand equations IDEMAND following (10.22).[6] The resource constraints are unchanged, but GDP is modified to equal the sum of net output value.

New variables are V(I), M(I), INT(II,I), which correspond to our three new equations. New parameters, in addition to the initial values of the variables, are the elasticity parameters at each level (RHOQ, RHOV and RHOI), which are free, and the shift and share parameters for each of the levels of the production function. The latter need to be calibrated. With initial prices set at unity, the process is exactly the same as with the CES functions we have been using for production thus far. Once the initial point is verified, the exogenous variables/parameters can be perturbed to see how the system reacts.

10.5   Exercises

(1) Consider an increase in the price of good 1, using the fixed proportions version of the model. You should find the return to one fixed factor rises while the return to the other fixed factor falls, in line with the results of the specific factors model. However, the nominal return to labor falls in the simulation. Why? Will this always happen?
(2) In the variable proportions model, try setting both RHOQ and RHOI to -10. Now conduct an experiment, a rise in the price of good 1 by 10 percent, say. Conduct the same experiment using the fixed proportions version of the model. What do you observe. Why?

---

[6]Note the use of exception handling in these equations is much the same as with factor demands.

Table 10.2   Partial GAMS Program for Intermediates (Variable Proportions).

```
EQUATIONS
PRODUCTION(I)      Production functions
VALUE(I)           Value added functions
INTERMED(I)        Intermediate functions
RESOURCE(J)        Resource constraints
FDEMAND(J,I)       Factor demand functions
IDEMAND(II,I)      Intermediate demands
INCOME             Gross domestic product;

PRODUCTION(I)..Q(I)=E=GAMMAQ(I)*(DELTAQ(I)*V(I)**RHOQ(I)+
  (1-DELTAQ(I))*M(I)**RHOQ(I))**(1/RHOQ(I));
INTERMED(I)..M(I)=E=GAMMAI(I)*(SUM(II$INTO(II,I), DELTAI(II,I)*
  INT(II,I)**RHOI(I)))**(1/RHOI(I));
VALUE(I)..V(I)=E=GAMMAV(I)*SUM(J$FO(J,I), DELTAV(J,I)*F(J,I)**
  RHOV(I))**(1/RHOV(I));
RESOURCE(J)..FBAR(J)=E=SUM(I, F(J,I));
FDEMAND(J,I)$FO(J,I)..R(J)=E=P(I)*Q(I)**(1-RHOQ(I))*V(I)**(RHOQ(I)-RHOV(I))*
  (GAMMAQ(I)**RHOQ(I))*(GAMMAV(I)**RHOV(I))*DELTAQ(I)*DELTAV(J,I)*F(J,I)**
  (RHOV(I)-1);
IDEMAND(II,I)$INTO(II,I)..P(II)=E=P(I)*Q(I)**(1-RHOQ(I))*M(I)**
  (RHOQ(I)-RHOI(I))*(GAMMAQ(I)**RHOQ(I))*(GAMMAI(I)**RHOI(I))*
  (1-DELTAQ(I))*DELTAI(II,I)*INT(II,I)**(RHOI(I)-1);
INCOME..GDP=E=SUM(I, P(I)*(Q(I)-M(I)));
```

(3) In the variable proportions case, when an industry uses its own output as an intermediate, the relevant marginal product must evaluate to 1 at an optimal choice. Why?

(4) The model presented in Table 10.1 assumes specific factors. By adjusting the underlying data, construct a version of the HOS model with intermediate inputs.

10.6   Further Reading

For early work on the role of intermediates see Vanek (1963). The properties of the one factor model we considered in section 10.1 are described in Melvin (1969a) and (1969b), while the two factor model with variable proportions is considered by Warne (1971). Casas (1972) looks at the implications of "pure" intermediates, which are only used in the production process.

Chapter 11

Autarky

The models of the preceding chapters have focused on the production/consumption decision independently, with prices exogenously given in all cases. We now turn to a complete general equilibrium model of both production and consumption in a single economy, where prices are determined within the system. In other words, we build a model of the autarkic (closed) economy in full. In the next chapter we will consider the small, open economy.

11.1 Formal Problem

We assume the existence of a representative consumer with a utility function $U(c_1, c_2)$. Hence, we can apply the same theory of consumer choice that we described in Chapter 3. The differences are that we think of the utility function as representing the preferences of all of society (we will consider the case where different groups in society have different preferences later) and that the constraint on consumption is not generated by a budget, but rather by the production capacity of society, in turn a function of technology and resources. The choice set is then generated by a production model, and the structure used in either Chapter 5 or 6 is appropriate, depending on whether our interest is in the long or the short run. We will assume the former and leave the latter as an exercise. As usual, the model can be described by a constrained maximization problem. The representative consumer maximizes their utility subject to the constraint of the production possibilities, determined by technology and resources. The Lagrangian is:

$$\mathcal{L} = \theta U(c_1, c_2) + \lambda_1[q_1(K_1, L_1) - c_1] + \lambda_2[q_2(K_2, L_2) - c_2]$$
$$+ \mu_K[\bar{K} - K_1 - K_2] + \mu_L[\bar{L} - L_1 - L_2]. \tag{11.1}$$

The first two constraints are the market clearing conditions for each good (i.e., production must equal consumption). The third and forth are the resource constraints. Taking the derivatives with respect to each of the choice variables and the multipliers we have:

$$\partial \mathscr{L}/\partial c_i = \theta \partial U/\partial c_i - \lambda_i = 0 \quad i = 1, 2 \tag{11.2}$$

$$\partial \mathscr{L}/\partial K_i = \lambda_i \partial q_i/\partial K_i - \mu_K = 0 \quad i = 1, 2 \tag{11.3}$$

$$\partial \mathscr{L}/\partial L_i = \lambda_i \partial q_i/\partial L_i - \mu_L = 0 \quad i = 1, 2 \tag{11.4}$$

$$\partial \mathscr{L}/\partial \lambda_i = q_i(K_i, L_i) - c_i = 0 \quad i = 1, 2 \tag{11.5}$$

$$\partial \mathscr{L}/\partial \mu_K = \bar{K} - K_1 - K_2 = 0 \tag{11.6}$$

$$\partial \mathscr{L}/\partial \mu_L = \bar{L} - L_1 - L_2 = 0. \tag{11.7}$$

Under competitive conditions, the multipliers λ_i are the prices of goods, and μ_j are the factor prices. θ is a positive constant. The expressions should be familiar. Equation (11.2) states that the marginal utility per dollar spent on consumption of all goods must be equal, (11.3) and (11.4) state that the factor prices must equal the marginal value products of the factors, while the remaining conditions replicate the constraints that consumption must equal production (11.5) and resource use is limited to resource availability (11.6) and (11.7). Simple manipulation of the first three conditions shows us that the condition for efficiency is:

$$\frac{\partial q_1}{\partial q_2} = \frac{\partial c_1}{\partial c_2} \tag{11.8}$$

where $\partial q_1/\partial q_2$ holds resources constant and $\partial c_1/\partial c_2$ holds utility constant. Thus the equation system (11.2)–(11.7) states that, to maximize utility, the marginal rate of transformation (the slope of the production possibilities frontier) must equal the marginal rate of substitution (the slope of an indifference curve), and resources must be fully employed.

Solving the system of equations yields the optimal autarky equilibrium values for factor use, consumption and the shadow prices, but there is an important problem. The system (11.2)–(11.7) gives us 10 equations in 11 variables, so we can pick one arbitrarily. As a consequence, we need to normalize the prices by setting one price as a numéraire, and interpret all other prices relative to the numéraire.[1] We arbitrarily set the price of good

---

[1]To understand the problem, consider exercise 2 from Chapter 5. When you changed both prices by 10 percent, you should have seen that the all factor prices also increased by 10 percent, but the input/output choices were unchanged. In other words, there are an infinite number of nominal prices consistent with the same equilibrium, for a given price ratio. Relative prices are what matters, not nominal prices.

1, λ_1, equal to unity. That means that each term in the Lagrangian (11.1) has dimensions \$ or good 1. Consequently, λ_2, μ_K and μ_L, become price and factor rewards measured either in \$ per item (good 2, machine, or worker) or good 1 per item. θ is measured in \$ per util or good 1 per util, the marginal cost of utility. Often it is convenient to label the utility level for each indifference curve as the minimum expenditure at initial prices that supports consumption on that indifference curve. Thus, any change in utility is measured as the equivalent variation in income, EV, where EV is the change in income at initial prices that supports the utility change. The utility function presented in Table 11.1 is normalized in this way, and it implies θ equals 1.

The μ's are shadow prices, representing how much the objective rises per unit increase in the exogenously determined resource supplies. Since $\lambda_1 = 1$, they represent how much of good 1 could be destroyed per unit increase in the resources, and still leave utility unchanged. Thus these shadow prices are measured in units of good 1. λ_2 is the shadow price of good 2 in the same sense. θ is the shadow price of utility, measuring how much of an exogenous jump in the supply of good 1 would be required to raise utility by one unit. Think of λ_2 and the μ's as the value of a gift to the country of good 2, capital, or labor, respectively, all measured in units of good 1. Tower and Pursell (1987) call these compensated shadow prices.

The geometry of the problem is shown in Figure 11.1, which combines the PPF from Chapter 5 (or in principle Chapter 6) and the indifference curve from Chapter 3. The production possibilities can be thought of as the consumption constraint under the autarky condition that only produced bundles can be consumed, and U^* is the highest indifference curve that can be reached given that constraint. The slope of the tangent line is minus the relative price of good 2. Tower (1979) discusses ways to rationalize community indifference curves, such as assuming all individuals in a country have identical tastes and identical factor ownership.

11.2 GAMS Implementation

The GAMS implementation of this problem essentially combines the models of Chapters 3 and 5, and is presented in Table 11.1. There is not much that is new, so we keep our description brief. We have taken all parameters, variables and equations from the model of Chapter 3, and added them in the appropriate sections of the combined model. Now the prices

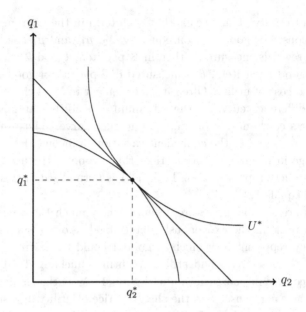

Fig. 11.1   Autarky Equilibrium.

are not exogenous, but endogenous, so we need new equations to determine them. These are the market clearing (also called material balance) equations (MAT_BAL) that we have introduced. They simply state that the quantity supplied will equal quantity demanded for each good, condition (11.5). The only other significant change is that rather than using an exogenous income level in the demand equations (DEMAND) as in Chapter 3, we have used the endogenously determined GDP value from the model of Chapter 5 instead.

Because the model can only determine relative prices, we need to create a numéraire. The way we have done this is by adding a new bounding condition for the price of good 1 (chosen arbitrarily). The code P.FX('1')=1;, just after declaring the initial levels and lower bounds for variables, defines the upper and lower bound for the price of good 1 at unity, thus keeping it fixed in the solution. An alternative would have been to add an additional equation to the model that determined the price (e.g., something like `NUMERAIRE..P('1')=E=1;`), but simply fixing the appropriate variable is somewhat easier in this case.[2]

11.3 Exercises

(1) Consider an increase in the value of the numéraire. What is the effect on the economic system?

(2) As you increase the amount of labor in the economy, what happens to factor prices? Why do they change now when in Chapter 5 they did not?

(3) As you increase both capital and labor by 10 percent, what is the change in the output of the two goods measured in percent?

(4) Build a version of the model in which the utility function of the representative household takes the CES form rather than Cobb–Douglas. This will allow you to explore the implications of different elasticities of substitution in consumption. (Hint: Look closely at the properties of the CES function that we developed in the context of production in Chapter 4).

(5) As you increase labor alone what is the relationship between the percentage changes in outputs of the two goods if the elasticity of substitution in consumption is close to zero?

(6) Now redo the preceding exercise for the case where the elasticity of substitution in consumption is large. Explain your results.

(7) As you increase the amount of capital in the economy, what happens to goods prices and factor prices? Explain why.

(8) Using the same approach we adopted here, can you create an autarky version of the specific factors model presented in Chapter 6?

(9) Can you adapt the techniques used here to construct an autarky model in which you have intermediate goods (as in Chapter 10)? (Hint: In addition to adjusting the production structure, you will need to ac-

---

[2]Using GAMS there are three distinct ways to fix a value. One way is to declare it as a parameter (this is what we have been doing for exogenous variables and terms in the various functions). Another is to declare it as a variable, but add an equation to the model that constrains it to be a particular value. A third is to declare it as a variable and then fix both the upper and lower bounds to the same value. Generally, either declaring as a parameter or fixing the bounds is more efficient. The latter is particularly useful if, for example, we want to frequently change which variables are exogenous/endogenous (i.e., the closure).

count for both final and intermediate demands in the market clearing
conditions.)

(10) Try extending the model to higher dimensions. See if you can create a
version with more goods than factors. Now change the technology for,
say, good 2, by altering GAMMA. In the model discussed in Chapter 9,
one of the goods disappears, but that does not happen here. Why is
it that we can generally have more goods than factors in this model,
when we could not in the model of Chapter 9?

Table 11.1   GAMS Program for Autarky.

```
SET I Goods /1,2/;
SET J Factors /K,L/;
ALIAS (J, JJ);

PARAMETERS
ALPHA                             Shift parameters in utility
BETA(I)                          Share parameters in utility
PO(I)                            Initial prices
UO                               Initial utility level
CO(I)                            Initial consumption levels
GAMMA(I)                         Shift parameters in production
DELTA(J,I)                       Share parameters in production
RHO(I)                           Elasticity parameters in production
FBAR(J)                          Endowments
QO(I)                            Initial output levels
RO(J)                            Initial factor prices
FO(J,I)                          Initial factor use levels
GDPO                             Initial gross domestic product;

PO(I)=1;
RO(J)=1;
QO(I)=100;
CO(I)=QO(I);
FO('L','1')=20;
FO('L','2')=80;
FO('K',I)=(QO(I)*PO(I)-FO('L',I)*RO('L'))/RO('K');
FBAR(J)=SUM(I, FO(J,I));
GDPO=SUM(I, PO(I)*QO(I));
RHO(I)=0.1;
DELTA(J,I)=(RO(J)/FO(J,I)**(RHO(I)-1))/(SUM(JJ, RO(JJ)
  /FO(JJ,I)**(RHO(I)-1)));
GAMMA(I)=QO(I)/(SUM(J, DELTA(J,I)*FO(J,I)**RHO(I)))**(1/RHO(I));
UO=GDPO;
BETA(I)=CO(I)*PO(I)/GDPO;
ALPHA=UO/PROD(I, CO(I)**BETA(I));

VARIABLES
U                                Utility level
P(I)                             Prices
C(I)                             Consumption levels
Q(I)                             Output levels
```

---

continued on next page

continued from previous page

```
R(J)                                    Factor prices
F(J,I)                                  Factor use levels
GDP                                     Gross domestic product;

U.L=UO;
P.L(I)=PO(I);
C.L(I)=CO(I);
Q.L(I)=QO(I);
R.L(J)=RO(J);
F.L(J,I)=FO(J,I);
GDP.L=GDPO;
P.LO(I)=0;
C.LO(I)=0;
Q.LO(I)=0;
R.LO(J)=0;
F.LO(J,I)=0;
GDP.LO=0;


P.FX('1')=1;


EQUATIONS
UTILITY                                 Utility function
DEMAND(I)                               Demand functions
MAT_BAL(I)                              Market clearing
PRODUCTION(I)                           Production functions
RESOURCE(J)                             Resource constraints
FDEMAND(J,I)                            Factor demand functions
INCOME                                  Gross domestic product;

UTILITY..U=E=ALPHA*PROD(I, C(I)**BETA(I));
DEMAND(I)..C(I)=E=BETA(I)*GDP/P(I);
MAT_BAL(I)..C(I)=E=Q(I);
PRODUCTION(I)..Q(I)=E=GAMMA(I)*SUM(J, DELTA(J,I)*F(J,I)**RHO(I))**(1/RHO(I));
RESOURCE(J)..FBAR(J)=E=SUM(I, F(J,I));
FDEMAND(J,I)..R(J)=E=P(I)*Q(I)*SUM(JJ, DELTA(JJ,I)*F(JJ,I)**RHO(I))**(-1)*
  DELTA(J,I)*F(J,I)**(RHO(I)-1);
INCOME..GDP=E=SUM(I, P(I)*Q(I));

MODEL AUTARKY /ALL/;
SOLVE AUTARKY USING NLP MAXIMIZING U;
```

Chapter 12

Small Country Trading Equilibrium

The previous chapter examined a closed (autarkic) economy. We now turn to a model of a small, open economy. The small economy takes prices on world markets as given, in much the same way as a competitive firm takes output and input prices as given. With free trade, the economy is free to export and import as much as it likes at the world price, subject to the constraint that the value of what it exports equals the value of what it imports. As in Chapter 11, we can construct the GAMS model by combining elements that we have already built — one of the models of production and the model of final demand.[1] The key difference is that it is not relative prices that adjust to equate quantity demanded to quantity supplied, but rather the volume of trade. This simple setup is widely used in the study of trade policy.

12.1 Formal Problem

As with other models we have seen, we can derive the equations we need by considering the underlying constrained optimization problem. The objective is again to maximize the utility of the representative household, subject to resource constraints, market clearing, and now the trade balance. Prices are fixed. For the long-run model, the Lagrangian can be written:

$$\mathcal{L} = \theta U(c_1, c_2) + \lambda_1[q_1(K_1, L_1) - c_1 - x_1] + \lambda_2[q_2(K_2, L_2) - c_2 - x_2]$$
$$+ \mu_K[\bar{K} - K_1 - K_2] + \mu_L[\bar{L} - L_1 - L_2]$$
$$+ \gamma[p_1^* x_1 + p_2^* x_2]. \tag{12.1}$$

---

[1] In fact, all of our models of production with prices fixed can be thought of as representations of the production problem for a small, open economy.

The changes relative to Chapter 11 are that rather than requiring consumption to equal production, we now require that the difference between production and consumption of each good be equal to the volume of net exports, x_i, which may be positive (exports) or negative (imports). World prices are denoted p_i^*. The final constraint is that the value of exports, at world prices, is equal to the value of imports at world prices. In other words, trade is balanced. Taking the derivatives with respect to the choice variables and the multipliers yields the following first-order conditions:

$$\partial \mathscr{L} / \partial c_i = \theta \partial U / \partial c_i - \lambda_i = 0 \quad i = 1, 2 \tag{12.2}$$

$$\partial \mathscr{L} / \partial x_i = -\lambda_i + \gamma p_i^* = 0 \quad i = 1, 2 \tag{12.3}$$

$$\partial \mathscr{L} / \partial K_i = \lambda_i \partial q_i / \partial K_i - \mu_K = 0 \quad i = 1, 2 \tag{12.4}$$

$$\partial \mathscr{L} / \partial L_i = \lambda_i \partial q_i / \partial L_i - \mu_L = 0 \quad i = 1, 2 \tag{12.5}$$

$$\partial \mathscr{L} / \partial \lambda_i = q_i(K_i, L_i) - c_i - x_i = 0 \quad i = 1, 2 \tag{12.6}$$

$$\partial \mathscr{L} / \partial \mu_K = \bar{K} - K_1 - K_2 = 0 \tag{12.7}$$

$$\partial \mathscr{L} / \partial \mu_L = \bar{L} - L_1 - L_2 = 0 \tag{12.8}$$

$$\partial \mathscr{L} / \partial \gamma = p_1^* x_1 + p_2^* x_2 = 0. \tag{12.9}$$

The interpretation of the multipliers is the same as in Chapter 11. The only exception is γ, which we interpret as the shadow price of foreign exchange, and which we normalize to unity. Equations (12.2), (12.4), (12.5), (12.7) and (12.8) are familiar, they are exactly the same optimality conditions that we have seen in preceding chapters on utility and production. Equation (12.3) has a very straightforward interpretation. It says that for optimality we require that the domestic price must equal the world price, i.e., free trade. Equations (12.6) and (12.9) merely replicate the material balance and trade balance constraints. Simple manipulation shows us that the overall condition for efficiency is:

$$\frac{\partial q_1}{\partial q_2} = \frac{\partial c_1}{\partial c_2} = -\frac{p_2^*}{p_1^*} \tag{12.10}$$

which states that, to maximize welfare, the marginal rate of transformation and the marginal rate of substitution must both equal the world price ratio (the foreign rate of transformation). The adaptations required to generate a short-run version of the model should be obvious.

In this chapter we did not set the shadow price of good 1 equal to unity. Instead we set the shadow price of foreign exchange equal to unity. This means that all shadow prices are measured in terms of foreign exchange. The μ's and λ's represent the amount of foreign currency that could be sacrificed per unit increase in the supply of resources or goods, and still leave utility unchanged. θ is the extra foreign exchange required to raise utility by one unit.

An alternative, sequential, way of thinking about the problem illustrates the tight connection between this model and those that we have already studied. Consider the maximization of income problem of Chapter 5. Solving the problem generates the maximum income possible given the prices and the technological/resource constraints. Society can then spend the income as it chooses, and how it spends it has no bearing on the income maximization problem. Using the same prices and the maximized income, we can therefore solve the utility maximization problem presented in Chapter 3. The difference between the consumption bundle and the production bundle is trade. It makes no difference whether we solve as one problem, as presented above, or as a sequence of two, because for a small, open economy the production and consumption decisions are independent.

Figure 12.1 illustrates condition (12.10) graphically. Think of the problem as two stages. First, national income at world prices is maximized, as in Chapter 5 (or Chapter 6 for the short run), by allocating resources so as to produce on the production possibilities at the point where the marginal rate of transformation is equal to (minus) the price ratio, i.e., q_1^* and q_2^*. The maximized value of income is Y^*. Given the maximized income, the economy selects its optimal consumption bundle along the budget constraint, just as in Chapter 3. As drawn, the consumption choice is c_1^* and c_2^*. This implies that good 1 is an exportable, and good 2 is an importable.

12.2 GAMS Implementation

Because we are essentially combining elements from previous chapters here, we skip the worked example and translation to set notation, and move directly to the GAMS implementation. The program is presented in Table 12.1 and is very similar to the preceding chapter, so we discuss only the changes. First, we introduce a new parameter XO(I) to hold the initial trade values, and calibrate it using the material balance condition XO(I)=QO(I)-CO(I). This ensures that the initial equilibrium is identical to the autarky equilibrium of the previous chapter.

Next we create a new variable X(I) to hold the solution values for the net exports. This replaces prices from the autarky model, since prices are now exogenous in the model, not endogenous. We assign levels for X(I)

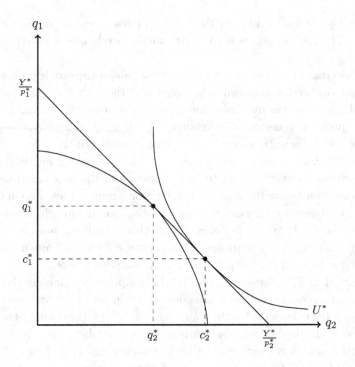

Fig. 12.1   Small Country Trading Equilibrium.

as usual, but note that we do not impose a lower bound. The reason is that, as defined, the net exports can be negative or positive, depending on whether the good in question is imported or exported. Hence, this variable should be left free.

Finally, the autarky market clearing condition, which is QO(I)=E=CO(I), is replaced by the open economy market clearing condition, i.e., X(I)=E=Q(I)-C(I). Note that we do not include the trade balance equation because we have set total consumption spending equal to GDP, and that implies trade balance. The trade balance is therefore not independent of the market clearing conditions, and so is not necessary. The model is then defined, and a benchmark simulation is run to test that everything works as expected. We now have a complete general equilibrium model of a small economy.

Table 12.1   GAMS Program for Small Country.

```
SET I Goods /1,2/;
SET J Factors /K,L/;
ALIAS (J, JJ);

PARAMETERS
ALPHA                                Shift parameters in utility
BETA(I)                              Share parameters in utility
P(I)                                 Prices
UO                                   Initial utility level
CO(I)                                Initial consumption levels
XO(I)                                Initial trade flows
GAMMA(I)                             Shift parameters in production
DELTA(J,I)                           Share parameters in production
RHO(I)                               Elasticity parameters in production
FBAR(J)                              Endowments
QO(I)                                Initial output levels
RO(J)                                Initial factor prices
FO(J,I)                              Initial factor use levels
GDPO                                 Initial gross domestic product;

P(I)=1;
RO(J)=1;
QO(I)=100;
CO(I)=QO(I);
XO(I)=QO(I)-CO(I);
FO('L','1')=20;
FO('L','2')=80;
FO('K',I)=(QO(I)*P(I)-FO('L',I)*RO('L'))/RO('K');
FBAR(J)=SUM(I, FO(J,I));
GDPO=SUM(I, P(I)*QO(I));
RHO(I)=0.1;
DELTA(J,I)=(RO(J)/FO(J,I)**(RHO(I)-1))/(SUM(JJ, RO(JJ)
  /FO(JJ,I)**(RHO(I)-1)));
GAMMA(I)=QO(I)/(SUM(J, DELTA(J,I)*FO(J,I)**RHO(I)))**(1/RHO(I));
UO=GDPO;
BETA(I)=CO(I)*P(I)/GDPO;
ALPHA=UO/PROD(I, CO(I)**BETA(I));

VARIABLES
U                                    Utility level
X(I)                                 Trade
```

continued on next page

continued from previous page

```
C(I)                              Consumption levels
Q(I)                              Output levels
R(J)                              Factor prices
F(J,I)                            Factor use levels
GDP                              Gross domestic product;

U.L=U0;
X.L(I)=X0(I);
C.L(I)=C0(I);
Q.L(I)=Q0(I);
R.L(J)=R0(J);
F.L(J,I)=F0(J,I);
GDP.L=GDP0;
C.LO(I)=0;
Q.LO(I)=0;
R.LO(J)=0;
F.LO(J,I)=0;
GDP.LO=0;


EQUATIONS
UTILITY                           Utility function
DEMAND(I)                         Demand functions
MAT_BAL(I)                        Market clearing
PRODUCTION(I)                     Production functions
RESOURCE(J)                       Resource constraints
FDEMAND(J,I)                      Factor demand functions
INCOME                            Gross domestic product;

UTILITY..U=E=ALPHA*PROD(I, C(I)**BETA(I));
DEMAND(I)..C(I)=E=BETA(I)*GDP/P(I);
MAT_BAL(I)..X(I)=E=Q(I)-C(I);
PRODUCTION(I)..Q(I)=E=GAMMA(I)*SUM(J, DELTA(J,I)*F(J,I)**RHO(I))**(1/RHO(I));
RESOURCE(J)..FBAR(J)=E=SUM(I, F(J,I));
FDEMAND(J,I)..R(J)=E=P(I)*Q(I)*SUM(JJ, DELTA(JJ,I)*F(JJ,I)**RHO(I))**(-1)*
  DELTA(J,I)*F(J,I)**(RHO(I)-1);
INCOME..GDP=E=SUM(I, P(I)*Q(I));


MODEL SMALL /ALL/;
SOLVE SMALL USING NLP MAXIMIZING U;
```

12.3 Exercises

(1) What is the numéraire in this model? Can you implement a numéraire shock?

(2) In the initial calibrated equilibrium, the volume of trade is zero (autarky). What happens if you increase the world price of good 1? What if you increase the world price of good 2? In particular what happens to factor prices?

(3) Can you calibrate a version of the model in which trade is already occurring?

(4) Holding prices constant, what happens to net exports of each good as you increase the stock of capital in the economy? What if you increase the stock of labor?

(5) Consider an increase in the stock of capital by 10 percent in the autarky model from the previous chapter. What happens to relative prices? Now conduct the same experiment in the open economy model. Given what you observed in the autarky model, how could you have predicted this outcome?

(6) In this model we dropped the trade balance equation. Can you use the model results to show that trade balance is in fact implied by the other equations in the system?

(7) Using the same approach we adopted here, can you create a small country version of the specific factors model presented in chapter 6? How about a version incorporating intermediate goods as in chapter 10? How about a version of the model in which there are also 'pure' intermediate goods, which do not appear in final consumption? (Hint: You will need to add exception handling to the demand side of the model.)

Chapter 13

Non-traded Goods

In Chapter 11 we considered an economy where no goods were traded, while in Chapter 12 we considered an economy where all goods were traded. We now turn to a case where an economy produces both tradable and non-tradable goods. Even if an economy is open, there may be some goods that society wishes to consume in positive quantities, but in which international trade is not feasible (an example might be raw milk, which is generally too costly to transport, or various services). The prices of such goods must be determined by domestic demand and supply conditions. Implementing such a model in GAMS requires only minor modifications to our previous examples, while greatly increasing the richness of the simulated economy.

13.1 Formal Problem

The appropriate constrained optimization problem combines elements from the autarky/open economy models that we have dealt with already. Let's consider an economy producing three goods. The first two are tradable and the last is not. The objective is to maximize the utility of the representative household, subject to resource constraints, market clearing, and the trade balance. However, market clearing for the non-traded good will set production equal to consumption, not to consumption plus trade. As before, the prices of the traded goods are fixed, and we assume a long-run model of production (with the usual technology restrictions). The Lagrangian is:

$$
\begin{aligned}
\mathscr{L} = {} & \theta U(c_1, c_2, c_3) + \lambda_1[q_1(K_1, L_1) - c_1 - x_1] \\
& + \lambda_2[q_2(K_2, L_2) - c_2 - x_2] + \lambda_3[q_3(K_3, L_3) - c_3] \\
& + \mu_K[\bar{K} - K_1 - K_2 - K_3] + \mu_L[\bar{L} - L_1 - L_2 - L_3] \\
& + \gamma[p_1^* x_1 + p_2^* x_2].
\end{aligned}
\tag{13.1}
$$

Everything looks pretty familiar. Taking the derivatives with respect to the choice variables and the multipliers yields the first-order conditions:

$$\partial \mathscr{L}/\partial c_i = \theta \partial U/\partial c_i - \lambda_i = 0 \quad i = 1,2,3 \tag{13.2}$$

$$\partial \mathscr{L}/\partial x_i = -\lambda_i + \gamma p_i^* = 0 \quad i = 1,2 \tag{13.3}$$

$$\partial \mathscr{L}/\partial K_i = \lambda_i \partial q_i/\partial K_i - \mu_K = 0 \quad i = 1,2,3 \tag{13.4}$$

$$\partial \mathscr{L}/\partial L_i = \lambda_i \partial q_i/\partial L_i - \mu_L = 0 \quad i = 1,2,3 \tag{13.5}$$

$$\partial \mathscr{L}/\partial \lambda_i = q_i(K_i, L_i) - c_i - x_i = 0 \quad i = 1,2 \tag{13.6}$$

$$\partial \mathscr{L}/\partial \lambda_i = q_i(K_i, L_i) - c_i = 0 \quad i = 3 \tag{13.7}$$

$$\partial \mathscr{L}/\partial \mu_K = \bar{K} - K_1 - K_2 - K_3 = 0 \tag{13.8}$$

$$\partial \mathscr{L}/\partial \mu_L = \bar{L} - L_1 - L_2 - L_3 = 0 \tag{13.9}$$

$$\partial \mathscr{L}/\partial \gamma = p_1^* x_1 + p_2^* x_2 = 0. \tag{13.10}$$

This is a system of 17 equations in 17 unknowns, the choice variables and the multipliers (once we have set a numéraire). Each of the equations has an interpretation that should be familiar from previous chapters (a set of marginal conditions for production and consumption, and equilibrium conditions for factors and goods). As in Chapter 12, we can use γ, the shadow value of foreign exchange, as the numéraire. We can then interpret λ_3/γ as the real exchange rate, or more simply the price of the non-traded good.

In fact, the model is not as difficult to solve as it may first appear. It is only a bit harder than the HOS model that we have already considered. If both tradable goods are produced in equilibrium, then factor prices are uniquely determined, as are factor proportions in all sectors.[1] Hence, the price of the non-traded good is also determined. Income is determined given factor prices and endowments, and with all prices known we can determine consumption levels for all goods. Market clearing for the non-traded good ensures production equals consumption for that good. We can then use the full employment conditions to determine the output levels of the two traded goods. Trade volumes follow immediately.

---

[1]The implication is that the real exchange rate will not respond to the changes in endowments or domestic demand, provided all goods continue to be produced. It will, however, respond to changes in production technology and/or shifts in international prices.

13.2 GAMS Implementation

Now consider the GAMS implementation. By using subsets and selectively fixing the values of variables, it is fairly straightforward to convert the model of the small open economy from Chapter 12 into a version that handles both traded and non-traded goods. The completed program is presented in Table 13.1, and we discuss only the new elements.

Since the smallest interesting case of non-traded goods involves three sectors, we begin by expanding the set of goods by changing the set statement to SET I /1,2,3/;. Good 3 will be our non-traded good. We then define two subsets SET T(I) /1,2/; and SET N(I) /3/;, where T is the subset of goods which are traded, and N is the subset of goods which are non-traded. Next we assign initial values for output, consumption and factor use to good 3.[2]

We have seen that we can assign values to parameters by a direct statement, or through the TABLE command, which both defines the parameter and assigns its value using a tabular format (see the discussion in Chapter 9). A third way of defining/assigning a parameter, which can be very convenient with large models, is presented in Table 13.1. The relevant code is:

```
PARAMETER FO(J,I) Initial factor use levels /
L.1 20
L.2 80
L.3 40 /;
```

The first part of the statement is the keyword PARAMETER, which tells GAMS that a parameter is being defined, followed by the parameter name and dimensions, then an optional description.[3] Next we have a list of data assignments, enclosed within forward slashes. As always, the statement is ended with a semicolon.

The data assignments take the form: element of the first set, dot, element of the second set, (followed by more dots and elements if needed), a space and then the value. Hence, the line L.1 20 is equivalent to the assignment FO('L','1')=20;. Each assignment is on a separate line. For relatively small, two-dimensional datasets the TABLE command is perhaps

---

[2] Just as in Chapter 12, we calibrate to an initial equilibrium in which trade in all goods is zero, but this is purely for convenience.

[3] If the sets are not provided, GAMS will try and guess them from the data, but it is good practice to specify them.

Table 13.1   GAMS Program for Small Country With Non-traded Goods.

```
SET I Goods /1,2,3/;
SET N(I) /3/;
SET T(I) /1,2/;
SET J Factors /K,L/;
ALIAS (J, JJ);

PARAMETERS
ALPHA                              Shift parameters in utility
BETA(I)                           Share parameters in utility
PO(I)                             Initial prices
UO                                Initial utility level
CO(I)                             Initial consumption levels
XO(I)                             Initial trade flows
GAMMA(I)                          Shift parameters in production
DELTA(J,I)                        Share parameters in production
RHO(I)                            Elasticity parameters in production
FBAR(J)                           Endowments
QO(I)                             Initial output levels
RO(J)                             Initial factor prices
GDPO                              Initial gross domestic product;

PO(I)=1;
RO(J)=1;
QO(I)=100;
CO(I)=QO(I);
XO(I)=QO(I)-CO(I);

PARAMETER FO(J,I)                  Initial factor use levels /
L.1 20
L.2 80
L.3 40 /;

FO('K',I)=(QO(I)*PO(I)-FO('L',I)*RO('L'))/RO('K');
FBAR(J)=SUM(I, FO(J,I));
GDPO=SUM(I, PO(I)*QO(I));
RHO(I)=0.1;
DELTA(J,I)=(RO(J)/FO(J,I)**(RHO(I)-1))/(SUM(JJ, RO(JJ)
  /FO(JJ,I)**(RHO(I)-1)));
GAMMA(I)=QO(I)/(SUM(J, DELTA(J,I)*FO(J,I)**RHO(I)))**(1/RHO(I));
UO=GDPO;
BETA(I)=CO(I)*PO(I)/GDPO;
ALPHA=UO/PROD(I, CO(I)**BETA(I));
```

continued on next page

continued from previous page

```
VARIABLES
U                               Utility level
X(I)                            Trade
P(I)                            Prices
C(I)                            Consumption levels
Q(I)                            Output levels
R(J)                            Factor prices
F(J,I)                          Factor use levels
GDP                             Gross domestic product;

U.L=UO; X.L(I)=XO(I); P.L(I)=PO(I); C.L(I)=CO(I);
Q.L(I)=QO(I); R.L(J)=RO(J); F.L(J,I)=FO(J,I); GDP.L=GDPO;
C.LO(I)=0; P.LO(N)=0; Q.LO(I)=0;
R.LO(J)=0; F.LO(J,I)=0; GDP.LO=0;

P.FX(T)=PO(T);
X.FX(N)=0;

EQUATIONS
UTILITY                         Utility function
DEMAND(I)                       Demand functions
MAT_BAL(I)                      Market clearing
PRODUCTION(I)                   Production functions
RESOURCE(J)                     Resource constraints
FDEMAND(J,I)                    Factor demand functions
INCOME                          Gross domestic product;

UTILITY..U=E=ALPHA*PROD(I, C(I)**BETA(I));
DEMAND(I)..C(I)=E=BETA(I)*GDP/P(I);
MAT_BAL(I)..X(I)=E=Q(I)-C(I);
PRODUCTION(I)..Q(I)=E=GAMMA(I)*SUM(J, DELTA(J,I)*F(J,I)**RHO(I))**(1/RHO(I));
RESOURCE(J)..FBAR(J)=E=SUM(I, F(J,I));
FDEMAND(J,I)..R(J)=E=P(I)*Q(I)*SUM(JJ, DELTA(JJ,I)*F(JJ,I)**RHO(I))**(-1)*
  DELTA(J,I)*F(J,I)**(RHO(I)-1);
INCOME..GDP=E=SUM(I, P(I)*Q(I));

MODEL NT /ALL/;
SOLVE NT USING NLP MAXIMIZING U;
```

more natural. However, this technique is useful to know. It is less cumbersome when dealing with data with three or more dimensions, and data in this format can be easily generated by other programs for use in GAMS.

Recall that in Chapter 11 prices were treated as endogenous, while in Chapter 12 they were treated as exogenous. In this model we need the prices of traded goods to be exogenous, but those of non-traded goods to be endogenous. As usual, there are a number of ways to accomplish this outcome. We will start by defining a parameter PO(I) to hold initial prices, which we normalize to unity. We then add a variable for prices, P(I), just as we did in Chapter 11. Notice that we have left the trade variables X(I) defined over all goods, and we also have the price variables defined over all goods. But, the prices of traded goods should not be variable, they are fixed by the small country assumption. Moreover, trade for non-traded goods should not be variable, it should be fixed at zero. We can accomplish this by selectively fixing elements of the trade/price vectors. Hence, we add the lines P.FX(T)=PO(T) and X.FX(N)=0, after the bounds. The material balance condition MAT_BAL(I)..X(I)=E=Q(I)-C(I); will now effectively set Q(N)=E=C(N), with P(N) adjusting for all goods in N as necessary. On the other hand P(T) will be fixed for all goods in T while X(T) adjusts, which is exactly what we want.[4]

Once we have verified the equilibrium, we can develop an understanding of the behavior of the model by changing the values of parameters, or the levels at which variables are fixed, and observing the results. Some suggested exercises follow.

13.3   Exercises

(1) Consider the implications of an increase in factor endowments. How do they compare to the model without non-traded goods?

(2) The model that we have built in this chapter has more goods produced than factors of production. Nonetheless, a change in the terms of trade will not (in general) lead to the disappearance of any industry. Why?

(3) How does an improvement in the technology used to produce non-traded goods affect the real exchange rate? Explain.

---

[4]Note just how convenient the approach of fixing variable values can sometimes be for adding constraints to the model — in this case we did not have to adjust the model equations to account for non-traded goods at all! Another way to accomplish the same result would have been to introduce two different material balance conditions, one for traded goods, and one for non-traded goods, along with an equation fixing the price of traded goods, which is much more work.

(4) How do changes in the prices of tradable goods affect factor prices? How do the results compare to the predictions of the Stolper–Samuelson theorem? What happens to the real exchange rate?

(5) Using the same approach we adopted here, can you create a version of the specific factors model with non-traded goods? How about a model incorporating both intermediate and non-traded goods? Can you make the model such that there are pure intermediate goods which are non-traded?

13.4 Further Reading

A comprehensive study of the three good, two factor model where one of the goods is non-traded is Komiya (1967), which includes discussion of trade policy in this context. Further discussion of the implications of non-traded goods in the presence of factor market distortions is contained in Batra (1973).

Chapter 14

Large Country Trading Equilibrium

For a small economy the world prices are treated as exogenous. In some cases we might be interested in economies that are large enough to influence world prices. There are two ways of incorporating this feature into our modeling approach. One way, which we present in the next chapter, is to explicitly model a system with multiple interacting economies. Another, which we present here, is to continue with a single country model, but to incorporate information on another implicit economy (or economies) through the use of partial international demand/supply functions. The latter approach is often adopted in large-scale CGE models of a single economy where the modeler is concerned with potential terms-of-trade effects. In a sense, it is not very different from what we have already been doing — a small country also faces international demand and supply functions, they just happen to be flat (i.e., perfectly elastic). Hence, we simply need to relax that assumption.

14.1 Formal Problem

At this stage we are very familiar with the problem of production in both the short and long run. Before considering the problem facing a large economy, let us introduce some economies in presentation. Consider the problem of maximizing the output of good 1 subject to a given level of output of good 2, given technology and resources. Through solving this problem we can express optimal output of good 1 as a function of output of good 2, and of course the available resources. We call this function the transformation locus or the production possibilities frontier $q_1 = \tilde{\psi}(q_2)$ (dropping the resource arguments for convenience). Under our technological assumptions $\tilde{\psi}$ is concave. It can summarize either a long-run or short-run production structure, both of which are ultimately a function of optimal use of technology and resources. We can rewrite the production possibilities in implicit form as $S - \psi(q_1, q_2) = 0$ (sometimes called the resource requirement function). Under our assumptions on technology, ψ is increasing in outputs and convex. Using this notation, the Lagrangian for the small economy problem we considered in Chapter 12 can be written:

$$\mathscr{L} = \theta U(c_1, c_2) + \lambda_1[q_1 - c_1 - x_1] + \lambda_2[q_2 - c_2 - x_2]$$
$$+ \delta[S - \psi(q_1, q_2)] + \gamma[p_1^* x_1 + p_2^* x_2].$$

It is easy to verify that the first order conditions for a maximum require $\partial c_1 / \partial c_2 = \partial q_1 / \partial q_2 = -p_2^* / p_1^*$, as we have seen.

For a large economy, the volume of imports the rest of the world is willing to offer in exchange for a unit of exports will depend on the total volume of trade, and this is an additional constraint on the economy. We call this the foreign offer, which we can write as, say, $x_1 = \tilde{\phi}(x_2)$, or in implicit form as $F - \phi(x_1, x_2) = 0$, where ϕ is increasing in exports and concave. The Lagrangian for the large economy maximization problem then becomes:

$$\mathscr{L} = \theta U(c_1, c_2) + \lambda_1[q_1 - c_1 - x_1] + \lambda_2[q_2 - c_2 - x_2]$$
$$+ \delta[S - \psi(q_1, q_2)] - \gamma[F - \phi(x_1, x_2)]. \tag{14.1}$$

Differentiating with respect to consumption, production and trade yields the first order conditions:

$$\partial \mathscr{L} / \partial c_i = \theta \partial U / \partial c_i - \lambda_i = 0 \quad i = 1, 2 \tag{14.2}$$

$$\partial \mathscr{L} / \partial q_i = \lambda_i - \delta \partial \psi / \partial q_i = 0 \quad i = 1, 2 \tag{14.3}$$

$$\partial \mathscr{L} / \partial x_i = -\lambda_i + \gamma \partial \phi / \partial x_i = 0 \quad i = 1, 2. \tag{14.4}$$

Differentiating with respect to the multipliers yields the original constraints, which also must hold at the optimum. Rearranging conditions (14.2) to (14.4) yields:

$$\frac{\partial q_1}{\partial q_2} = \frac{\partial c_1}{\partial c_2} = \frac{\partial x_1}{\partial x_2}. \tag{14.5}$$

This looks fairly familiar. In words, the marginal rate of transformation (the slope of the transformation locus) must equal the marginal rate of substitution (the slope of the indifference curve) and the foreign rate of transformation (the slope of the offer). If the foreign offer takes the form $0 - (p_1^* x_1 + p_2^* x_2)$, where p_1^* and p_2^* are fixed, then the foreign rate of transformation is simply $-p_2^* / p_1^*$, and the problem and the solution collapse to the small country case. In general, however, since ϕ is concave, it is not possible for a large country to satisfy the condition unless foreign relative prices differ from home relative prices, implying that it cannot optimally follow a policy of free trade. We will return to this point when we introduce tariffs and other interventions into the model.

The typical geometry of a large country outcome is presented in Figure 14.1. The only difference relative to Figure 12.1 is the addition of a curve passing through the optimal production point q_1^*, q_2^* and the optimal consumption point c_1^*, c_2^* under conditions of free trade. This represents the foreign offer.[1] With free trade the value of output and the value of consumption at world prices are equal. The foreign offer represents the trading partner's willingness to exchange at various relative prices. At relative prices where the offer coincides with the home country's trade triangle, we have an equilibrium solution. Since foreign is willing to accept any points along its offer, and some lie above the indifference curve passing through c_1^*, c_2^*, this geometry makes it immediately evident that free trade is not optimal policy for a country facing a concave offer curve.

14.2 The Foreign Offer

Allowing for a large country requires replacing the fixed world prices with functions representing the foreign offers. We do this by introducing a foreign demand/supply function for each good except the numéraire. While any appropriate function can be used, the constant elasticity of demand/supply function is typical. This takes the form:

$$x_i = \xi_i p_i^{*\varepsilon_i} \tag{14.6}$$

where ε_i is the trade elasticity (negative for exportables, positive for importables), and ξ_i is a constant (positive for exportables and negative for importables, since we have defined the latter as negative exports). The elasticities are free parameters. We can set them to any appropriate values that we wish. As $\varepsilon_i \to -\infty$ for all exportables and ∞ for all importables, the economy is effectively a small economy. Given an initial trade flow and normalized price, the calibration of ξ_i is straightforward.

---

[1] We discuss the offer curve further in the next chapter.

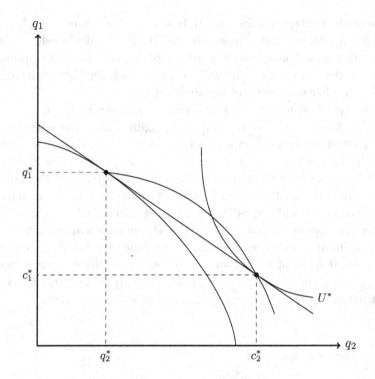

Fig. 14.1   Large Country Trading Equilibrium.

14.3   GAMS Implementation

The GAMS program is very similar to that from Chapter 12, so we present only the changes. As always, the full program is available for download. We start with the HOS model structure. First, under the sets, we explicitly define a subset of the goods to represent the numéraire, and then a subset holding all other goods:

```
SET N(I) Numeraire Good /1/;
SET G(I) Other goods /2/;
```

Next, under `PARAMETERS`, we replace the exogenous price we used in the small country model with an initial value for the now endogenous prices (much like in the autarky model of Chapter 11), and we add names for the parameters of the export demand/import supply functions:

```
EPSILON(G) Trade elasticities
XI(G)      Shifts on foreign offers
PO(I)      Initial prices
```

Note how the latter are defined over G rather than I. We will be fixing the price of the numéraire good. In the model calibration, we set the system up so that trade occurs in the starting point, with good 1 arbitrarily chosen to be an exportable:

```
QO(I)=100;
CO('1')=150;
CO('2')=50;
XO(I)=QO(I)-CO(I);
```

We then calibrate the parameters of the foreign demand function, using exception handing to ensure that they are defined only for the good that is not the numéraire:

```
EPSILON(G)$(XO(G) > 0)=-3;
EPSILON(G)$(XO(G) < 0)=2;
XI(G)=XO(G)/(PO(G)**EPSILON(G));
```

Note the use of the set G to control assignment only to goods other than the numéraire, and the use of exception handling to assign a negative elasticity if the good is an exportable, and a positive value if importable.[2]

Next, under the **VARIABLES** heading, we have to add terms for the now endogenous prices:

```
P(I) Prices
```

As usual, the level for this variable is set with its initial value. As in Chapter 11, we define a numéraire by fixing the value of one of the prices:

```
P.FX(N)=1;
```

Finally, under **EQUATIONS** we assign a name and define the foreign demand, using the subset to ensure that it is defined only for the non-numéraire goods:

```
OFFER(G) Foreign offer functions
```

---

[2]With only two goods we do not need the second equation, since no non-numéraire good is imported. The equation is necessary if more traded goods are introduced into the model, or if you decide to switch the choice of the numéraire good to the exportable good.

```
OFFER(G)..X(G)=E=XI(G)*P(G)**EPSILON(G);
```

The rest of the model remains the same. Running the script should verify the initial equilibrium, and then we are again free to begin experimenting with the model parameters and exogenous variables to see how the economy responds.

14.4   Exercises

(1) What happens to world prices when the capital stock grows? What about when the stock of labor grows? How do you explain the difference in the results that you observe relative to the model of Chapter 12?

(2) Does it matter which good is the numéraire? Try switching the numéraire good and re-running exercise 1. Do the results change? What if you change the values of the trade elasticities? Can you work out why we used the $-3/+2$ pair for the export demand/import supply elasticities in the program?

(3) Is it possible to set up the model such that an increase in the capital stock in fact lowers economic welfare (as measured by the utility index) for the economy? Explain.

(4) Try setting the elasticities at a very large number (say -100 and 99 for exports and imports, respectively). How do the results of exercise 1 compare with the small country model now? Explain.

(5) Using the same approach we adopted here, can you create a large country version of the specific factors model presented in Chapter 6? How about a version featuring non-traded goods and/or intermediates?

(6) Suppose the stocks of capital and labor both grow by 10 percent, and foreign demand for the exportable also shifts outward by 10 percent. What do you expect will happen? Is this supported by your simulation?

14.5   Further Reading

To find out more about the potential effect of growth on the terms of trade, and how it may sometimes lower welfare, read the classic papers by Johnson (1955a) and Bhagwati (1958).

Chapter 15

Two Country Trading Equilibrium

In previous chapters we have looked at trade from the perspective of a single economy, first small relative to the rest of the world and then large. Many questions require us to move beyond this simplification to explicitly introduce a second economy. In this chapter and the following we show how our model can be adapted to handle two (or more) economies, and to describe the pattern and consequences of international trade between them. We begin with the two sector case.

15.1 Formal Problem

Consider the first order conditions for the long run version of the autarky model developed in Chapter 11, which we replicate below, replacing the multipliers with the appropriate market prices:

$$\theta \partial U / \partial c_i - p_i = 0 \quad i = 1, 2 \tag{15.1}$$

$$p_i \partial q_i / \partial K_i - r = 0 \quad i = 1, 2 \tag{15.2}$$

$$p_i \partial q_i / \partial L_i - w = 0 \quad i = 1, 2 \tag{15.3}$$

$$q_i(K_i, L_i) - c_i = 0 \quad i = 1, 2 \tag{15.4}$$

$$\bar{K} - K_1 - K_2 = 0 \tag{15.5}$$

$$\bar{L} - L_1 - L_2 = 0. \tag{15.6}$$

Clearly, these equations must hold for any autarkic economy, assuming non-satiation in both goods, so by indexing the variables for a set of countries, we can easily create a system of two or more identical economies. We could then allow endowments, technology and/or preferences to vary across economies too, by indexing the parameters and exogenous variables. This would allow us to create a set of autarkic economies with the same basic structure, but potentially differing in terms of some key economic characteristics.

Now consider the small economy model from Chapter 12. There is a great deal of overlap between the small country model and the autarky model of Chapter 11. In essence, we take the market clearing conditions (11.5) and replace them with the open economy market clearing conditions (12.6), replicated below:

$$q_i(K_i, L_i) - c_i - x_i = 0 \quad i = 1, 2. \tag{15.7}$$

Also, rather than having (relative) prices determined endogenously as with autarky, they are exogenous (they are simply determined by the world market prices, as in equation (15.8), with the exchange rate normalized at unity):

$$p_i - p_i^* = 0 \quad i = 1, 2. \tag{15.8}$$

The volume of trade in each commodity takes the place of the domestic autarky prices in the model, keeping the system of equations square (i.e., we have the same number of equations as unknowns). In other words, the key difference between the autarky and small open economy models is that in the former, prices adjust to ensure consumption equals production, whereas in the latter, excess demand and supply adjust to ensure domestic prices equal world prices.

Again, if we index the model of Chapter 12 by a set of countries, we can very easily represent a series of small economic systems, perhaps differing in terms of some characteristics, that can be thought of as small parts of some larger global economy.

But what if the economies are large relative to one another? Then we need to think of the world prices as being endogenously determined within world markets, not as exogenous, and we need an equation with which they are determined. Let the set of all countries be **R** with elements indexed by r. If we then let the exports of each economy be indexed by country such that x_i^r represents the excess supply of good i in country r, the equations we need to determine the world prices are:

$$\sum_{r \in \mathbf{R}} x_i^r = 0 \quad i = 1, 2 \tag{15.9}$$

i.e., market clearing. In words, the world prices are those where the total excess supply of all exporting countries is equal to the total excess demand of all importing countries. Of course, Walras' law applies here, the equilibrium conditions are not independent. Moreover, we must set the world price of one good equal to unity to act as a numéraire. We have enough information, though, to determine a set of relative prices.

For the case of two countries and two goods, the equilibrium in traded good space can be depicted using the same offer curves that we introduced in the preceding chapter.[1] These are the general equilibrium equivalent of excess demand functions. In Figure 15.1, the offer labeled O^h is that of the home economy, which, as drawn, imports good 2 and exports good 1. In the two sector/two factor model, the pattern of trade follows the Heckscher-Ohlin pattern. That is, home must be relatively abundant in the factor which is used intensively in the production of good 1. The offer labeled O^f is that of the foreign economy, which exports good 2 and imports good 1. Where the offers intersect, the equilibrium relative price is determined (labeled p), along with the volume of trade (denoted x_1 and x_2).

In the case of the 2×2 model, we can also usefully represent the equilibrium in terms of outcomes in factor markets, using a geometric device introduced by Dixit and Norman (1980). Imagine that the global economy consists of a single country. The dimensions of the production box in Figure 15.2 are the endowments of capital and labor in this single or "integrated" economy, the total amount of capital and labor available in the world.

Since we are considering one closed economy, using our model of autarky from Chapter 11 we could determine the equilibrium relative prices, outputs, the associated factor allocations, and the corresponding returns to factors of production in this "integrated" equilibrium. The factor intensity rays drawn in Figure 15.2 are those that arise in the equilibrium. As drawn, good 1 is capital intensive. The factor allocations to the two goods are given by the intersections of the solid lines.

Now suppose that the global economy is split into two separate countries, which we call home and foreign. Samuelson (1949) invokes an 'angel' who divides up the world's capital and labor between the countries, and restricts them from moving from one country to the other. Graphically, we

---

[1]The offer curve plots each countries desired imports against its desired imports at various relative prices. The slope of the offer curve at the origin must be the relative price (of good 2) at autarky, the relative price at which the economy does not want to trade. The offer curves extend into the negative quadrant, but do not cross in that region provided preferences are well behaved. Since the offer curves are derived from the optimal production and consumption choices, their shape will depend on the shape of the transformation locus and preferences, so they need not be as regular as drawn. In particular, we have drawn the offers upward sloping across their range, implying an elastic import demand. If import demand is inelastic across some range, the offer curves may be downward sloping. A small economy faces an offer that is a straight line.

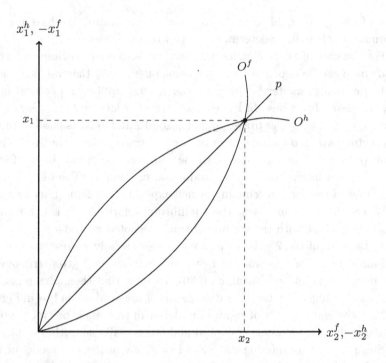

Fig. 15.1 Two Country Trading Equilibrium.

can represent the new state of affairs in Figure 15.2 by considering O^h to be the origin with respect to home, O^f the origin respect to foreign, and denoting the division of the factors by a point in the box, say E.

Since both new countries were formed from the same original country, they both have the same constant returns to scale technology and the same homothetic preferences. Suppose that the angel does not restrict the movement of *goods* between the countries (i.e., international trade is allowed). In that case arbitrage ensures that goods prices are the same in both countries. Moreover, with relative prices the same in both countries, provided both countries produce both goods in positive quantities, because they are using the same constant returns to scale technology, factor prices and factor proportions must be the same.[2]

To be consistent with full employment of resources in both countries (and therefore in the global economy overall), the inputs to each sector

---

[2]Strictly, we must also assume that the factor intensity ranking of industries never reverses. Both countries will produce both goods only if E lies within the shaded region of Figure 15.2.

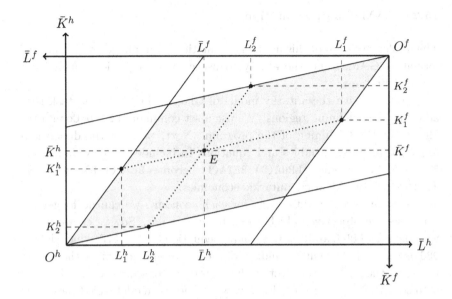

Fig. 15.2   Factor Allocation in Equilibrium.

must lie on the same factor intensity rays that we derived from the integrated equilibrium, as drawn. But this means that the trading equilibrium not only causes factor prices to be the same in each country, but exactly replicates the integrated equilibrium in terms of total production, factor allocations, and good/factor prices! In a real sense then, under certain conditions, international trade "integrates" economies in the same way as allowing factors of production to move across national borders, or equivalently eliminating borders altogether, would do.

While we have framed our discussion in terms of the HOS (2×2) model, the general approach we have outlined and the offer curve geometry applies equally to the specific factors model, and indeed to the other two-sector variations that we have considered. Once relative prices are known, we can represent the solution for the rest of the economic system (production, factor prices, etc.) using the same geometric devices that we have used in previous chapters. The "integration" argument would not hold in the specific factors case, however, since in that model factor prices depend not only on goods prices, but also on factor endowments.

15.2   GAMS Implementation

The implementation of this model is dramatically simplified by the indexed format of GAMS, and the ability to use common equations in multiple model definitions.

We begin with the autarky model of Chapter 11. The first task is to add a new set defining regions. We use a set command SET D Countries /H,F/; at the beginning of the program. Next, we alter the dimensions of all parameters, variables and equations to include the new dimension. Hence, ALPHA becomes ALPHA(D), BETA(I) becomes BETA(I,D), and so on. This creates two identical autarkic economies.

Since we have a utility index for each economy, we can no longer use utility as the objective, which needs to be a scalar. So, we create a new variable called OBJ, and a corresponding equation OBJECTIVE, which defines OBJ as the sum of the utility indices of the two economies. Since the system is square, the particular objective chosen is of no consequence (try changing it to something else to see). Finally, we define the model, this time listing all the equations individually as follows:

```
MODEL AUTARKY /UTILITY, DEMAND, PRODUCTION, RESOURCE, FDEMAND,
    INCOME, OBJECTIVE, CLEAR /;
```

Solving at this point generates two identical equilibria, one for each economy. The code is presented in Table 15.1, and is very similar to what we saw in Chapter 11.

The code for implementing a model in which trade can occur between the economies is presented in Table 15.2, which can be appended directly to the autarky model. Note that we can have multiple assignment statements, and they do not have to be placed together. So, in this part of the model we define and assign new parameters, variables and equations as usual, but only for those components of the model that differ between the autarkic and open economies. Hence, the new parameters are the initial world prices and trade flows, new variables are the world prices and trade flows, and new equations are the open economy material balance conditions, the price arbitrage conditions, and the world market clearing conditions.

Because the other parts of the model with trade (production, consumption, etc.) maintain the same structure as in the autarky model, we can avoid replication simply by creating another GAMS model that includes only the relevant components. Hence we have:

Table 15.1 GAMS Program for HOS Model (Autarky).

```
SET I Goods /1,2/;
SET J Factors /K,L/;
SET D Countries /H,F/;
ALIAS (J, JJ);

PARAMETERS
ALPHA(D)                        Shift parameters in utility
BETA(I,D)                       Share parameters in utility
PO(I,D)                         Initial domestic prices
UO(D)                           Initial utility level
CO(I,D)                         Initial consumption levels
GAMMA(I,D)                      Shift parameters in production
DELTA(J,I,D)                    Share parameters in production
RHO(I,D)                        Elasticity parameters in production
FBAR(J,D)                       Endowments
QO(I,D)                         Initial output levels
RO(J,D)                         Initial factor prices
FO(J,I,D)                       Initial factor use levels
GDPO(D)                         Initial gross domestic product;

PO(I,D)=1;
RO(J,D)=1;
QO(I,D)=100;
CO(I,D)=QO(I,D);
FO('L','1',D)=20;
FO('L','2',D)=80;
FO('K',I,D)=(QO(I,D)*PO(I,D)-FO('L',I,D)*RO('L',D))/RO('K',D);
FBAR(J,D)=SUM(I, FO(J,I,D));
GDPO(D)=SUM(I, PO(I,D)*QO(I,D));
RHO(I,D)=0.1;
DELTA(J,I,D)=(RO(J,D)/FO(J,I,D)**(RHO(I,D)-1))/(SUM(JJ, RO(JJ,D)
   /FO(JJ,I,D)**(RHO(I,D)-1)));
GAMMA(I,D)=QO(I,D)/(SUM(J, DELTA(J,I,D)*FO(J,I,D)**RHO(I,D)))**(1/RHO(I,D));
UO(D)=GDPO(D);
BETA(I,D)=CO(I,D)*PO(I,D)/GDPO(D);
ALPHA(D)=UO(D)/PROD(I, CO(I,D)**BETA(I,D));

VARIABLES
U(D)                            Utility indices
P(I,D)                          Prices
C(I,D)                          Consumption levels
Q(I,D)                          Output levels
```

---

continued on next page

continued from previous page

```
R(J,D)                          Factor prices
F(J,I,D)                        Factor use levels
GDP(D)                          Gross domestic product
OBJ                             Objective;


U.L(D)=UO(D);
P.L(I,D)=PO(I,D);
C.L(I,D)=CO(I,D);
Q.L(I,D)=QO(I,D);
R.L(J,D)=RO(J,D);
F.L(J,I,D)=FO(J,I,D);
OBJ.L=SUM(D, UO(D));
GDP.L(D)=GDPO(D);
P.LO(I,D)=0;
C.LO(I,D)=0;
Q.LO(I,D)=0;
R.LO(J,D)=0;
F.LO(J,I,D)=0;
GDP.LO(D)=0;
P.FX('2',D)=1;


EQUATIONS
UTILITY(D)                      Utility functions
DEMAND(I,D)                     Demand functions
CLEAR(I,D)                      Market clearing
PRODUCTION(I,D)                 Production functions
RESOURCE(J,D)                   Resource constraints
FDEMAND(J,I,D)                  Factor demand functions
INCOME(D)                       Gross domestic products
OBJECTIVE                       Objective function;

UTILITY(D)..U(D)=E=ALPHA(D)*PROD(I, C(I,D)**BETA(I,D));
DEMAND(I,D)..C(I,D)=E=BETA(I,D)*GDP(D)/P(I,D);
CLEAR(I,D)..C(I,D)=E=Q(I,D);
PRODUCTION(I,D)..Q(I,D)=E=GAMMA(I,D)*SUM(J, DELTA(J,I,D)*F(J,I,D)**
  RHO(I,D))**(1/RHO(I,D));
RESOURCE(J,D)..FBAR(J,D)=E=SUM(I, F(J,I,D));
FDEMAND(J,I,D)..R(J,D)=E=P(I,D)*Q(I,D)*SUM(JJ, DELTA(JJ,I,D)*F(JJ,I,D)**
  RHO(I,D))**(-1)*DELTA(J,I,D)*F(J,I,D)**(RHO(I,D)-1);
INCOME(D)..GDP(D)=E=SUM(I, P(I,D)*Q(I,D));
OBJECTIVE..OBJ=E=SUM(D, U(D));


MODEL AUTARKY /UTILITY, DEMAND, PRODUCTION, RESOURCE, FDEMAND,
  INCOME, OBJECTIVE, CLEAR/;
SOLVE AUTARKY USING NLP MAXIMIZING OBJ;
```

Table 15.2   GAMS Program Modifications for HOS Model (Trade).

```
PARAMETERS
PWO(I)                                  Initial world prices
XO(I,D)                                 Initial trade flows;

PWO(I)=1;
XO(I,D)=QO(I,D)-CO(I,D);

VARIABLES
PW(I)                                   World prices
X(I,D)                                  Trade;

PW.L(I)=PWO(I);
X.L(I,D)=XO(I,D);
PW.LO(I)=0;
PW.FX('2')=1;

EQUATIONS
MAT_BAL(I,D)                            Open economy material balance
INT_CLEAR(I)                           International market clearing
ARBITRAGE(I,D)                         International price arbitrage;

MAT_BAL(I,D)..X(I,D)=E=Q(I,D)-C(I,D);
INT_CLEAR(I)..SUM(D, X(I,D))=E=0;
ARBITRAGE(I,D)..P(I,D)=E=PW(I);

MODEL TRADE /UTILITY, DEMAND, PRODUCTION, RESOURCE, FDEMAND,
  INCOME, OBJECTIVE, MAT_BAL, INT_CLEAR, ARBITRAGE /;
SOLVE TRADE USING NLP MAXIMIZING OBJ;
```

MODEL TRADE /UTILITY, DEMAND, PRODUCTION, RESOURCE, FDEMAND, INCOME, OBJECTIVE, MAT_BAL, INT_CLEAR, ARBITRAGE /;

That is, the model with trade is the same as for autarky, but we drop the autarky market clearing condition and replace it with the open economy material balance conditions, then add international market clearing and price arbitrage (law of one price) conditions. This method is a very efficient way of combining common model elements into multiple different models. Solving the trade model generates an equilibrium solution for an integrated world economy, with free trade.

Of course, at the initial point, no trade takes place because the economies are identical, and trade (at least of the comparative advantage type with perfect competition and no product differentiation) makes no sense in this context. However, you should find that if you change either economy in terms of endowments, technology or preferences, that trade will arise.

15.3   Exercises

(1) In the initial calibration, when we shift from a pair of closed economies to a trading world, no trade occurs in the solution. Verify and explain.

(2) Using the autarky model, increase the capital stock in home and the labor stock in foreign. How does this change factor prices and the prices of goods? How is this related to the concept of comparative advantage?

(3) Using the trade model, what happens when you increase the factor endowments in the same way as in the question above. What exactly is the pattern of trade, and why? What happens to factor prices?

(4) What is the pattern of trade if you implement an improvement in technology in one sector of one economy? Do factor prices still equalize?

(5) See if you can adjust the model to allow for an exogenous transfer from home to foreign, defined in units of the numéraire good. For a positive transfer from foreign to home, what happens to the terms of trade? Is it possible for home to be made worse off by the transfer?

(6) Using the specific factors model, can you build a two country model of international trade along the same lines presented here? Using the model, does international trade equalize factor prices? What is your explanation?

(7) Try building and calibrating a model in which trade is already occurring in the initial equilibrium.

(8) Krugman (1982) argues that under certain circumstances if the foreign economy becomes uniformly more efficient, the domestic economy will not suffer. Can you demonstrate that this is true if the utility functions of all the actors are identical and homothetic?

15.4   Further Reading

The HOS model is one of the most important models in international trade theory. A good place to start is Bhagwati *et al.* (1998), especially Chapters 5 and 6. After that you might want to go back and read some of the classic articles, including Samuelson (1949) and (1953), and Jones (1956).

Dixit and Norman (1980) provide a thorough treatment from the dual perspective, in addition to elucidating the "integrated equilibrium" approach to factor price equalization. Exercise 5 above involves what is known as the "transfer problem." Classic readings on the problem include Samuelson (1952) and Johnson (1955b). Generalizations can be found in Bhagwati *et al.* (1983).

Chapter 16

Higher Dimensions and Trade

The preceding chapter examined the $2 \times 2 \times 2$ (2 goods, two factors, two countries), or HOS, model of international trade. You should be able to easily extend the analysis to handle the $2 \times 3 \times 2$ case. With the HOS model we can show that the pattern of trade is determined by the pattern of factor abundance and the pattern of factor intensity. However, these concepts are fundamentally two-dimensional in nature. A natural question then is what happens to the pattern of trade in higher dimensional models? This is the question we address in the current chapter.

16.1 Formal Problem

Consider the dual representation of the higher dimensional production problem that we introduced in Chapter 9:

$$\mathbf{AR} = \mathbf{P} \tag{16.1}$$

$$\mathbf{A^T Q} = \mathbf{V} \tag{16.2}$$

where $\mathbf{A}$ is the matrix of the optimal unit factor demands, $\mathbf{R}$ is the vector of factor prices, $\mathbf{P}$ is the vector of good prices, $\mathbf{Q}$ is the vector of outputs and $\mathbf{V}$ is the vector of endowments. The system may be even, i.e., the number of factors equals the number of goods, or the number of goods may exceed the number of factors. Using the material balance condition, we can define a vector of net exports $\mathbf{X}$:

$$\mathbf{X} = \mathbf{Q} - \mathbf{C}. \tag{16.3}$$

With identical and homothetic preferences, we have:

$$\mathbf{C} = \alpha[\mathbf{C} + \mathbf{C^*}] = \alpha[\mathbf{Q} + \mathbf{Q^*}] \tag{16.4}$$

where an asterisk denotes foreign. This states that the vector of home consumption is equal to α, the home country's share of world income, multiplied by the vector of world consumption, which must also equal the vector of world production. Now, if factor price equalization obtains, then with the same technology in both countries and full employment we must have:[1]

$$\mathbf{A}^{\mathbf{T}}[\mathbf{Q} + \mathbf{Q}^*] = \mathbf{V} + \mathbf{V}^* \tag{16.5}$$

since the matrix of optimal inputs $\mathbf{A}$ must be the same for both countries. This simply states that resources are fully employed at the global level. Multiplying both sides of (16.3) by $\mathbf{A}^{\mathbf{T}}$ and substituting from (16.2), (16.4) and (16.5) we have the following expression for the factor content of trade:

$$\mathbf{A}^{\mathbf{T}}\mathbf{X} = \mathbf{V} - \alpha[\mathbf{V} + \mathbf{V}^*] \tag{16.6}$$

The left-hand side measures the factor content of the trade vector. Hence, a positive element for, say, capital means that the services of capital are exported by home. The right-hand side tells us that this can be true if and only if the home economy is abundant in capital in the sense that its share of the world endowment of capital exceeds its share of world income, evaluated at the integrated equilibrium. This result is called the Heckscher–Ohlin–Vanek theorem. Note that we cannot say exactly which goods will be exported; the proposition tells us only about the factor content of trade. Nonetheless, since we can usefully think of trade in goods as being merely packages for transporting factors, the result is an informative one.

In Chapter 9 we noted that if the number of goods exceeds the number of factors; for arbitrarily given prices there is generally not an equilibrium solution in which all goods are produced. Why do we not face a similar issue here? The key difference is that here prices are not determined arbitrarily. We can think of them being determined in the integrated equilibrium as described in Chapter 15.[2] Hence, all goods will be produced in the global economy. However, even if factor price equalization occurs, it is not necessary for all goods to be produced in all countries. In general, there will be multiple production patterns consistent with the integrated equilibrium. See Dixit and Norman (1980) for further discussion.

---

[1] Dixit and Norman (1980) provide a detailed description of the conditions under which this will be true.

[2] If you tried exercise 10 in Chapter 11, you found that an autarky equilibrium with more goods than factors did not pose any particular problem.

16.2   GAMS Implementation

Implementing a model to illustrate the HOV theorem in GAMS is really just a matter of combining the higher dimensional production structure we introduced in Chapter 9 with the two country model we used in Chapter 15. There are only a few new things of note, so we will forgo a complete presentation.

The first step is to increase the dimensions of the sets. We will consider a 3 × 3 × 2 model. Next we provide values for initial factor inputs FO(J,I,D). Because this is three dimensional, we combine the TABLE and list methods that we used in Chapters 9 and 13, respectively. To enter three dimensional data we use the following form:

```
TABLE FO(J,I,D) Initial factor use levels
            H       F
L.1        20      20
K.1        80      80
L.2        80      80
K.2        20      20
L.3        10      10
K.3        15      15;
```

The first two dimensions are indicated by the format INDEX1.INDEX2, and the third dimension is in the columns. Hence, the first entry in the table is equivalent to the statement FO('L','1','H')=20. The remainder of the program is essentially unchanged from Chapter 15. Running the model should verify the initial equilibrium. Tweaking the endowments should result in trade occurring.

A final question is how to easily observe the factor content of trade in the solution. Of course, we could calculate it manually, but it is easier to use GAMS to make the calculations for us. First we define a new parameter to hold the factor contents:

```
PARAMETER
CONTENT(J,D) Factor content of trade;
```

Next, we make the required calculation from the equilibrium solution. The solution is held in the levels for the variables, and we can use it as we would any other fixed value:

```
CONTENT(J,D)=SUM(I, (F.L(J,I,D)/Q.L(I,D))*X.L(I,D));
```

```
DISPLAY CONTENT;
```

The first line calculates the content, on the basis of the solution values. The second line uses the `DISPLAY` command, which forces GAMS to display the values of the listed items at the current point. The format is the keyword `DISPLAY`, followed by the item or items to be displayed (separated by commas), and a concluding semicolon. Note that the indices of the values are not used in the statement. GAMS will display a listing of the values.

16.3 Exercises

(1) Can you verify that the HOV theorem is holding in this experiment by comparing the factor endowment pattern to the income shares, and matching the pattern to the factor content index?
(2) Is it possible for a country to be a net exporter of the services of all factors of production? Why or why not?

16.4 Further Reading

The classic reference on higher dimensional trade theory is Vanek (1968). For detailed discussion on the conditions under which factor price equalization will arise in these models see Dixit and Norman (1980).

Chapter 17

Reciprocal Dumping

Our modeling so far has concentrated on the "standard" trade theory with perfect competition and constant returns to scale. Of course, there is an extensive literature on how imperfect competition and scale economies can be incorporated into models of international trade, and in particular used to explain intra-industry trade, or two-way trade in the same product category. This literature is often called the "new" trade theory. The two main branches of the literature explore how strategic rivalry can lead to trade in models of oligopoly, and how product differentiation can lead to trade in models of monopolistic competition. GAMS programs can be developed to explore these structures in much the same way as with the standard theory. In this chapter we consider a simple example of trade arising from strategic rivalry, while in Chapter 18 we examine a case of monopolistic competition.

17.1   Reciprocal Dumping

The reciprocal dumping model (Brander and Krugman, 1983) illustrates how oligopolistic rivalry can generate international trade of the intra-industry variety. The critical assumption underlying the model is the segmented markets perception, whereby firms make distinct quantity decisions for each market. What is particularly interesting about the model is that international trade is in products that are identical — not different varieties within the same category. In that sense, trade is wasteful, although it can work to reduce the economic efficiency costs associated with firms exploiting their market power.

The basic setup is fairly simple. The model is partial equilibrium, and assumes the existence of two identical markets, with a single firm in each producing a homogeneous commodity for sale (potentially) in both markets.

Transporting goods from one country to the other is assumed to be costly. Finally, each firm behaves in accordance with the Cournot perception (i.e., it chooses its sales in each country under the assumption that the firm from the other country will hold its sales constant).

Let's denote the countries "home" (h) and "foreign" (f). The quantity of the good produced by the home firm for home consumption is q_{hh}, while the quantity of the good produced by the home firm for foreign consumption is q_{hf}. The marginal cost of production is assumed to be a constant, c, and transportation costs are of the iceberg type, so the cost of selling an additional unit in the foreign country is c/g, where $0 \leq g \leq 1$.[1] The foreign country is symmetric, hence q_{ff} is foreign production for sale in the foreign market, and q_{fh} is foreign production for sale in the home market.

Suppose that the inverse demand function in the home country is given by $p_h(q_{hh} + q_{fh})$, and in the foreign country by $p_f(q_{ff} + q_{hf})$. We can define the profit function for the home firm as:

$$\pi_h = p_h(q_{hh} + q_{fh})q_{hh} + p_f(q_{ff} + q_{hf})q_{hf} - c[q_{hh} + q_{hf}/g] - F_h \quad (17.1)$$

where F_h represents fixed costs. Similarly, for the foreign firm we have:

$$\pi_f = p_h(q_{hh} + q_{fh})q_{fh} + p_f(q_{ff} + q_{hf})q_{ff} - c[q_{ff} + q_{fh}/g] - F_f. \quad (17.2)$$

Now, with each firm maximizing profit with respect to its own output, the first order conditions for an optimal choice by each firm with respect to its sales in each market are:

$$\partial\pi_h/\partial q_{hh} = (\partial p_h/\partial q_{hh})q_{hh} + p_h - c = 0 \qquad (17.3)$$

$$\partial\pi_h/\partial q_{hf} = (\partial p_f/\partial q_{hf})q_{hf} + p_f - c/g = 0 \qquad (17.4)$$

$$\partial\pi_f/\partial q_{ff} = (\partial p_f/\partial q_{ff})q_{ff} + p_f - c = 0 \qquad (17.5)$$

$$\partial\pi_f/\partial q_{fh} = (\partial p_h/\partial q_{fh})q_{fh} + p_h - c/g = 0. \qquad (17.6)$$

Equations (17.3)–(17.6) are best response functions. They represent four equations in the four unknown quantities, the q_{ij}'s, and the solution represents an equilibrium provided that the second order conditions are satisfied (i.e., the derivatives of each best response function with respect to own sales are negative). A necessary condition for the solution to be stable is that the best response functions are downward sloping (i.e., the derivatives of each best response function with respect to rival sales are negative.)

---

[1]Iceberg transportation costs can be thought of as meaning that of the goods sent, only the proportion g arrives, the rest having melted away. Hence, to ensure that one unit arrives it is necessary to ship $1/g$ units.

Once we have solved for the Nash equilibrium quantities as functions of the costs of production, the costs of transportation, and the characteristics of demand, we can solve for the prices and the profit levels. If q_{hf} and q_{fh} are positive in the solution, international trade of the reciprocal dumping variety is occurring.

17.2   GAMS Implementation

To operationalize the model as a GAMS program we need to choose a functional form for demand. Brander (1981) uses linear demand functions, which satisfy the second order and stability conditions globally. Brander and Krugman (1983) use the constant elasticity of demand function that we introduced in Chapter 14. In this case home demand would be $p_h = \alpha_h[q_{hh} + q_{fh}])^{1/\varepsilon_h}$, where $\varepsilon_h < 0$ is the elasticity of demand and α_h is a positive constant. The demand function in foreign takes the same form. The profit functions are therefore written:

$$\pi_h = \alpha_h[q_{hh} + q_{fh}]^{1/\varepsilon_h} q_{hh} + \alpha_f[q_{ff} + q_{hf}]^{1/\varepsilon_f} q_{hf}$$
$$- c_h[q_{hh} + q_{hf}/g_h] - F_h \tag{17.7}$$
$$\pi_f = \alpha_f[q_{ff} + q_{hf}]^{1/\varepsilon_f} q_{ff} + \alpha_h[q_{hh} + q_{fh}]^{1/\varepsilon_h} q_{fh}$$
$$- c_f[q_{ff} + q_{fh}/g_f] - F_f. \tag{17.8}$$

We have generalized the Brander–Krugman model somewhat by allowing for differences in the demand and cost parameters, including transportation costs, across the economies. The first-order conditions for an optimal choice of sales by both firms in the home market are:

$$q_{hh}\alpha_h\varepsilon_h^{-1}[q_{hh} + q_{fh}]^{\frac{1-\varepsilon_h}{\varepsilon_h}} + \alpha_h[q_{hh} + q_{fh}]^{1/\varepsilon_h} - c_h = 0 \tag{17.9}$$
$$q_{fh}\alpha_h\varepsilon_h^{-1}[q_{hh} + q_{fh}]^{\frac{1-\varepsilon_h}{\varepsilon_h}} + \alpha_h[q_{hh} + q_{fh}]^{1/\varepsilon_h} - c_f/g_f = 0. \tag{17.10}$$

These are the best response functions applying in the home market. Similar conditions apply for each firm's choice in the foreign market. The second order conditions are globally satisfied provided that demand in each country is elastic (i.e., $\varepsilon_i < -1$), so marginal revenue for total sales in each market is positive.

We can rewrite the best response functions in the following form, which will be helpful when we calibrate the model:

$$p_h = c_h\varepsilon_h/[\varepsilon_h + \theta_{hh}] \tag{17.11}$$
$$p_h = c_f\varepsilon_h/[g_f(\varepsilon_h + \theta_{fh})] \tag{17.12}$$

where θ_{hh} is the share of the home firm in the home market, and θ_{fh} is the share of the foreign firm in the home market. The stability conditions are locally satisfied provided that $(1 - 1/\varepsilon_i)\theta_{ii} < 1$.[2]

Now let's consider a welfare function. Under appropriate assumptions we can use the consumer surplus plus the profit of the firm. Let $Z_h = q_{hh} + q_{fh}$, i.e., total sales in the home market. Then home welfare can be measured by:

$$W_h = \int_0^{Z_h} p_h(Z_h)dZ_h - p_h Z_h + \pi_h. \tag{17.13}$$

The constant elasticity of demand function has a vertical asymptote at zero and so its integral is improper. However, it is convergent provided that $\varepsilon < -1$, which is the same condition we require to ensure the second order conditions are globally satisfied. The welfare function for home in this case can be written:

$$W_h = \alpha_h \frac{\varepsilon_h}{\varepsilon_h + 1} Z_h^{\frac{\varepsilon_h+1}{\varepsilon_h}} - p_h Z_h + \pi_h. \tag{17.14}$$

A similar expression can be derived to describe welfare for the foreign economy.

We are now ready to build the GAMS model. The completed program is presented in full in Table 17.1. As usual, we begin by defining the SETS (here countries/firms). We then use the ALIAS command to generate two more sets with the same elements.

Next we define the PARAMETER names, ALPHA(D) and EPSILON(D) for the demand parameters, C(D) and F(D) for the cost parameters, and G(D,DD) for the transportation costs. Notice that we have defined G with dimensions country × country for convenience (this allows us generalize the model more easily). We also define initial values for sales, Q0(D,DD), prices, P0(D), profits, PROFIT0(D), and welfare, WELFARE0(D), along with two other convenience parameters: Z0(D) representing total sales in each market and SHARE(D,DD) representing the share of each firm in each market. Finally we have defined a parameter CONTROL(D,DD), the utility of which will become clear in due course.

Under the VARIABLES heading we define the endogenous variable names P(D), Q(D,DD), PROFIT(D) and WELFARE(D). We also define OBJ, a scalar variable that we will use as the objective. As in Chapter 15, since the system is square, the particular objective chosen is of no consequence.

---

[2]To see this, take the derivative of (17.9) with respect to q_{fh} and express in share form.

Table 17.1   GAMS Program for Reciprocal Dumping.

```
SET D Countries /H,F/;
ALIAS (D,DD,DDD);

PARAMETERS
ALPHA(D)                    Shift parameters in demand
EPSILON(D)                  Elasticities of demand
G(D,DD)                     Iceberg parameters
C(D)                        Marginal costs
F(D)                        Fixed costs
Q0(D,DD)                    Initial firm sales by market
Z0(D)                       Initial total sales by market
SHARE(D,DD)                 Initial market shares
P0(D)                       Initial prices
PROFIT0(D)                  Initial profits
WELFARE0(D)                 Initial welfare
CONTROL(D,DD)               Control matrix;

P0(D)=1;
Z0(D)=500;
EPSILON(D)=-4;
ALPHA(D)=P0(D)/Z0(D)**(1/EPSILON(D));
CONTROL(D,DD)=1;
CONTROL(D,D)=0;
G(D,D)=1;
SHARE(D,D)=0.75;
SHARE(D,DD)$CONTROL(D,DD)=1-SHARE(D,D);
C(D)=P0(D)*G(D,D)*(EPSILON(D)+SHARE(D,D))/EPSILON(D);
G(D,DD)$CONTROL(D,DD)=EPSILON(DD)*C(D)/(P0(DD)*(EPSILON(DD)+SHARE(D,DD)));
Q0(D,DD)=Z0(D)*SHARE(D,DD);
PROFIT0(D)=50;
F(D)=SUM(DD, P0(DD)*Q0(D,DD))-SUM(DD, C(D)/G(D,DD)*Q0(D,DD))-PROFIT0(D);
WELFARE0(D)=ALPHA(D)*EPSILON(D)/(1+EPSILON(D))*Z0(D)**((1+EPSILON(D))/
  EPSILON(D))-P0(D)*Z0(D)+PROFIT0(D);

VARIABLES
PROFIT(D)                   Firm profits
P(D)                        Prices
Q(D,DD)                     Firm sales by market
WELFARE(D)                  Welfare measures
OBJ                         Objective;
```

continued on next page

continued from previous page

```
PROFIT.L(D)=PROFIT0(D);
P.L(D)=P0(D);
Q.L(D,DD)=Q0(D,DD);
WELFARE.L(D)=WELFARE0(D);
PROFIT.LO(D)=0;
P.LO(D)=0;
Q.LO(D,DD)=0;
WELFARE.LO(D)=0;

EQUATIONS
DEMAND(D)                    Demand functions
PROF(D)                      Profit functions
BEST(D,DD)                   Best response functions
PEWELFARE(D)                 Welfare function
OBJECT                       Objective ;

DEMAND(D)..P(D)=E=ALPHA(D)*SUM(DD, Q(DD,D))**(1/EPSILON(D));
PROF(D)..PROFIT(D)=E=SUM(DD, P(DD)*Q(D,DD))-SUM(DD, C(D)/G(D,DD)*Q(D,DD))
 -F(D);
BEST(D,DD)..Q(D,DD)*P(DD)/EPSILON(DD)*SUM(DDD,Q(DDD,DD))**(-1)+P(DD)
 -C(D)/G(D,DD)=E=0;
PEWELFARE(D)..WELFARE(D)=E=ALPHA(D)*EPSILON(D)/(1+EPSILON(D))*
 SUM(DD,Q(DD,D))**((1+EPSILON(D))/EPSILON(D))-P(D)*SUM(DD,Q(DD,D))+PROFIT(D);
OBJECT..OBJ=E=0;

MODEL RECIPROCAL /ALL/;
SOLVE RECIPROCAL USING NLP MAXIMIZING OBJ;
```

The equations are then defined and assigned. We have the demand functions, the profit functions, the best response functions and the welfare functions, each of which correspond to the forms defined above. The model is defined as consisting of all of the equations.

Now let's consider the calibration section of the model. As in our previous models, the objective of calibration is to fit the model to a particular set of base data and any free parameters, and we do that in effect by solving the model for the parameters that are consistent with a solution.

We begin by normalizing all prices to unity. We then set a value for the initial total sales in each market, and a value for the elasticity of demand in each market. This must be less than −1 for the reasons discussed above. We can then use the inverse demand functions to calibrate the shifts on the inverse demand curves.

The next step is to determine the cost and transportation cost values that are consistent with the solution we want to generate. This is where we need the CONTROL parameter that we defined earlier. The statement CONTROL(D,DD)=1 sets the parameter value to 1 for all country pairs. The next statement, CONTROL(D,D)=0, overwrites the values where the first element is the same as the second with a zero.[3] Hence, for home CONTROL('H','H')=0, while CONTROL('H','F')=1, and so on. Next we set the values of iceberg parameters when the sales are in the country in which production takes place at 1 with the statement G(D,D)=1, and similarly, we use the statement SHARE(D,D)=0.75 to assign a share of each country in its own market of 75 percent.[4] Using the CONTROL parameter and exception handling technique that we introduced in Chapter 6, we can then define the corresponding share of the rival firm in each market.

Next we can use equation (17.11) to determine the value of marginal cost for each firm, and (17.12) to determine the value of the iceberg parameter for each firm. Again, we use CONTROL to ensure that the assignment occurs only for the iceberg parameters on flows from H→F and F→H, since there are no transportation costs within each economy.

Finally, we can determine the value of each firm's sales in each market using the total sales and the market shares. We then assign a value to profit, and use the profit functions to determine the values of fixed costs for each firm. We can then use the welfare function to determine the initial level of the welfare index. The model is now fully calibrated, and we can assign the calibrated values to the levels of the endogenous variables, set the lower bounds, and solve the model as usual to generate the initial solution. Once you have verified that the model is working correctly, the exercises below contain some suggestions for exploring the properties of the model and extending it in various directions.

17.3 Exercises

(1) What happens in the model when transportation costs drop to zero (i.e., the iceberg parameters are all unity)?

---

[3] Note that even though the set DD has the same elements as D, it is not the same set. So the first assignment applies to all elements of the Cartesian product of D and DD, while the second applies only to the diagonal elements.

[4] Assuming the transportation costs are symmetric, the own shares should be greater than 50 percent. To ensure local stability the own shares must be less than $\varepsilon/(\varepsilon - 1)$, which in the example is 80 percent.

(2) Can you find the values of the iceberg parameters at which trade ceases? From the perspective of the firms, which scenario is better, no transportation costs or prohibitive transportation costs? How about from the perspective of society overall? Explain.

(3) In an earlier paper by Brander (1981) a similar analysis to the reciprocal dumping model was presented which assumed linear demand curves. See if you can alter the GAMS model for linear demands.

(4) See if you can extend the model to allow for more countries engaging in reciprocal dumping.

(5) Brander and Krugman also describe an extension of the model to free entry. See if you can modify the GAMS model and replicate their results.

17.4 Further Reading

The classic articles are of course Brander (1981) and Brander and Krugman (1983). There have been many extensions and generalizations.

Chapter 18

Monopolistic Competition

In the preceding chapter we built a GAMS model to illustrate the idea that imperfect competition in the form of international oligopoly can lead to trade in the absence of comparative advantage, through the strategic inter-actions of firms. The other main branch of the "new" trade theory considers the implications of monopolistically competitive market structures.

In monopolistic competition, firms produce a differentiated product (horizontally or vertically) and face a downward-sloping demand for their product.[1] They thus have some degree of market power. Nonetheless, they make zero profit in the long run because of free entry to the industry. Hence, in monopolistic competition, strategic trade drivers of the type described in the preceding chapter do not exist.

Monopolistically competitive market structures can still lead to intra-industry trade, however, and that trade can lead to gains through the exploitation of economies of scale and/or making more varieties available for consumption. As with oligopolistic models, there are many different ways of modeling monopolistic competition in the literature. In this chapter we consider a simple example and GAMS program based on the seminal paper by Krugman (1980).

18.1 Closed Economy

Krugman's model of monopolistic competition and trade illustrates a case where increasing returns to scale and monopolistic competition leads to international trade even when the pattern of technology, preferences and

---

[1]Horizontal product differentiation refers to the case where goods differ in terms of characteristics other than quality. Vertical differentiation is where the goods can be unambiguously ordered along a quality dimension.

factor abundance is the same across countries. The trade is beneficial because it increases the number of varieties available to households, who value variety (i.e., the model features horizontal product differentiation). While the volume of trade is determinate within the model, the pattern of trade is not.

The model that Krugman sets out has a simple and elegant structure. We start with the autarkic case. Assume that all consumers have the same preferences, described by the representative utility function $U = \sum_i c_i^\theta$, where $0 < \theta < 1$, and i indexes the v available varieties, which is assumed to be a large number but small relative to the potential range.[2] Consumers maximize utility subject to their budget constraint $Y = \sum_i p_i c_i$. We can solve this problem by setting up the Lagrangian. Using the first order conditions (we leave the details to you) we obtain the individual demand functions:

$$p_i = \frac{\theta c_i^{\theta-1}}{\lambda} \qquad \forall i \tag{18.1}$$

where λ is the multiplier, which has the usual interpretation. Notice that each consumer's demand for each variety is independent of their demand for all of the other varieties.

For simplicity, Krugman (1980) assumes that each consumer corresponds to a unit of labor (the only factor of production in the model). Let the stock of labor be denoted $\bar{L}$. Total consumption of each variety, C_i, is then equal to $\bar{L}c_i$. For a closed economy, at equilibrium total consumption has to equal total production, q_i, implying that $c_i = q_i/\bar{L}$. Substituting this expression into (18.1) gives us:

$$p_i = \frac{\theta \left(\frac{q_i}{L}\right)^{\theta-1}}{\lambda} \qquad \forall i. \tag{18.2}$$

This is the market demand curve faced by each firm.

Each firm is assumed to have the same increasing returns to scale production technology, represented by $l_i = \alpha + \beta q_i$, where l_i is the amount of labor used in industry i, and α and β are positive constants. Using (18.2), the firm's profit function is therefore:

$$\pi_i = \frac{\theta \left(\frac{q_i}{L}\right)^{\theta-1}}{\lambda} q_i - w[\alpha - \beta q_i] \qquad \forall i \tag{18.3}$$

[2]This is obviously a rather special functional form. The approach can generalized somewhat. See Helpman and Krugman (1985).

where the economy-wide wage is denoted w. Firms choose their output level to maximize profits. The first order condition for profit maximization allows us to solve for the profit maximizing price:

$$p_i = p = \frac{\beta w}{\theta} \qquad \forall i. \tag{18.4}$$

Hence every variety has the same price. We denote this p.[3]

In monopolistically competitive markets, free entry implies that firms must make zero profits. Using (18.3) and (18.4), and solving for where profit is equal to zero we have:

$$q_i = q = \frac{\alpha \theta}{\beta[1-\theta]} \qquad \forall i. \tag{18.5}$$

Hence, all firms produce the same quantity, q. Dividing q by $\bar{L}$ yields the solution for individual consumption of any variety, and the technological assumptions allow us to determine l_i, which again is the same for every firm. We can denote this as l.

The final step is to solve for the number of varieties produced, v. As Krugman (1980) notes, since firms can costlessly differentiate their product, and each variety has the same demand, no two firms will want to occupy the same product space. So the number of firms and the number of varieties is the same. Full employment of labor requires that $\sum_i l_i = vl = \bar{L}$. This implies that:

$$v = \frac{\bar{L}[1-\theta]}{\alpha}. \tag{18.6}$$

Solving for the number of varieties completes the model of the closed economy.

18.2 Open Economy

We now consider the case when trade is allowed. As in Krugman (1980), imagine that there exists another economy that is identical in every respect to the one that we have just examined. Clearly, relative prices will be the same in both economies in autarky, so comparative advantage-based trade cannot occur.

If transportation costs are zero, then with trade allowed the representative consumer faces the problem of maximizing $U = \sum_i c_i^\theta + \sum_j c_j^\theta$ where i

---

[3] An assumption used in deriving this expression is that since v is large, the pricing decision of any one firm does not impact the marginal utility of income (i.e., λ is treated as a constant in the firm's decision).

indexes the v goods produced at home, and j indexes the v^* goods produced in foreign, subject to the budget constraint $Y = \sum_i p_i c_i + \sum_j p_j^* c_j$.

The range of goods produced in each country is distinct, for the same reason that no two firms in either country produce the same product. Given the demand assumptions, consumers will allocate half (more generally $v/[v + v^*]$ if the stock of labor is allowed to vary across countries) of their income to consumption of varieties from each country. Total world demand for any variety remains unchanged, so the firm's problem is unchanged. Hence, equations (18.4) and (18.5) continue to determine the price (in wage units) and the output of each good. Equation (18.6) and its foreign equivalent then determine the number of varieties produced.

Is this trade beneficial? Trade in Krugman's model does not alter the real wage in terms of any produced good. Welfare does increase, however, because of the increased range of consumption.[4] There are no scale economy effects, because the level of output of every variety is the same in both autarky and with trade. Generalizing the demand structure can allow scale effects to arise.

18.3   GAMS Implementation

A GAMS program illustrating the features of the closed economy model is presented in Table 18.1. As usual, we begin by defining names for all of the model parameters, including initial values of the variables. Next we calibrate to a convenient equilibrium (in this case one that normalizes all initial prices to unity). Calibration of the model is quite straightforward given the closed form solution to the model; we leave the details to you.

Next we define names for the variables of the model, and assign lower bounds and levels. Note that we fix the wage rate as the numéraire.

The equation name assignments follow, along with the definitions, and finally MODEL and SOLVE statements. Once you have verified the initial equilibrium, you can perturb the model parameters to see how it behaves.

To extend the model to illustrate the effects of opening up to trade, we adopt an approach similar to the one we used in Chapter 15. First, we define a set to hold the countries with the statement SET R /H,F/. Next we

---

[4]To see this, note that the utility index of an individual consumer in autarky is $v[q/\bar{L}]^\theta$ whereas with trade it is $2v[q/2\bar{L}]^\theta$ (assuming the economies have the same labor stock). Since $\theta < 1$, the latter is larger than the former. Consumers give up some consumption of each good, since some must be exported to obtain other varieties, but that is more than made up for by the increase in the range of choices.

define an **ALIAS** for R with the statement **ALIAS(R,RR)**. We then index all of the variables, parameters and equations of the model by R. If we run the model (adding an arbitrary scalar objective) it will generate two identical autarkic economies.

Table 18.1   GAMS Program for Monopolistic Competition.

```
PARAMETERS
THETA                           Utility parameter
LBAR                            Labor endowment
ALPHA                           Cost function parameter
BETA                            Cost function parameter
W0                              Initial wage
V0                              Initial number of varieties
Q0                              Initial output
C0                              Initial consumption
P0                              Initial price
U0                              Initial utility index
L0                              Initial labor use ;

ALPHA=5;
BETA=0.5;
THETA=0.5;
LBAR=1000;
W0=1;
V0=LBAR*(1-THETA)/ALPHA;
Q0=ALPHA*THETA/(BETA*(1-THETA));
C0=Q0/LBAR;
L0=ALPHA+BETA*Q0;
P0=BETA*W0/THETA;
U0=V0*C0**THETA;

VARIABLES
V                               Varieties
Q                               Output
C                               Consumption
P                               Prices
U                               Utility index
L                               Labor used
W                               Wage;
```

continued on next page

continued from previous page

```
W.FX=WO;
V.LO=0; Q.LO=0; C.LO=0; P.LO=0; L.LO=0;
V.L=VO; Q.L=QO; C.L=CO; P.L=PO; U.L=UO; L.L=LO;

EQUATIONS
UTILITY                                          Utility function
CLEARING                                         Good market clearing
PRICE                                            Profit maximization
COST                                             Cost function
ENTRY                                            Free entry condition
RESOURCE                                         Full employment;

UTILITY..U=E=V*C**THETA;
CLEARING..C=E=Q/LBAR;
PRICE..P=E=BETA*W/THETA;
COST..L=E=ALPHA+BETA*Q;
ENTRY..P*Q-L*W=E=0;
RESOURCE..LBAR=E=V*L;

MODEL MONOP /ALL/;
SOLVE MONOP USING NLP MAXIMIZING U;
```

To allow for trade, we add a new variable called VT(R) to hold the total number of varieties available for consumption. We initialize this at the number of domestically produced varieties (i.e., the autarkic solution). We then let VT(R) take the place of V(R) in the utility functions, i.e:

```
UTILITY(R)..U(R)=E=VT(R)*C(R)**THETA(R);
```

Next we add two new equations to determine the values of VT(R):

```
VARIETY_A(R)..VT(R)=E=V(R);
VARIETY_T(R)..VT(R)=E=SUM(RR, V(RR));
```

The first states that the number of available varieties is the number produced domestically, and applies in autarky. The second states that the number of available varieties is the number produced globally, and applies with trade. We also need to adjust the market clearing conditions:

```
CLEARING_A(R)..C(R)=E=Q(R)/LBAR(R);
CLEARING_T(R)..C(R)=E=Q(R)/SUM(RR, LBAR(RR));
```

The first equation holds in autarky, and is the same as above. With trade, the product is spread across consumers globally rather than domestically.

Finally we define two models. One represents autarky, and consists of VARIETY_A, CLEARING_A, the adjusted utility function, and the other equations from Table 18.1 (plus a scalar objective). The other represents trade, and replaces VARIETY_A and CLEARING_A with the open economy counterparts. Solving the models sequentially reveals the impact of opening to trade. A complete version of the GAMS code is available for download.

18.4 Exercises

(1) In the closed economy model, evaluate the consequences of (a) reductions/increases in the fixed cost of production, (b) reductions/increases in the marginal cost of production, (c) and expansions/contractions of the stock of labor.

(2) In the trade model, what happens if one economy is larger than the other in terms of its labor stock?

(3) In the model with trade there is no explicit trade balance condition. Is trade balanced?

(4) How do the gains from trade in this model vary with the THETA parameter?

(5) See if you can construct a model in with a more general demand function along the lines of Krugman (1979).

18.5 Further Reading

The seminal paper on this form of monopolistic competition is Dixit and Stiglitz (1977). This chapter has focused on the implementation of monopolistic competition in a trade context presented in Krugman (1980). An earlier paper, Krugman (1979), explores a similar structure. Ethier (1979) is another influential paper in the area. Rather than introducing the product differentiation in final demand, his paper introduces it in the firm's demand for intermediates. The classic text by Helpman and Krugman (1985) gives a very detailed exposition of these types of models, and how they are related to the "standard" trade theory.

PART 2
Commercial Policy and Distortions

Chapter 19

Tariffs and Other Trade Interventions

So far we have considered economies that are free from policy-induced distortions to the economic system. In the next three chapters we will explore how various distortions can be modeled, and their consequences. First, we will consider how trade taxes, subsidies, and other interventions can be incorporated into the models of the small and large economy that we developed in Chapters 12 and 14, and the two country model we developed in Chapter 15. This will allow us to examine the production, consumption, trade, income distribution (domestic and international), and economic welfare implications of interventions. Since almost all real world trade patterns are riddled with distortions of various kinds, introducing these types of distortions is also a crucial step in building the components we need for a CGE model applied to an actual economic system.

19.1 Formal Problem for Small Country

Recall the optimization problem underlying the small country model. We will use the version with factor markets compressed into the resource requirement function that we introduced in Chapter 14. All of the standard assumptions apply, and the Lagrangian for the maximization problem can be written:

$$\mathscr{L} = \theta U(c_1, c_2) + \lambda_1[q_1 - c_1 - x_1] + \lambda_2[q_2 - c_2 - x_2]$$
$$+ \delta[S - \psi(q_1, q_2)] + \gamma[p_1^* x_1 + p_2^* x_2].$$

We can normalize γ (the exchange rate) to unity, and optimality requires relative consumer and producer prices equal relative world prices (the marginal rate of substitution and the marginal rate of transformation both equal the foreign rate of transformation).

In Chapter 12 we showed that we can break the analysis into two steps and still reach the same result; first find the levels of output that maximize the value of output, then maximize utility subject to the budget constraint, where the latter is determined by the value of income generated through production. This stepwise procedure is a particularly useful way of dealing with the problem with trade taxes/subsidies.

A trade tax/subsidy has the effect of driving a wedge between domestic and world prices. We can define the wedge in percentage (more precisely proportional or *ad valorem*) terms as $t_i = (p_i - p_i^*)/p_i^*$, $i = 1, 2$, with the price of foreign exchange normalized to unity. For an importable good (i.e., $x_i < 0$) a positive value of t_i represents a tariff, while a negative value represents an import subsidy. For an exportable good $(x_i > 0)$ a positive t_i represents an export subsidy while a negative value represents an export tax.[1]

First consider the production side of the economy. The maximization problem in production is represented by the following Lagrangian:

$$\mathscr{L} = p_1^*(1 + t_1)q_1 + p_2^*(1 + t_2)q_2 + \delta[S - \psi(q_1, q_2)]. \qquad (19.1)$$

Notice we are maximizing the value of output at domestic (tariff inclusive) prices, since those are the prices faced by the firms. Taking the derivatives of the Lagrangian with respect to q_1, q_2 and δ yields three equations in three unknowns:

$$\partial \mathscr{L}/\partial q_1 = p_1^*(1 + t_1) - \delta \partial \psi/\partial q_1 = 0 \qquad (19.2)$$

$$\partial \mathscr{L}/\partial q_2 = p_1^*(1 + t_2) - \delta \partial \psi/\partial q_2 = 0 \qquad (19.3)$$

$$\partial \mathscr{L}/\partial \delta = S - \psi(q_1, q_2) = 0. \qquad (19.4)$$

We can solve for the output levels as functions of the world prices, the trade tax rates, and of course the technology and resources implicit in the resource requirement function $S = \psi(q_1, q_2)$. As usual, only relative prices matter here, so the solution will be the same for any pair of world prices in the same ratio (a proportional rise in both world prices is just like a rise in the price of foreign exchange, γ, which is the numéraire). The condition for an optimal choice in production is familiar: the marginal rate

---

[1]While this might seem like a confusing way of defining things, the logic is that both a tariff and an export subsidy push the domestic price up relative to the world price, while an import subsidy or export tax pushes the domestic price down relative to the world price. It is important to note that tariffs and export taxes can drive the relative domestic price no further away from the relative world price than the relative autarky price. Beyond that point they are said to contain "water". We are considering only cases where there is no water.

of transformation must equal (minus) the price ratio. The only change is that the price ratio that matters is the domestic one, not the world one.

Now consider the demand side of the economy. Since consumers also face domestic prices, we can write their problem in the same way as in Chapter 3. They will maximize utility at domestic prices subject to their income constraint. The Lagrangian is:

$$\mathscr{L} = U(c_1, c_2) + \lambda[Y - p_1^*(1 + t_1)c_1 - p_2^*(1 + t_2)c_2]. \tag{19.5}$$

Taking the derivatives with respect to consumption quantities and the multiplier yields the familiar conditions for an optimum:

$$\partial\mathscr{L}/\partial c_1 = \partial U/\partial c_1 - \lambda p_1^*(1 + t_1) = 0 \tag{19.6}$$

$$\partial\mathscr{L}/\partial c_2 = \partial U/\partial c_2 - \lambda p_2^*(1 + t_2) = 0 \tag{19.7}$$

$$\partial\mathscr{L}/\partial \lambda = Y - p_1^*(1 + t_1)c_1 - p_2^*(1 + t_2)c_2 = 0. \tag{19.8}$$

We can solve for the consumption levels and λ as functions of the world prices, the trade taxes, and the level of income. At an optimum, the representative consumer will spend all of their income, and the marginal rate of substitution will equal the domestic price ratio.

To complete the model we need to determine Y. With free trade, Y is simply equal to the value of production at world prices (which is the same as the value of production at domestic prices). With trade taxes, if we assume that all tax revenue is returned in lump-sum fashion to households (and all subsidy expenditure is likewise taken from households), income is defined as the value of production at domestic prices plus the revenue generated by taxes, net of expenditures on trade subsidies. That is:

$$Y = p_1^*(1 + t_1)q_1 + p_2^*(1 + t_2)q_2 - p_1^* t_1(q_1 - c_1) - p_2^* t_2(q_2 - c_2). \tag{19.9}$$

Using equations (19.2) to (19.4), (19.6) to (19.8), and (19.9), we have enough information to determine the solution in terms of world prices and the taxes.[2]

---

[2]Condition (19.9) implies the trade balance conditions directly. Recognizing that Y is equal to consumption at domestic prices, and that net exports equal production minus consumption yields the trade balance condition. Notice that we do not use (19.9) directly in formulating the Lagrangian (19.5). To do so would imply that consumers factor into their decision how their changes in consumption will affect trade tax/subsidy revenues/expenditures. But, consumer choices affect revenues and expenditures only in the aggregate: each individual consumer is too small to have any appreciable effect on them, and so does not take changes in them into account. If there truly were a single consumer, as opposed to a representative one, then they would factor in changes in revenue, and the solution would be to equate the marginal rate of substitution to the world price ratio.

Figure 19.1 illustrates the typical geometry of the equilibrium outcome with a tariff. As drawn, good 2 is the importable. The tariff raises the relative price of good 2 on domestic markets, inducing firms to produce at point a (increasing production of the importable, and decreasing production of the exportable, relative to free trade). There are two isovalue lines drawn through point a. The isovalue line that is tangent to the transformation locus (dotted) represents the value of production at domestic, tariff inclusive, prices. The solid isovalue line represents the value of production at world prices.

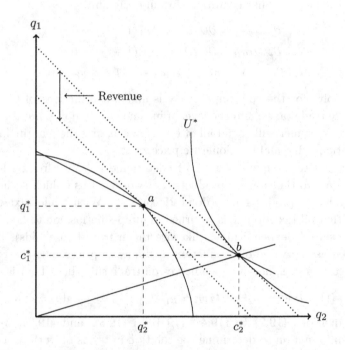

Fig. 19.1   Small Country Tariff/Export Tax.

Since trade takes place at world prices, the production bundle can be exchanged for one of equal value at world prices, hence under balanced trade the consumption bundle must lie on the solid isovalue line through a. However, since consumers face domestic prices, the indifference curve at the consumption point must be tangent to an isovalue line drawn for the domestic relative price. The point labeled b is the optimal choice. The line drawn through the origin and point b is the income consumption curve —

the locus of tangencies between indifference curves and budget constraints for all levels of income at constant relative prices.[3] The excess height of the dotted isovalue passing through b above the dotted isovalue passing through a is the tariff revenue. Since an export tax will shift domestic relative prices in the same way, Figure 19.1 can equally represent the effect of an export tax.[4]

Constructing a diagram to show the effect of an export subsidy (or import subsidy) proceeds in much the same way. First, determine how domestic relative prices will differ from world relative prices (the domestic relative price of the exportable will be higher). Given the domestic relative price, next determine the optimal production choice by finding the tangency with the production possibility frontier. The isovalue at world prices through the production point represents the consumption bundles for which the production bundle can be traded. Where the income-consumption curve cuts through this isovalue line we have the consumption solution. The excess height of the domestic price isovalue passing through the production point above that passing through the consumption point (measured in terms of good 1) represents the tax revenue collected and disbursed as expenditure on the subsidy.

19.2   GAMS Implementation

To incorporate tariffs and other interventions we need to introduce a distinction between world and domestic prices, with the wedge between them determined by the intervention, and incorporate the revenues/expenditures into income.

Starting with the model from Chapter 12, introduce a new parameter PW(I) to hold the fixed world prices, and a parameter T(I) to hold the taxes. Because domestic prices will now be endogenous (determined by the world prices and trade taxes) we change P(I) in the parameters section to PO(I), representing the initial domestic price. We then normalize all prices to unity, set the tax rates at zero, and calibrate the model to an initial free trade equilibrium.

Next we add P(I) as a variable in the model, and set its level and lower bound. Corresponding to the new variable we add a

---

[3] For homothetic preferences the income-consumption curve is linear as drawn, but this is not necessary.

[4] This result is called the Lerner symmetry theorem, see exercise 2.

new equation name, TRADE_TAX(I), and assign to it the expression
TRADE_TAX(I)..P(I)=E=(1+T(I))*PW(I). Finally, we alter the INCOME
equation to incorporate revenues/expenditures:[5]

INCOME..GDP=E=SUM(I, P(I)*Q(I))-SUM(I, T(I)*PW(I)*X(I));

Note that because we have defined X(I) such that exports are positive and
imports are negative, we need to subtract the SUM. All other equations in the
model are unchanged, as they already reflect firm and consumer behavior
in response to domestic prices.

Once you have the model working, you can use simulations to improve
your understanding of the implications of trade interventions. Exercises
1–8 at the end of the chapter provide some directions to explore.

19.3   Quotas

The model that we developed in the preceding section is able to handle any
price-based intervention in trade. But in some cases countries may instead
choose to limit the quantity of goods imported or exported. These types
of interventions are called quantitative restrictions or quotas. Under competitive conditions, including competitive allocation of the quota licenses,
an import quota and an import tax will be equivalent in effect, as will an
export tax and export quota.[6]

Nonetheless, the economy may respond differently to changes in the
economic system when distorted by a trade quota rather than a trade tax,
so it is useful to think about how to transform the model to describe an
economy distorted by quotas.[7] This is fairly straightforward to do. Rather
than introducing T(I) to the model as a parameter, introduce it instead
as a variable. Do this prior to the calibration, and then fix the level at
zero with the statement T.FX(I)=0. In the calibration of the model you
need replace appearances of T(I) with T.L(I). Even though T(I) is a
variable, because its value is fixed, it performs the same function as the
original parameter. After you have made the modifications, run the model
and verify that the free trade equilibrium is generated. You might also
want to try introducing a tariff to check the behavior of the model matches
with your expectations.

---

[5]We continue to denote this as GDP in the programs, although it is not GDP in the
national accounts sense but rather spending at domestic prices.

[6]This is often referred to as the quota licenses being auctioned off.

[7]See exercise 12.

We can now introduce quotas into the model by switching the import quantity of one good with the associated trade tax. That is, with good 2 the importable, an import quota of, say, 20 units can be implemented by imposing `X.FX('2')=-20`, along with `T.UP('2')=INF` and `T.LO('2')=-INF`. The value chosen for the quota should be less than the free trade volume.[8] In effect, we are fixing the level of imports, and freeing the associated trade tax. The number of equations and (unfixed) variables remains the same. If we solve the model it will generate the domestic price associated with the quota, and the quota's tariff equivalent, `T.L('2')`. Exercises 9–12 below relate to this model.

19.4   Large Countries

As we saw in Chapter 14, the key difference between a large and a small economy is that for the former the terms of trade (i.e., relative world prices) depend on the trade volume. Since tariffs and other trade taxes affect the trade volume by design, they affect the terms of trade in the large economy case. By imposing a tariff (or an export tax), a large economy is able to exploit its monopsony power to push the relative price of the importable down. Similarly an export subsidy (or import subsidy) would have the effect of pushing the world relative price of the exportable down. Analysis of trade interventions must factor in these price movements.

In fact, again as we saw in Chapter 14, free trade is not optimal policy for the large economy. A tariff/export tax is required for the large economy to achieve an optimal outcome. The geometry is presented in Figure 19.2. An optimal outcome requires that the marginal rate of substitution equal the marginal rate of transformation, and both must equal the foreign rate of transformation (the slope of the offer curve). To achieve this outcome a wedge must be driven between the prices paid in the domestic market (represented by the slopes of the dotted lines through a and b) and those received in the world market (represented by slope of the solid line through a and b). The difference between the slopes represents the required tariff.

The mechanics of incorporating trade taxes/subsidies into the GAMS model of a large country that we developed in Chapter 14 are essentially the same as for the small country. In this model prices are already endogenous, but we still need to introduce a new variable to represent world prices,

---

[8] In other words, the quota should be binding. If this is not the case the quota will have no effect on the model, and should not be introduced as an equality constraint.

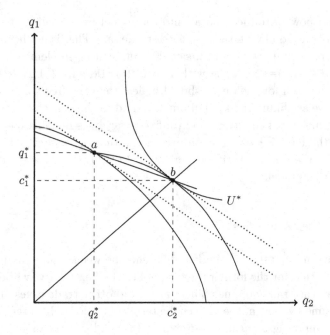

Fig. 19.2   Large Country Optimal Tariff/Export Tax.

PW(I), and a parameter to hold its initial value, PWO(I). We also introduce the tariff rates T(I), either as a parameter or as a variable, in the latter case also making sure to fix the value. As before, we then normalize all prices to unity, set the tax rates at zero, and calibrate the model to an initial free trade equilibrium.

Because we have a new endogenous variable (domestic and world prices are now distinct) we need to add the equation TRADE_TAX(I), and assign it with TRADE_TAX(I)..P(I)=E=(1+T(I))*PW(I), just as in the small country case. We also adjust the income to include revenues/expenditures. The change is the same as in Section 19.2. Finally, we need to alter the offer function to read:

OFFER(G)..X(G)=E=XI(G)*PW(G)**EPSILON(G);

The offer is representing what the rest of the world is willing to pay/wants to receive, so must be expressed in terms of world prices not domestic ones. All other equations in the system remain unchanged.

Once you have the model working, you can use simulations to see how tariffs and other interventions affect the large economy. Note that interventions should only be applied to goods other than the numéraire good, which is acting as our unit of account in this model. If you simulate a small tariff in the large country model you will find that, in contrast to the small country model, the index of economic welfare increases.

How high should the tariff be to maximize the welfare index? If you implement the tariff as a fixed variable rather than a parameter, try removing the bounds on the tariff for the imported good and running the model again. Now the model has one more unknown (the tariff rate). GAMS is free to find the value of the tariff that maximizes the index of welfare, the "optimal" tariff.[9] In effect, we have solved the maximization problem for the large economy that we presented in Chapter 14. For further directions to explore with this model see exercises 13–15.

19.5   Two Countries

Using the large country model we can analyze how changes in a country's own trade policy might affect the terms of trade. We can also indirectly assess how changes in a trading partner's trade policy might affect the economy, by shifting the foreign offer. To directly assess changes in another country's trade policy on the economy of interest we can implement tariffs and other interventions into the two country model that we developed in Chapter 15.

The basic geometry of tariffs in this context can be illustrated in the offer curve diagram, as in Figure 19.3, following the method of Lerner (1936).[10] As drawn, the home economy imports good 1 and foreign imports good 2, with the free trade relative price of good 2 denoted by the line labeled p. Suppose that foreign imposes an import tax. This will drive a wedge between prices paid on the foreign market (p_f) and those received in the home market (p_h). The magnitude of the tariff determines the angle between p_f and p_h. Geometrically, we can form the cone between the dotted lines in Figure 19.3. As drawn, the tariff is of magnitude ab/ax_2. The exact position of the cone depends on the manner in which the tariff revenue (ab

---

[9]GAMS will search for the point where $dU/dt = 0$, subject to the other constraints in the system.

[10]Figure 19.3 follows Lerner in assuming that the government spends the tariff revenue rather than giving it away as a non-distorting subsidy. The effects are the same if the government spends in the same manner as the households. Lerner's idea that the effects of an import tariff can be replicated by the same export tax holds regardless of whether the revenue is spent by the government or redistributed to the private sector.

measured in units of good 1) is spent. The right angle *acd*, where the
slope of the line *ad* represents the ratio in which tariff revenue is spent on
consumption of good 1 to good 2, must fit exactly between the two offers
for markets to clear. As more of the revenue is spent on good 1, the cone
is rotated downward, while as more is spent on good 2 the cone is rotated
upward. The tariff-inclusive offer of foreign will pass through point *d*.[11]

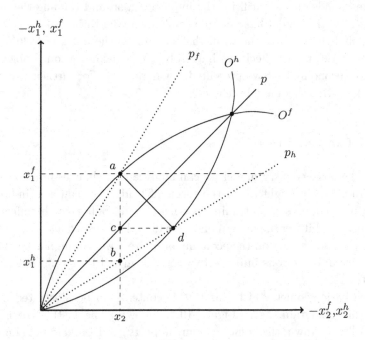

Fig. 19.3   Offer Curve Geometry With Tariff/Export Tax.

The adjustments to the GAMS code for the two country model that we
need to incorporate trade taxes are much the same as in the small/large
country case. First, we set up the two country model to calibrate to a free
trade equilibrium.[12] Once we have verified the equilibrium, we introduce
trade taxes, either as parameters or as fixed variables. The trade taxes are

---

[11] We have drawn the offer curves of both countries as elastic throughout most of their
ranges. See if you can construct the same diagram when the offer of one or more countries
is inelastic over the relevant range. For more on how a tariff can affect both home and
foreign prices, including the possibility that an increase in the tariff on a good may causes
its relative home price to fall, see Metzler (1949).

[12] Alternatively, you could generate a trading equilibrium from autarky using simulation
prior to introducing changes in the trade taxes.

now defined as T(I,D), since they will differ across countries. A distinction between world and domestic prices is already made in the model, so all we need to do next is adjust the ARBITRAGE and INCOME equations to reflect the trade taxes in each country:

```
ARBITRAGE(I,D)..P(I,D)=E=(1+T(I,D))*PW(I);
INCOME(D)..GDP(D)=E=SUM(I, P(I,D)*Q(I,D))
   -SUM(I, PW(I)*T(I,D)*X(I,D));
```

The completed model is presented in Table 19.1. With it you can explore the implications of tariffs and other interventions on both trading partners. Some suggested exercises are at the end of the chapter (see in particular numbers 16–18). As with the large country model, because the price of one of the goods (the numéraire) is acting as a unit of account, we can only apply trade taxes to the other goods.

Also, recall that the objective in this model is defined as the sum of the utility indices of the two economies. This is arbitrary, since we have the same number of independent equations as we have unknowns, the purpose of the objective is only to provide a scalar value to use in the SOLVE statement. However, if we want to conduct an experiment as in the previous section, where we free the value of a trade tax in one country to determine the optimal tariff, the objective takes on new importance. The optimal tariff should be chosen to maximize the utility index of the economy imposing the tariff.

If you are interested in exploring issues of optimal tariffs and/or retaliation then, you might try defining two objective functions, one corresponding to the home utility index, and the other corresponding to the foreign utility index. You can then use two model statements to define two versions of the model, one containing each objective. These can be used to determine the optimal trade tax for each country, given that of the other. See also exercise 18.

19.6   Exercises

(1) Using the small country model developed in Section 19.2, implement a series of small incremental increases in the tariff (you might want to set up a LOOP). As the tariff increases, what happens to the index of utility? Is moving from a zero tariff to a 10 percent tariff more or less damaging than moving from a 10 percent tariff to a 20 percent tariff in welfare terms? Explain.

Table 19.1   GAMS Program for HOS Model With Trade Taxes.

```
SET I Goods /1,2/;
SET J Factors /K,L/;
SET D Countries /H,F/;
ALIAS (J, JJ);

PARAMETERS
ALPHA(D)                          Shift parameters in utility
BETA(I,D)                         Share parameters in utility
PO(I,D)                           Initial domestic prices
PWO(I)                            Initial world prices
XO(I,D)                           Initial trade
UO(D)                             Initial utility levels
O(I,D)                            Initial consumption levels
GAMMA(I,D)                        Shift parameters in production
DELTA(J,I,D)                      Share parameters in production
RHO(I,D)                          Elasticity parameters in production
BAR(J,D)                          Endowments
RO(J,D)                           Initial factor prices
GDPO(D)                           Initial gross domestic products;

PARAMETER QO(I,D)                 Initial output levels /
1.H 200
1.F 75
2.H 75
2.F 200 /;

PARAMETER FO(J,I,D)               Initial factor use levels /
K.1.H 160
K.1.F 60
K.2.H 15
K.2.F 40
L.1.H 40
L.1.F 15
L.2.H 60
L.2.F 160 /;

PWO(I)=1;
PO(I,D)=PWO(I);
RO(J,D)=1;
CO(I,D)=137.5;
XO(I,D)=QO(I,D)-CO(I,D);
FBAR(J,D)=SUM(I, FO(J,I,D));
GDPO(D)=SUM(I, PO(I,D)*QO(I,D));
```

---

continued on next page

continued from previous page

```
RHO(I,D)=0.1;
DELTA(J,I,D)=(RO(J,D)/FO(J,I,D)**(RHO(I,D)-1))/(SUM(JJ, RO(JJ,D)
  /FO(JJ,I,D)**(RHO(I,D)-1)));
GAMMA(I,D)=QO(I,D)/(SUM(J, DELTA(J,I,D)*FO(J,I,D)**RHO(I,D)))**(1/RHO(I,D));
UO(D)=GDPO(D);
BETA(I,D)=CO(I,D)/GDPO(D);
ALPHA(D)=UO(D)/PROD(I, CO(I,D)**BETA(I,D));


VARIABLES
U(D)                Utility indices
T(I,D)              Trade taxes
P(I,D)              Prices
C(I,D)              Consumption levels
Q(I,D)              Output levels
R(J,D)              Factor prices
F(J,I,D)            Factor use levels
PW(I)               World prices
X(I,D)              Trade levels
GDP(D)              Gross domestic products
OBJ                 Objective;


U.L(D)=UO(D); P.L(I,D)=PO(I,D); C.L(I,D)=CO(I,D); Q.L(I,D)=QO(I,D);
R.L(J,D)=RO(J,D); F.L(J,I,D)=FO(J,I,D); PW.L(I)=PWO(I); X.L(I,D)=XO(I,D);
GDP.L(D)=GDPO(D); OBJ.L=SUM(D, UO(D));


P.LO(I,D)=0; C.LO(I,D)=0; Q.LO(I,D)=0; R.LO(J,D)=0;
F.LO(J,I,D)=0; GDP.LO(D)=0; PW.LO(I)=0;


T.FX(I,D)=0; PW.FX('1')=1;


EQUATIONS
UTILITY(D)          Utility functions
DEMAND(I,D)         Demand functions
PRODUCTION(I,D)     Production functions
RESOURCE(J,D)       Resource constraints
FDEMAND(J,I,D)      Factor demand functions
INCOME(D)           Gross domestic products
MAT_BAL(I,D)        Open economy material balance
INT_CLEAR(I)        International market clearing
ARBITRAGE(I,D)      International price arbitrage
OBJECTIVE_H         Home objective function
OBJECTIVE_F         Foreign objective function;
```

---

continued on next page

continued from previous page

```
UTILITY(D)..U(D)=E=ALPHA(D)*PROD(I, C(I,D)**BETA(I,D));
DEMAND(I,D)..C(I,D)=E=BETA(I,D)*GDP(D)/P(I,D);
MAT_BAL(I,D)..X(I,D)=E=Q(I,D)-C(I,D);
INT_CLEAR(I)..SUM(D, X(I,D))=E=0;
ARBITRAGE(I,D)..P(I,D)=E=(1+T(I,D))*PW(I);
PRODUCTION(I,D)..Q(I,D)=E=GAMMA(I,D)*SUM(J, DELTA(J,I,D)*F(J,I,D)**
  RHO(I,D))**(1/RHO(I,D));
RESOURCE(J,D)..FBAR(J,D)=E=SUM(I, F(J,I,D));
FDEMAND(J,I,D)..R(J,D)=E=P(I,D)*Q(I,D)*SUM(JJ, DELTA(JJ,I,D)*F(JJ,I,D)**
  RHO(I,D))**(-1)*DELTA(J,I,D)*F(J,I,D)**(RHO(I,D)-1);
INCOME(D)..GDP(D)=E=SUM(I, P(I,D)*Q(I,D))-SUM(I, PW(I)*T(I,D)*X(I,D));
OBJECTIVE_H..OBJ=E=U('H');
OBJECTIVE_F..OBJ=E=U('F');

MODEL TRADE_H / UTILITY, DEMAND, MAT_BAL, INT_CLEAR, ARBITRAGE, PRODUCTION,
  RESOURCE, FDEMAND, INCOME, OBJECTIVE_H /;
MODEL TRADE_F / UTILITY, DEMAND, MAT_BAL, INT_CLEAR, ARBITRAGE, PRODUCTION,
  RESOURCE, FDEMAND, INCOME, OBJECTIVE_F /;

SOLVE TRADE_H USING NLP MAXIMIZING OBJ;
```

(2) Using the small country model, implement a tariff of 10 percent. Now remove the tariff and implement an export tax of 9.09 percent (as modeled here this will be a negative value of T). Compare the results. Explain your observations.

(3) We have introduced tariffs as a percentage of value, but they can also be introduced as dollar values (i.e., specific duties). See if you can alter the model to express the tariffs as specific duties. Does the form of expression matter for the solution? What if a tariff is in place and world prices fall?

(4) Using the small country model, implement a tariff of 10 percent and simultaneously an export subsidy of 10 percent. What happens? Explain.

(5) If the underlying production model is specific factors, which factors of production would you expect to be in favor of a tariff? How about an export subsidy? How would your answer change if the production structure was HOS?

(6) Again using the small country model, introduce a tariff. With the tariff in place, simulate growth of the importable sector by changing either technology or factor endowments. Note the change in the welfare index. Now consider the same growth scenario without introducing the tariff first. Again note the change in the welfare index. What do you observe?

(7) How would the results of your analysis in exercise 6 change if the growth were to occur through capital accumulation in the importable good, and the increment to capital was assumed to be owned by foreign interests who repatriate the earnings?

(8) See if you can calibrate the small country model to an initial tariff ridden equilibrium. (Hint: It is easier to normalize domestic rather than world prices.)

(9) In Section 19.3 we introduced an import quota to the model. Can you use the same technique to simulate an export quota?

(10) What is the effect of an import/export quota of zero?

(11) Can you use the information you obtained in the preceding exercise to determine the value of the prohibitive tariff for the small country? Simulate the tariff to verify your result.

(12) Using the quota model, implement a binding quota and a subsequent fall in the world price of the importable. How do the results compare to the same price fall in the presence of the tariff that is equivalent to the initial quota? Explain.

(13) Using the large country model developed in Section 19.4, try changing the values of the trade elasticities and simulating the optimal tariff. How does the optimal tariff vary with the elasticities?

(14) What happens in the large country model if the economy imposes an export subsidy? Explain.

(15) Using the large country model, change the objective function to tariff revenue. Can you find the value of the revenue maximizing tariff? How does it compare to the optimal tariff?

(16) Using the two country model developed in Section 19.5, simulate an export subsidy in one economy. What happens if the other country responds with a tariff (i.e., a countervailing duty)?

(17) Using the same techniques we developed in Section 19.4, see if you can modify the two country model to determine the optimal tariff for home, assuming foreign does not impose a tariff. What do you know about the trade elasticities faced by home at that point?

(18) Simulate a retaliatory trade war between home and foreign, with each country imposing optimal trade taxes in turn. Does it matter who starts the war?

19.7   Further Reading

The literature on tariffs and other trade interventions is vast, and Bhagwati *et al.* (1998) is a good place to start. For discussion of the symmetry between import tariffs and export taxes see the classic paper by Lerner (1936). Also see Kaempfer and Tower (1982). On the equivalence of tariffs and quotas under certain circumstances see Bhagwati (1965) and Sweeney *et al.* (1977). The classic treatment of the relationship between domestic and international prices in the presence of tariffs is Metzler (1949). On the structure of optimal tariffs you might want to read Graaff (1949), while Johnson (1953) considers the issues of tariff retaliation. For a discussion of the issue of countervailing export subsidies with tariffs see Copeland *et al.* (1989). Tower (1977) compares the maximum revenue and the optimal tariff. Johnson (1967) and Brecher and Diaz-Alejandro (1977) consider growth in the presence of tariffs.

Chapter 20

Domestic Taxes and Subsidies

In this chapter we introduce other price based distortions into the model: production taxes and subsidies, consumption taxes/subsidies, and factor taxes/subsidies. We discuss only the case of the small economy; extension to the large economy or to models with multiple economies is straightforward.

20.1 Production Taxes/Subsidies

Dealing with production and consumption taxes/subsidies is not very difficult now that we understand how to deal with tariffs and other trade taxes as in Chapter 19. The reason is that trade taxes can be usefully thought of as combinations of domestic policies. For example, an import tariff raises the relative price of the importable. From the perspective of firms producing the importable, this is analogous to a production subsidy, while from the perspective of consumers it is analogous to a consumption tax on the importable. Hence, we can think of a tariff as being the same as a production subsidy and a consumption tax, implemented at the same time and at the same percentage rate. All other trade taxes can be thought of in much the same way.

In the preceding chapter, we considered the problem of the trade tax/subsidy first from the perspective of the firms, and subsequently from the perspective of the consumer. We can take the same approach here. Consider a production subsidy/tax. The relative producer prices are distorted and firms maximize the value of output subject to those distorted prices. Hence, the maximization problem in production is represented by the following Lagrangian:

$$\mathscr{L} = p_1^*(1 + s_1)q_1 + p_2^*(1 + s_2)q_2 + \delta[S - \psi(q_1, q_2)] \qquad (20.1)$$

where s_i is the percentage subsidy offered to industry i (more precisely, the subsidy expressed as a proportion of the world price). Aside from replacing the t_i with s_i, this is the same as the maximization problem presented in equation (19.1), and has the same attendant first order conditions.

Once production quantities are known, the value of output at world prices can be determined. Consumers, who are left to face world prices, then maximize their utility as usual. The Lagrangian is:

$$\mathscr{L} = U(c_1, c_2) + \lambda[Y - p_1^* c_1 - p_2^* c_2]. \tag{20.2}$$

The first-order conditions require equating the marginal rate of substitution with the world price ratio.

The geometry of the problem is presented in Figure 20.1 (for a production subsidy to good 2, or equivalently a production tax on good 1). The subsidy raises the relative producer price of good 2, inducing firms to increase their production of good 2 and decrease production of good 1 (point a), relative to no intervention. The isovalue line at world prices through a (the solid line) represents those bundles that can be exchanged for the production bundle. The best of those is point b, where an indifference curve is just tangent to the constraint. The expenditure on the subsidy is the value of the production bundle measured at producer prices minus that at world prices and expressed in units of good 1. That is the vertical intercept of the dotted line minus that of the solid line. That same amount must be levied as a lump-sum tax to give consumers the solid-line budget constraint.

20.2   Consumption Taxes/Subsidies

The case of a consumption tax/subsidy can be analyzed in much the same way. Producers are now left facing world prices, so the Lagrangian for the production maximization problem is:

$$\mathscr{L} = p_1^* q_1 + p_2^* q_2 + \delta[S - \psi(q_1, q_2)] \tag{20.3}$$

which implies tangency of the production possibilities and an isovalue line at world prices. Consumers maximize utility given their income and the distorted prices they face:

$$\mathscr{L} = U(c_1, c_2) + \lambda[Y - p_1^*(1 + t_1^c)c_1 - p_2^*(1 + t_2^c)c_2] \tag{20.4}$$

where t_i^c is the consumption tax on good i. The first-order conditions require equating the marginal rate of substitution with the consumer (distorted) price ratio. Assuming that the tax revenue is redistributed to the consumers, income is:

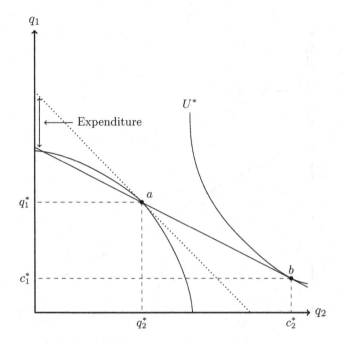

Fig. 20.1   Small Country Production Subsidy.

$$Y = p_1^* q_1 + p_2^* q_2 + p_1^* t_1^c c_1 + p_2^* t_2^c c_2. \tag{20.5}$$

Note that, just as in the tariff case, the consumer does not consider how a change in their consumption affects tax revenue when making their consumption choice. Also notice that if both a subsidy and a consumption tax are introduced at the same time, and $s_i = t_i^c$, then the problem is the same as the tariff.

The geometry of a consumption tax/subsidy is presented in Figure 20.2, for a tax on good 2 (or equivalently a subsidy to good 1). Producers maximize the value of output at world prices by producing at a. Consumers face the tax-distorted prices, implying consumption along the income consumption path through b. Combining this with the balance of trade, consumption is at b, with the difference between b evaluated at tax-inclusive prices and b valued at world prices representing the consumption tax revenue, which is remitted in a lump-sum.

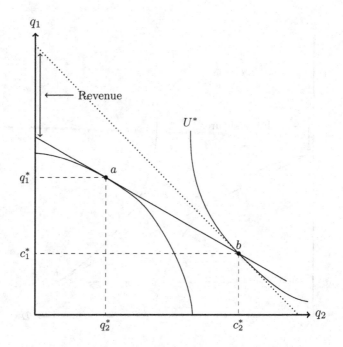

Fig. 20.2   Small Country Consumption Tax.

20.3   Factor Taxes and Subsidies

Now we consider the implications of taxes and subsidies applied to the firm's usage of factors of production. First take the case of a subsidy or tax applied to both capital and labor in industry 2, assuming a Heckscher-Ohlin production structure.

Let the price that the firm pays for labor, inclusive of the tax/subsidy, be defined as $w/(1+s_2^L)$ and the price paid for capital be defined as $r/(1+s_2^K)$. Hence, positive values indicate subsidies (they lower the price paid relative to the market price) and negative values indicate taxes. We can then write the firm's profit function as:

$$\pi_2 = p_2 q_2(K_2, L_2) - r/(1+s_2^K)K_2 - w/(1+s_2^L)L_2. \qquad (20.6)$$

Maximizing profit requires the firm set the value of the marginal product of each factor equal to the price paid. This is the same condition we have seen before, the only difference being that now the price paid incorporates the factor taxes/subsidies.

Evidently, if we replace the uniform factor subsidies with a production subsidy at the same level ($s_2 = s_2^K = s_2^L$), we can rewrite the profit function as:

$$\pi_2 = p_2(1 + s_2)q_2(K_2, L_2) - wL_2 - rK_2. \tag{20.7}$$

But this means that a uniform tax/subsidy on the firm's inputs is equivalent to a production tax/subsidy, for the second profit function is simply a multiple of the first. With no intervention in the other industry, the outcome would look the same as in Figure 20.1 (for a subsidy).

If we have a subsidy or tax to a single factor in industry 2, say capital, and no intervention in sector 1, then the profit functions are:

$$\pi_1 = p_1 q_1(K_1, L_1) - rK_1 - wL_1 \tag{20.8}$$

$$\pi_2 = p_2 q_2(K_2, L_2) - r/(1 + s_2^K)K_2 - wL_2. \tag{20.9}$$

Taking the first order conditions for a maximum in each industry, it is easy to see that the marginal rate of technical substitution will equal w/r in sector 1, but $w(1 + s_2^K)/r$ in sector 2. That is to say, the economy will be drawn off the production efficiency locus, and hence off the production possibility frontier.

The geometry is in Figure 20.3. The dotted line through a represents the newly feasible production possibilities with the factor market distortion, which lies inside the unconstrained production possibilities. Production is at point a, showing an increase in output of good 2 relative to free trade with undistorted factor markets. World prices are not tangent to the production possibilities at a because producers of good 2 are paying less for capital than producers of good 1. Consumers pay world prices, and so consume at point b, where an indifference curve is tangent to the budget constraint.

20.4 GAMS Implementation

Incorporating domestic taxes and subsidies is much the same as incorporating trade taxes and subsidies. Starting from the small country model with trade taxes that we developed in Chapter 19, we add in domestic interventions, TC(I) for consumption taxes or subsidies, TP(I) for production taxes or subsidies, and TF(J,I) for factor taxes or subsidies. These can be added as either parameters or as variables. In the latter case we also fix their initial values at zero.

Next we need to adjust the model itself. Rather than introducing a new variable for each distorted price, we introduce the price distortions directly

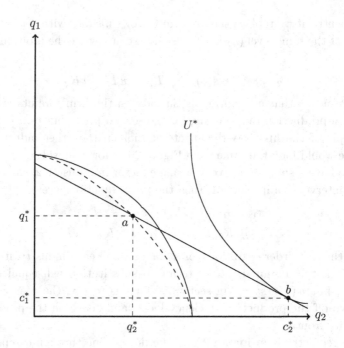

Fig. 20.3 Small Country Factor Subsidy.

into the model equations. Hence, consumption taxes/subsidies alter the prices faced by consumers, so the demand functions become:

```
DEMAND(I)..C(I)=E=BETA(I)*GDP/(P(I)*(1+TC(I)));
```

As defined, a positive value of TC(I) represents a consumption tax; a negative value a subsidy. Similarly, the factor demand equations have two adjustments:

```
FDEMAND(J,I)$FO(J,I)..R(J)/(1+TF(J,I))=E=(P(I)*(1+TP(I)))*
    Q(I)*SUM(JJ$FO(JJ,I),DELTA(JJ,I)*F(JJ,I)**
    RHO(I))**(-1)*DELTA(J,I)*F(J,I)**(RHO(I)-1);
```

On the left hand side we have introduced the factor taxes/subsidies. Positive values of TF(J,I) indicate a subsidy as defined. On the right hand side we introduce production taxes/subsidies, again with positive values of TP(I) representing subsidies.

The final step is to adjust income to properly reflect the various distortions. Consumers spend all of their income (GDP). So GDP is consumption at consumer prices. For trade balance, consumption equals production, all at world prices. The tariff is an implicit subsidy on production and implicit tax on consumption. Consequently GDP equals production at domestic prices, minus the implicit subsidy on production plus the implicit tax on consumption plus the explicit tax on consumption. The implicit tax on consumption minus the implicit subsidy on production is the tariff revenue. Thus GDP equals production at domestic prices plus the tariff revenue plus the consumption tax revenue. Consequently, GDP is defined as:

```
INCOME..GDP=E=SUM(I, P(I)*Q(I))-SUM(I, T(I)*PW(I)*X(I))
    +SUM(I, TC(I)*P(I)*C(I));
```

Notice that P(I) in the model is inclusive of trade taxes, but not of producer taxes/subsidies, hence we do not need to add/subtract producer tax/subsidy revenues/expenditures (if we defined GDP in terms of the value of output at producer prices we would). Similarly, factor taxes/subsidies are already accounted for in the first term. However, we do need to factor in trade tax revenues/expenditures and consumption tax revenues/expenditures.

If our starting point involves no distortions we are done. However, if the starting point may contain distortions (e.g., if you are interested in the effect of removing a distortion rather than adding one), we need to adjust the calibration part of the model to reflect any existing distortions. A completed program, including the calibration, is presented in Table 20.1. Once you have it working, try some of the exercises below.

20.5   Exercises

(1) Try imposing a tariff of 10 percent. Now try imposing a combination of production subsidy and consumption tax. Can you replicate the effect of the tariff?

(2) Try imposing a subsidy to production of one good. Can you replicate the effect of the policy with a tax on production of the other good?

(3) Conduct the same experiment as above with a consumption tax/subsidy.

(4) Show that you can replicate a production subsidy with an appropriate combination of factor subsidies.

(5) Can you express the model in terms of taxes/subsidies defined in currency units rather than as percentages of value?

Table 20.1   GAMS Program for Small Country With Domestic Taxes.

```
SET I Goods /1,2/;
SET J Factors /K,L/;
ALIAS (J, JJ);

PARAMETERS
ALPHA                   Shift parameter in utility
BETA(I)                 Share parameters in utility
PO(I)                   Initial domestic prices
PW(I)                   World prices
U0                      Initial utility level
CO(I)                   Initial consumption levels
XO(I)                   Initial net exports
GAMMA(I)                Shift parameters in production
DELTA(J,I)              Share parameters in production
RHO(I)                  Elasticity parameters in production
FBAR(J)                 Endowments
QO(I)                   Initial output levels
RO(J)                   Initial factor prices
FO(J,I)                 Initial factor use levels
GDPO                    Initial gross domestic product;

VARIABLES
T(I)                    Trade taxes or subsidies
TC(I)                   Consumption taxes or subsidies
TP(I)                   Production taxes or subsidies
TF(J,I)                 Factor taxes or subsidies;
T.FX(I)=0;
TC.FX(I)=0;
TP.FX(I)=0;
TF.FX(J,I)=0;

PO(I)=1;
PW(I)=PO(I)/(1+T.L(I));
RO(J)=1;
QO(I)=100;
CO('1')=50;
CO('2')=150;
XO(I)=QO(I)-CO(I);
FO('L','1')=20*(1+TF.L('L','1'))*(1+TP.L('1'));
FO('L','2')=80*(1+TF.L('L','2'))*(1+TP.L('2'));
FO('K','2')=20*(1+TF.L('K','2'))*(1+TP.L('2'));
FO('K','1')=80*(1+TF.L('K','1'))*(1+TP.L('1'));
FBAR(J)=SUM(I, FO(J,I));
GDPO=SUM(I,PO(I)*QO(I))-SUM(I,T.L(I)*PW(I)*XO(I))+SUM(I,TC.L(I)*PO(I)*CO(I));
```

continued on next page

continued from previous page

```
RHO(I)=0.1;
DELTA(J,I)$FO(J,I)=((RO(J)/(1+TF.L(J,I)))/FO(J,I)**(RHO(I)-1))/
  (SUM(JJ$FO(JJ,I),(RO(JJ)*(1+TF.L(JJ,I)))/FO(JJ,I)**(RHO(I)-1)));
GAMMA(I)=QO(I)/(SUM(J$FO(J,I), DELTA(J,I)*FO(J,I)**RHO(I)))**(1/RHO(I));
UO=GDPO;
BETA(I)=(PO(I)*(1+TC.L(I))*CO(I))/GDPO;
ALPHA=UO/PROD(I, CO(I)**BETA(I));


VARIABLES
U               Utility index
X(I)            Trade levels
P(I)            Domestic prices
C(I)            Consumption levels
Q(I)            Output levels
R(J)            Factor prices
F(J,I)          Factor use levels
GDP             Gross domestic product;

U.L=UO; X.L(I)=XO(I); C.L(I)=CO(I); Q.L(I)=QO(I); R.L(J)=RO(J);
F.L(J,I)=FO(J,I); P.L(I)=PO(I); GDP.L=GDPO;
C.LO(I)=0; Q.LO(I)=0; R.LO(J)=0; F.LO(J,I)=0; P.LO(I)=0; GDP.LO=0;


EQUATIONS
UTILITY         Utility function
DEMAND(I)       Demand functions
TRADE_TAX(I)    Trade taxes
MAT_BAL(I)      Market closure
PRODUCTION(I)   Production functions
RESOURCE(J)     Resource constraints
FDEMAND(J,I)    Factor demand functions
INCOME          Gross domestic product;

UTILITY..U=E=ALPHA*PROD(I, C(I)**BETA(I));
DEMAND(I)..C(I)=E=BETA(I)*GDP/(P(I)*(1+TC(I)));
TRADE_TAX(I)..P(I)=E=(1+T(I))*PW(I);
MAT_BAL(I)..X(I)=E=Q(I)-C(I);
PRODUCTION(I)..Q(I)=E=GAMMA(I)*SUM(J$FO(J,I), DELTA(J,I)*F(J,I)**
  RHO(I))**(1/RHO(I));
RESOURCE(J)..FBAR(J)=E=SUM(I, F(J,I));
FDEMAND(J,I)$FO(J,I)..R(J)/(1+TF(J,I))=E=(P(I)*(1+TP(I)))*Q(I)*SUM(JJ$
  FO(JJ,I),DELTA(JJ,I)*F(JJ,I)**RHO(I))**(-1)*DELTA(J,I)*F(J,I)**(RHO(I)-1);
INCOME..GDP=E=SUM(I,P(I)*Q(I))-SUM(I,T(I)*PW(I)*X(I))+SUM(I,TC(I)*P(I)*C(I));


MODEL SMALL /ALL/;
SOLVE SMALL USING NLP MAXIMIZING U;
```

(6) In Chapter 19 we showed how to adjust the model to analyze import/export quotas as opposed to tariffs/export taxes. Can you modify this model in a similar way to describe production, consumption and/or employment quotas?

(7) Suppose that the government had the objective of increasing output of one of the goods to a particular level, say 120 units. Can this be achieved with a trade tax? How about a production or factor subsidy? Which technique has the lowest welfare cost? (Hint: If you fix the value of output, you can free up a policy instrument, much like the technique we used to find the optimal tariff.)

(8) See if you can incorporate domestic taxes and subsidies into the large country and two country models.

20.6   Further Reading

Bhagwati *et al.* (1998) has a good description of the basic effects of interventions, focusing on geometry and the various equivalences (Chapter 17). For classic studies of how domestic policies can be optimally used to achieve various objectives see Bhagwati and Srinivasan (1969) and Bhagwati (1971). Vandendorpe (1974) discusses the extension of this theory to the case of the large economy.

Chapter 21

Factor Market Distortions

In this chapter we consider the implications of distortions in factor markets. These can take a wide variety of forms. For example, wage (or more generally, factor price) differential models can be used to represent the effect of sector specific unionization or regulation, and sticky wage models can be used to examine the effect of binding minimum wage regulations or other wage rigidities (general or sector specific). Incorporating these features into our models requires only relatively minor modifications to the GAMS codes that we have developed already. Another interesting case is imperfect factor mobility. We have already examined the extreme version of this distortion, since the specific factors model treats one factor of production as completely immobile across sectors. In this chapter we generalize to allow for limited factor mobility.

21.1 Wage Differentials

A wage differential model is one where labor is paid a higher return when it is employed in one sector than the other. The differential may be defined in percentage form, or as a fixed differential expressed in terms of the numéraire.

The implications of this type of distortion are most easily seen using the dual approach we introduced in Chapter 7. First consider the short run, as represented by the specific factors model. With a wage differential the production system for a small economy is written:

$$c_1(w_1, r_1) = p_1 \tag{21.1}$$

$$c_2(w_2, r_2) = p_2 \tag{21.2}$$

$$w_1 = \alpha w_2 \tag{21.3}$$

$$a_{K1}(w_1, r_1)q_1 = \bar{K}_1 \tag{21.4}$$

$$a_{K2}(w_2, r_2)q_2 = \bar{K}_2 \tag{21.5}$$

$$a_{L1}(w_1, r_1)q_1 + a_{L2}(w_2, r_2)q_2 = \bar{L}. \tag{21.6}$$

The first two equations are the zero profit conditions in each industry, with the wages paid to labor and rental rates on capital differentiated, the former by policy the latter by lack of mobility. Equation (21.3) defines the wedge between the wages paid in each industry, where $\alpha > 1$ if workers in industry 1 are favored and $\alpha < 1$ if workers in industry 2 are favored. Given goods prices and endowments, we can solve equations (21.1)–(21.6) for the factor prices and output levels. With $\alpha = 1$ the model will collapse to the standard model.

The implications of the wage distortion can be seen from Figure 21.1, using the quadrant geometry. Suppose that the undistorted equilibrium outcome is represented by the points labeled a. With a wage differential, industry 2 (say) is forced to pay a higher wage relative to industry 1. With goods prices fixed, industry 2 will hire less labor, moving down the total product curve. The labor released will be employed in industry 1, moving up the total product curve. The new equilibrium is at b. The slopes of the total product curves of each industry at b measure the marginal products of labor in each sector, the real wage in terms of each good.

Notice that in the specific factors model, the economy is not drawn off the short-run production possibilities by this type of factor market distortion, as resources continue to be fully employed and firms continue to minimize costs. However, because firms are not paying the same prices for labor, the world price ratio is not tangent to the production possibilities at the production point b. Hence, the value of output at world prices must fall, as indicated by the dotted isovalue line through b.

If our interest is in the long-run implications of a wage differential, we can use the HOS production model as the base. The economic system with a wage differential is written:

$$c_1(w_1, r) = p_1 \tag{21.7}$$

$$c_2(w_2, r) = p_2 \tag{21.8}$$

$$w_1 = \alpha w_2 \tag{21.9}$$

$$a_{K1}(w_1, r)q_1 + a_{K2}(w_2, r)q_2 = \bar{K} \tag{21.10}$$

$$a_{L1}(w_1, r)q_1 + a_{L2}(w_2, r)q_2 = \bar{L}. \tag{21.11}$$

The first two equations are the zero profit conditions in each industry, with only the wages paid differentiated, since capital is now mobile. Equation

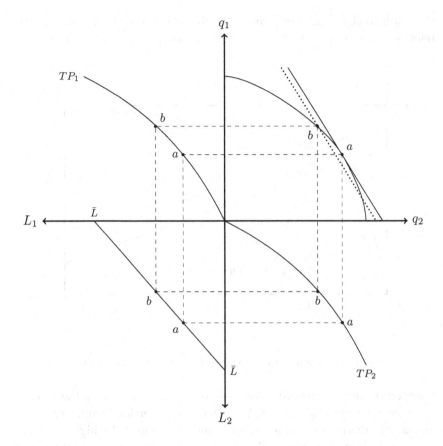

Fig. 21.1   Short-Run Production With a Wage Differential.

(21.9) again defines the wedge between the wages paid in each industry.
Given goods prices, we can solve equations (21.7)–(21.9) for the factor
prices. Optimal unit factor demands then follow by Shepherd's lemma.
The last two equations are the resource constraints, which can be used to
determine outputs. With $\alpha = 1$ the model will collapse to the standard
HOS model.

The implications of the wage differential in the long run can be viewed
in the Edgeworth box framework that we developed in Chapter 5. In Figure
21.2, the solid line connecting the origins is the efficiency locus. Efficiency
requires that the isoquants of each industry be tangent to each other. As
we have seen, under competitive conditions this is guaranteed if each industry pays the same factor prices, since profit maximizing behavior leads

to each firm choosing inputs such that the MRTS is equal to (minus) the
relative factor prices. With the wage differential, each firm faces a distinct

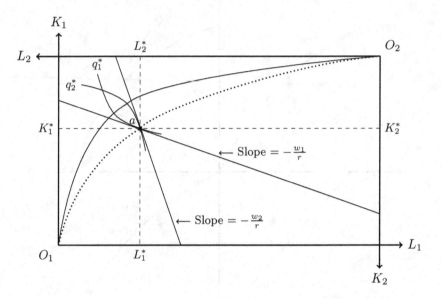

Fig. 21.2   Long-Run Factor Allocation With a Wage Differential.

wage/rental ratio. Suppose output of good 2 is described by the level of
the isoquant labeled q_2^*. If $\alpha < 1$, so that the distortion favors workers in
industry 2, the relative wage/rental in industry 2 must be higher than in
industry 1. Suppose it is given by the slope of the isoquant at a. Resources
continue to be fully employed, and the isoquant for good 1 that passes
through a represents output of good 1. The slope of the isoquant for good
1 at a represents the relative wage in industry 1, and the difference between
the slopes of the isoquants represents the extent of the differential.

As noted, with a wage differential factors of production remain fully
employed. However, relative to the absence of the distortion, they are
employed inefficiently. The wage differential induces industry 2 to use a
more capital-intensive technique than it otherwise would, while industry
1 uses a more labor-intensive technique.[1] The economy is pulled off the

---

[1]At constant output prices a wage differential favoring the labor-intensive sector (as
illustrated) causes wages in both sectors to fall and rents in both sectors to rise. The
output of the labor-intensive sector falls and the output of the capital-intensive sector
rises, with full employment of all the factors being maintained by both sectors becoming
more labor intensive. Can you prove this?

efficiency locus. The dotted locus, drawn through a, represents the input points where the wage differential holds.

The outcome in output space is described in the same way as Figure 20.3. The dotted efficiency locus corresponds to a new feasible production possibilities frontier that lies within the unconstrained one except at the end points. World prices are not tangent to the production possibilities at the equilibrium because producers of good 2 are paying more for labor than producers of good 1, just as in the specific factors case.

We have in fact already built a GAMS model that can be used to demonstrate the implications of wage differentials. Consider the factor tax/subsidy model that we developed in Chapter 20. Clearly, a tax on labor used in industry 2, assuming the revenue is redistributed to the household, is equivalent to setting a value of $\alpha < 1$, and hence a wage differential defined in percentage terms. Some further suggestions for experimenting with the model can be found at the end of the chapter.

21.2   Sticky Wages

Another type of factor market distortion is wage rigidity. There is a significant literature examining the consequences of downwardly inflexible wages, applying to all or some sectors. We consider the former in this section and turn to the latter in the next.

We begin with the small, open economy in the short run. Let the minimum wage be binding and denote it $\bar{w}$. The model is:

$$c_1(\bar{w}, r_1) = p_1 \tag{21.12}$$

$$c_2(\bar{w}, r_2) = p_2 \tag{21.13}$$

$$a_{K1}(\bar{w}, r_1)q_1 = \bar{K}_1 \tag{21.14}$$

$$a_{K2}(\bar{w}, r_2)q_2 = \bar{K}_2 \tag{21.15}$$

$$a_{L1}(\bar{w}, r_1)q_1 + a_{L2}(\bar{w}, r_2)q_2 + L_U = \bar{L} \tag{21.16}$$

assuming that production in both industries remains profitable at the fixed goods prices. This is a very simple structure. Equations (21.12) and (21.13) determine the return to capital in each sector. Once these are known, we can use Shephard's lemma to determine the optimal unit factor demands. Equations (21.14) and (21.15) then determine output of each good. With the minimum wage binding, each industry will seek to lower its use of labor, resulting in unemployment. The equilibrium volume of unemployment is determined by equation (21.16) as the difference between the endowment and the optimal demands of each industry, denoted L_U.

The effect of the minimum wage is easily seen in the labor market equilibrium diagram. In Figure 21.3, the market clearing solution is a. With a binding minimum wage at $\bar{w}$, each industry reduces their purchases of labor until the value of the marginal product is equal to its price. The horizontal distance between the two labor demand curves at the minimum wage represents labor that is unemployed.

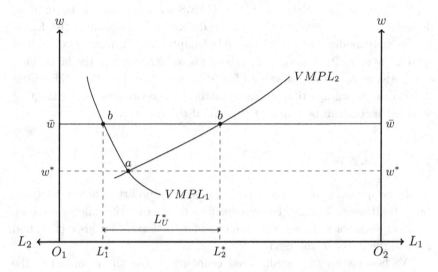

Fig. 21.3   Short-Run Labor Market With a Sticky Wage.

The implications for the production possibilities can be seen in Figure 21.4. Suppose at the prevailing world prices the undistorted equilibrium in production is at point a. The minimum wage reduces both outputs wherever it is binding. The new equilibrium output is point b. If the minimum wage is defined in units of good 1 any change in the relative price of good 2 will cause output of good 2 to change in the same direction, while output of good 1 stays constant. Thus the distorted production possibilities frontier is a flat line through point b, and it rejoins the undistorted production possibilities frontier below that height.

Now consider the long-run case using the HOS structure. This is a more complex proposition, as there are a number of different possible outcomes. The long-run zero profit conditions are:

$$c_1(\bar{w}, r) \geq p_1 \qquad\qquad (21.17)$$

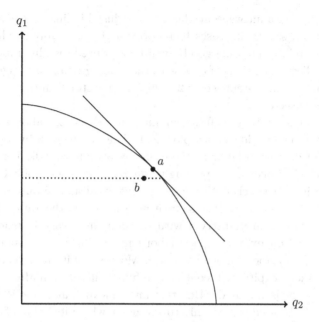

Fig. 21.4   Short-Run Production Possibilities With a Sticky Wage.

$$c_2(\bar{w}, r) \geq p_2 \qquad (21.18)$$

Notice that we have used the inequality form. The equations must hold with equality if the relevant production is non-zero. Suppose that the minimum wage is not binding. In that case it is obviously of no consequence and the model reduces to the standard HOS structure. If the wage is binding there are two possibilities. First, it may be "just" binding, such that both conditions hold with equality. There can only be one relative price at which this occurs. Given p_1, equation (21.17) determines a rental rate on capital, and given p_2, equation (21.18) determines another, so usually both cannot hold as equalities. In other words, only one good can be produced in equilibrium.[2]

The issue can be illustrated using the isoprice diagram shown in Figure 21.5. As illustrated, good 2 is labor intensive, so the isoprice line for good 2 is flatter than for good 1 at point a. Given goods prices p_1 and p_2, the market clearing wage and rental rate are determined by the intersection of the isoprice curves at point a. A minimum wage below this point is not

---

[2]The result is essentially the same as the case of more goods than factors with fixed prices that we examined in Chapter 9. We have two goods, but only one (flexible) factor.

binding. A minimum wage at this point is just binding. At a minimum wage above a, say $\bar{w}$, it ceases to be possible to profitably produce both goods. At equilibrium, only good 1 will be produced (as illustrated).

Point b lies to the right of c, so with the binding minimum wage, capital will migrate from low-rent sector 2 to high-rent sector 1, until the economy specializes in sector 1.

If the minimum wage is fully binding, as in this case, labor will not be fully utilized, i.e., we have unemployment. This can be seen by noting that the ratio of capital to labor in the economy overall must lie between the slopes of the isoprice curves passing through a, since that point represents an equilibrium in which both goods are produced and resources are fully employed. The slope of the isoprice at b indicates the ratio of capital to labor employed in industry 1 with the minimum wage in place. Since the isoprice is convex, the capital/labor employment ratio must be higher than the capital/labor endowment ratio. Moreover, with no intervention in capital markets, capital will continue be fully utilized even after a binding minimum wage is imposed. But this must mean that labor is not fully utilized at b. It is employed only to the point where its value of marginal product in industry 1 equals the binding minimum wage.

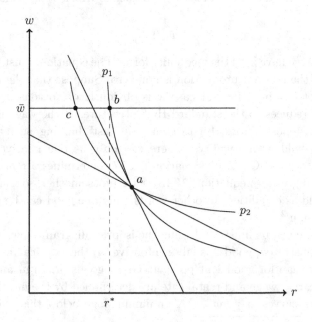

Fig. 21.5   Long-Run Factor Prices With a Sticky Wage.

We assume the minimum wage is defined in terms of commodity 2. A proportional increase in p_2 causes p_2 to shift outward by that same proportion, $\bar{w}$ to rise by that same proportion, and a to rise by a larger proportion, eventually making the minimum wage non-binding.

The implications of the minimum wage for the production possibilities are shown in Figure 21.6. The full-employment production possibilities is the solid line through c, a, e, and f. Good 1 is the capital-intensive good. With a minimum wage in place, the range fe represents possible production points where the wage constraint is not binding (i.e., at relatively high prices of the labor-intensive good, unless the minimum wage is so high that even when the economy is specialized in good 2 there is not enough capital to keep labor fully employed).

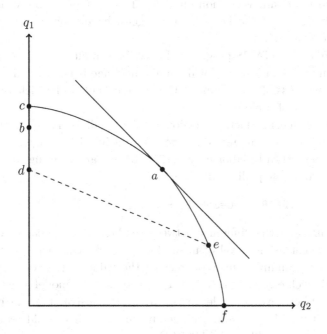

Fig. 21.6   Long-Run Production Possibilities With a Sticky Wage.

Suppose the minimum wage and prices are such that at point e, the minimum wage is just binding. Equilibrium production may be at e, in which case full employment is maintained. However, as Brecher (1974a) notes, there are multiple production equilibria that are consistent with this particular price ratio, all the points along the Rybczynski line, ed. This reflects the idea that as unemployment rises, so employed labor falls, output of the labor-intensive good 2 falls, and output of capital-intensive good 1 rises. If the relative price of good 2 is any lower, but still above a critical level, producing any of good 2 is unprofitable, the minimum wage is fully binding, and equilibrium production lies along the range dc (say, at b), with complete specialization in good 1 and unemployment.

Once the relative price of good 2 falls below the critical level, the minimum wage measured in good 1 falls enough to induce industry 1 to hire enough workers to restore full employment, with the economy specialized at c.

The idea is that a rise in the relative price of labor-intensive good 2 raises the full-employment wage measured in both goods and eventually makes the minimum wage non-binding. Thus perturbations which raise the relative price of the labor-intensive good have a beneficial effect via employment on welfare.

Modifying the GAMS programs that we have built in previous chapters to accommodate an economy-wide minimum wage is not too difficult. We consider two possible techniques. There are others, and which you use is really a matter of preference.

Taking a specific factors version of the small economy model from Chapter 12 as the starting point, we can add in sticky wages very easily by fixing the return to labor using R.FX('L')=1, and altering the resource constraint to an inequality form, i.e:

```
RESOURCE(J)..FBAR(J)=G=SUM(I, F(J,I));
```

Here we interpret the difference between the labor used in each sector and the endowment as the level of unemployment. We can then simulate the effect of a minimum wage by increasing the value of the wage above its calibrated level, e.g., R.FX('L')=1.1, and solving the model as usual.

Alternatively, we could leave the resource constraint as an equality, but explicitly add in a term for unemployment. This would require setting up a new variable, say UNEMP(J), setting initial levels at zero using UNEMP.L(J)=0, and then fixing the levels at zero for the factors that are fully employed, i.e., UNEMP.FX('K')=0 and UNEMP.FX('N')=0.[3] We would then set a lower bound of zero for unemployed labor using UNEMP.LO('L')=0, and an upper bound using UNEMP.UP('L')=FBAR('L'), and fix the return

---

[3]If you are setting up a model in which unemployment is present in the initial equilibrium, you would also need to incorporate the appropriate changes into the model calibration.

to labor in the same way as above using R.FX('L')=0. The resource constraint becomes:

```
RESOURCE(J)..FBAR(J)=E=SUM(I, F(J,I))+UNEMP(J);
```

We can deal with the long run case in a similar fashion. To get started, take the HOS model of a small economy from Chapter 12, fix the return to labor as above, then change the resource constraint to an inequality (or add unemployment explicitly), just as we did in the specific factors case.

Unfortunately, when you simulate a binding minimum wage by increasing the fixed wage level above its initially calibrated level and solving the model as it stands, GAMS will fail with the ominous message **Domain errors in nonlinear functions**.

The problem, as you have probably guessed, is related to complete specialization. GAMS is heading toward a corner and failing. In this particular case, the issue is that the first order conditions for profit maximization as we have written them are not defined in the case of complete specialization. As we saw in Chapter 9, one way to deal with this problem is to drop the first order conditions entirely and obtain the factor prices from the marginal values on the resource constraints. This is not satisfactory here though, as we have a constraint applying to the factor prices, so we want them in the model. Another possible solution is to rewrite the problematic equation. The original form for the factor demand equations is:

```
FDEMAND(J,I)..R(J)=E=P(I)*Q(I)*SUM(JJ, DELTA(JJ,I)*F(JJ,I)**
    RHO(I))**(-1)*DELTA(J,I)*F(J,I)**(RHO(I)-1);
```

We have set RHO=0.1, so as factor usage approaches zero two of the terms in the expression are undefined (zero brought to a negative power). We can eliminate the problem by rewriting the condition in a form which avoids negative powers:

```
FDEMAND(J,I)..R(J)*SUM(JJ, DELTA(JJ,I)*F(JJ,I)**RHO(I))*F(J,I)
    =E=P(I)*Q(I)*DELTA(J,I)*F(J,I)**RHO(I);
```

Written this way, the equations remain well behaved even if some factor demands approach zero, and the model will solve correctly. Of course, there are other possible ways of dealing with the problem too. The general lesson is that when dealing with numerical simulation models we need to think carefully about potential problems that might arise as we search for the solution numerically. Having a good idea from theory about what the solution will be can often help us to pinpoint and fix numerical solution problems.[4] Some suggested exercises can be found in Section 21.5.

21.3   Sector-Specific Sticky Wages

In some cases it may be that wages are downward inflexible only in part of the economy. A classic model at the interface of international trade theory and development economics is the Harris and Todaro (1970) characterization of a dual economy, in which urban production activities are subject to a binding minimum wage, but the wage in rural production activities is determined competitively.

The nature of the distortion can again easily be seen using the dual description of a small, open economy. Let sector 1 be the urban industry, which pays a fixed wage $\bar{w}_1$, and sector 2 be the rural industry. Again starting with the short run, the distortion manifests in the following way:

$$c_1(\bar{w}_1, r_1) = p_1 \tag{21.19}$$

$$c_2(w_2, r_2) = p_2 \tag{21.20}$$

$$w_2 = \pi \bar{w}_1 \tag{21.21}$$

$$a_{K1}\bar{w}_1, r_1)q_1 = \bar{K}_1 \tag{21.22}$$

$$a_{K2}(w_2, r_2)q_2 = \bar{K}_2 \tag{21.23}$$

$$a_{L1}(\bar{w}_1, r)q_1 + \pi a_{L2}(w_2, r)q_2 = \pi \bar{L}. \tag{21.24}$$

The key new component in addition to the fixed urban wage is the introduction of a new variable labeled π. Equation (21.21) states that the rural wage will have to equal the urban wage multiplied by π. This is similar to a wage differential as examined in Section 21.1. The difference is that π is endogenous, and also appears in equation (21.24). Rearranging the latter reveals that $\pi = L_1/(\bar{L} - L_2)$, i.e., the proportion of workers in the urban region who are employed. If the urban minimum wage is binding $\pi < 1$. This is effectively a wage subsidy to urban workers, but only those that are in fact employed. We can interpret (21.24) as saying that the rural wage is equal to the expected urban wage.[5]

The effect of this distortion can be seen in Figure 21.7. The point labeled a represents the undistorted equilibrium. The wage constraint is $\bar{w}_1$, and the intersection of the horizontal line at this level with the labor demand

---

[4]For more tips on what to do when a model fails to solve, see Appendix B.

[5]The specification implies random turnover in the urban labor market and that the unemployed can live on their savings. See Corden and Findlay (1975) for details.

curve for industry 1 (point b) determines employment in the urban region, i.e., industry 1 will hire until the value of the marginal product of labor is equal to the institutionally determined wage. The return to capital in industry 1 is determined residually via product exhaustion.

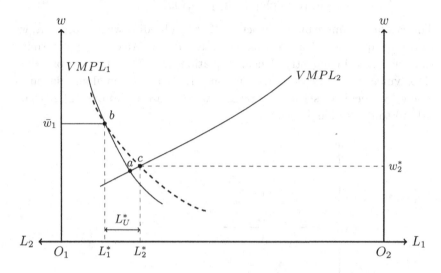

Fig. 21.7   Short Run Labor Market With a Sticky Wage in Sector 1.

Note from equations (21.21) and (21.24) that $w_2(\bar{L} - L_2) = \bar{w}_1 L_1$. Geometrically, this implies that the allocation of labor to industry 2 must lie on the rectangular hyperbola passing through b, the dashed line. Profit maximization implies that industry 2 will pay labor the value of its marginal product, hence the allocation of labor to industry 2, and the wage paid, are determined at point c.[6] Open unemployment arises at the equilibrium, unless the minimum wage is just binding. Unemployment is given by the horizontal distance labeled L_U^*.

To investigate the long-run consequences of this form of distortion we turn once again to the HOS production structure. The minimum wage continues to be imposed only in sector 1, which is assumed to be capital-intensive.[7] The equations representing the economic system are:

$$c_1(\bar{w}_1, r) = p_1 \qquad (21.25)$$

---

[6]As drawn, the wage in industry 2 rises relative to no distortion. This need not be the case, point c may lie to the left or right of a. See Corden and Findlay (1975) for further discussion.

[7]As shown by Neary (1978) this is a necessary condition for stability of the model.

$$c_2(w_2, r) = p_2 \tag{21.26}$$

$$w_2 = \pi \bar{w}_1 \tag{21.27}$$

$$a_{K1}(\bar{w}_1, r)q_1 + a_{K2}(w_2, r)q_2 = \bar{K} \tag{21.28}$$

$$a_{L1}(\bar{w}_1, r)q_1 + \pi a_{L2}(w_2, r)q_2 = \pi \bar{L}. \tag{21.29}$$

This is a fairly simple model structure. Given a binding wage constraint, we can solve equation (21.25) for the return to capital. We can then determine the wage rate in industry 2 using equation (21.26). The rate of urban employment then follows using equation (21.27), and optimal unit demands follow by Shepherd's lemma. Finally we can use equations (21.28) and (21.29) to determine outputs.

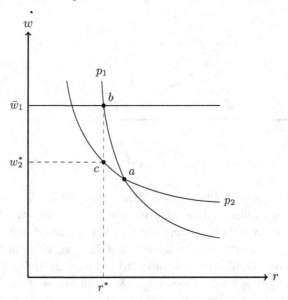

Fig. 21.8   Long-Run Factor Prices With a Sticky Wage in Sector 1.

Figure 21.8 illustrates the equilibrium outcome in factor price space. The intersection of the isoprice curves at a indicates the undistorted equilibrium. With a sticky wage of $\bar{w}_1$ applying in industry 1, the return to capital is determined (point b). Since capital is paid the same return in both sectors, the wage in industry 2 must be w_2^* (point c). The ratio of w_2^* to $\bar{w}_1$ is the urban employment rate. Once factor prices are known, so are factor intensities — geometrically they are the slopes the tangent lines at b and c. The distortion causes both industries to use more capital intensive techniques than they otherwise would.

The equilibrium outcome with respect to factor employment can be illustrated using the Edgeworth box geometry as in Figure 21.9. The solid line drawn through d represents the capital to labor ratio in industry 1. Similarly, the solid line through point c is the ratio of capital to labor in industry 2. The dotted line through point c is the ratio of capital to labor in the urban region (i.e., including the unemployed). Equilibrium factor allocations to industry 2 are determined by the intersection of the factor intensity rays at c. Point d represents equilibrium factor allocations to industry 1, and the horizontal distance between the two points the level of unemployment. The isoquants passing through c and d are, obviously, not tangent to each other. Hence, the economy has been drawn off the efficiency locus.

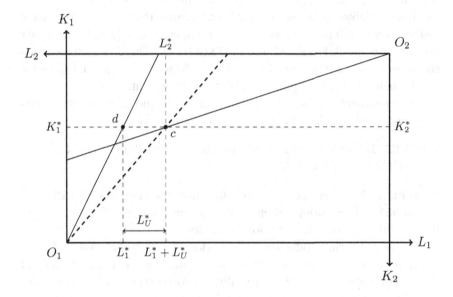

Fig. 21.9   Long-Run Factor Allocation With a Sticky Wage in Sector 1.

To implement the model in GAMS we start with the HOS model from Chapter 12 (the adjustments for the specific factors model are similar). We begin the modifications by partitioning both the set of goods and the set of factors into two groups. The set ST(J) references those factors subject to a constraint on the return (here L), while the set NST(J) references factors that are not regulated (in this case K). Similarly, URBAN(I) references goods produced in the urban region, and hence subject to factor price restrictions

(i.e., good 1), and RURAL(I) those produced in the rural region (good 2).
The elements of these sets are mutually exclusive, and fully exhaust the
elements of the originating sets.

Next we introduce two new PARAMETERS to hold the initial values of
the two new variables that we will introduce to the model. The first is
RIO(J,I), which we will use to represent the initial factor prices paid in
each industry (since these will now differ in general). The second is PIO(J)
which will represent the initial rate of urban factor employment. We then
calibrate to a full employment equilibrium for convenience, so all factor
prices are the same across industries and the employment rates are 100
percent.

Under the VARIABLES heading we define the names of the two new variables RI(J,I) and PI(J). We then set the initial levels and lower bounds
on these variables as usual. In addition, because the rate of employment
cannot exceed 100 percent, we impose an upper bound on PI(J) of 1. We
also need to add R.FX(ST)=1 and PI.FX(NST)=1. The first statement has
the effect of fixing the return to regulated factors. The second fixes the
employment rate of unregulated factors at 100 percent.

To accommodate potential unemployment, we need to modify the resource constraints. The new version of the equation is:

```
RESOURCE(J)..FBAR(J)*PI(J)=E=SUM(URBAN, F(J,URBAN))+PI(J)*
    SUM(RURAL, F(J,RURAL));
```

Since PI(J) has been fixed to unity for all of the elements of J that are
also in NST, this equation will generate the equivalent of (21.29) for labor,
but the full employment condition for capital.

To complete the model we need to close the factor markets. This is
tricky because factor prices paid are determined in a number of different
ways. For those factors that are fully employed, the price paid in each
industry must equal a single market price. Hence we have the equation:

```
LABNST(NST,I)..RI(NST,I)=E=R(NST);
```

For the other factors, the wage will depend on where it is being employed.
For regulated factors employed in the urban region we have:

```
LABSTU(ST,URBAN)..RI(ST,URBAN)=E=R(ST);
```

This just states that the industry level factor payment is equal to R(ST),
which we fixed above. On the other hand, in the rural region we have:

```
LABSTR(ST,RURAL)..RI(ST,RURAL)=E=PI(ST)*R(ST);
```

Which states that the industry wage is equal to the expected wage. Of course, the three equation names must be added to the EQUATIONS section of the program. Running the model generates a full employment equilibrium, which can then be perturbed to generate urban unemployment. The modifications for the specific factors model are essentially the same. Once you have the model working, some suggested exercises can be found in Section 21.5.[8]

21.4 Imperfect Factor Mobility

As noted in the previous section, one way of thinking about the Harris-Todaro model structure is that it combines a sticky wage model with a particular endogenization of a wage differential. Another mechanism for endogenizing a factor price differential is by introducing imperfect factor mobility. We have already examined the extreme case — the specific factors model. In that model, as we have seen, each specific factor is paid a distinct return.

In some situations we may want to allow for factors of production to be less than perfectly mobile, but not perfectly immobile. To see how this works, consider the case where capital is fully mobile, as in the HOS model, but labor is less than perfectly mobile. The GDP maximization problem can be represented by the following Lagrangian:

$$\mathscr{L} = p_1 q_1(K_1, L_1) + p_2 q_2(K_2, L_2) + \lambda[\bar{K} - K_1 - K_2]$$
$$+ \mu[\bar{L} - \ell(L_1, L_2)]. \qquad (21.30)$$

The terms $\bar{K}$ and $\bar{L}$ represent the given endowment of capital and labor, respectively, and the production functions are assumed to exhibit the usual neoclassical properties, just as before. The new element is the replacement of the labor resource constraint with a labor allocation function $\ell(L_1, L_2)$, where ℓ is convex, and homogeneous of degree one (implying that a proportional increase in the labor allocated to each sector requires the same proportional increase in the labor endowment).[9] Obviously one special case corresponding to the standard model is where $\ell = L_1 + L_2$. Taking the

---

[8]See in particular exercises 7–11.

[9]We can think of this as a shorthand way of modeling the phenomenon that gives rise to the sluggish labor.

derivatives of the Lagrangian yields the following first-order conditions:

$$\partial \mathscr{L}/\partial K_1 = p_1 \partial q_1/\partial K_1 - \lambda = 0 \tag{21.31}$$

$$\partial \mathscr{L}/\partial L_1 = p_1 \partial q_1/\partial L_1 - \mu \partial \ell/\partial L_1 = 0 \tag{21.32}$$

$$\partial \mathscr{L}/\partial K_2 = p_2 \partial q_2/\partial K_2 - \lambda = 0 \tag{21.33}$$

$$\partial \mathscr{L}/\partial L_2 = p_2 \partial q_2/\partial L_2 - \mu \partial \ell/\partial L_2 = 0 \tag{21.34}$$

$$\partial \mathscr{L}/\partial \lambda = \bar{K} - K_1 - K_2 = 0 \tag{21.35}$$

$$\partial \mathscr{L}/\partial \mu = \bar{L} - \ell(L_1, L_2) = 0. \tag{21.36}$$

These look quite similar to the standard model. We can interpret $\mu \partial \ell/\partial L_i$ as the industry specific wage that arises in the equilibrium. The multiplier μ continues to be interpreted as the increment to GDP from a one unit rise in the labor endowment. Clearly, if $\ell = L_1 + L_2$ then $\partial \ell/\partial L_i = 1$, and the conditions for an optimum are the same as those we derived in Chapter 5. More generally, the wage will differ across sectors, and as in the exogenous wage differential model, the economy is pulled off of the production possibility frontier. We can introduce imperfect mobility for other factors of production in the same way, with similar implications.

To operationalize the theory we need to choose a functional form for the factor allocation function(s). The constant elasticity of transformation function (CET) is usually used. This takes the form $\ell = \gamma_L[\delta_L L_1^{\rho_L} + (1 - \delta_L)L_2^{\rho_L}]^{1/\rho_L}$, and can easily be generalized to more goods. This is the same as the CES function that we have used in a number of contexts. The difference is that with the CES function we have $-\infty < \rho < 1$, which ensures the function is concave, whereas with the CET we have $1 < \rho_L < \infty$, which ensures that the function is convex (the linear case, where $\rho = 1$ is both convex and concave).

To implement the model in GAMS, we can start with the small country version of the HOS model from Chapter 12. The first step is to add an ALIAS for the set of goods with the command ALIAS(I,II). We will allow for imperfect mobility of all factor of production, so next we define parameters RHO_F(J) to control the degree of immobility, DELTA_F(J,I) for the factor allocation shares, and GAMMA_F(J) for the shift parameter on the factor allocation functions. We also define a parameter RIO(J,I) to hold the initial industry-level factor prices.

The next step is calibration. We begin by normalizing all factor prices to unity, and then set values (greater than one) for RHO_F(J). Next we calibrate the shares parameters DELTA_F(J,I) and the shift parameters GAMMA_F(J). The calibration is very similar to previous examples:

```
DELTA_F(J,I)=(RIO(J,I)/FO(J,I)**(RHO_F(J)-1))/(SUM(II,
    RIO(J,II)/FO(J,II)**(RHO_F(J)-1)));
GAMMA_F(J)=FBAR(J)/(SUM(I, DELTA_F(J,I)*FO(J,I)**RHO_F(J)))**
    (1/RHO_F(J));
```

Under the VARIABLES heading, we define the new variable RI(J,I) for the industry-level factor prices, and set the initial level and a lower bound of zero as usual. Under EQUATIONS we define the new equation FSUPPLY(J,I).

Next we make some adjustments to the model equations. The standard (additive) resource constraint is replaced by the more general resource allocation function of the CET form:

```
FBAR(J)=E=GAMMA_F(J)*(SUM(I, DELTA_F(J,I)*F(J,I)**RHO_F(J)))**
    (1/RHO_F(J));
```

We also adjust the factor demand equations to account for the fact that firms now pay differentiated factor prices:

```
FDEMAND(J,I)..RI(J,I)=E=P(I)*Q(I)*SUM(JJ, DELTA(JJ,I)*
    F(JJ,I)**RHO(I))**(-1)*DELTA(J,I)*F(J,I)**(RHO(I)-1);
```

Finally, we define the factor supply equations:

```
FSUPPLY(J,I)..RI(J,I)=E=R(J)*FBAR(J)*SUM(II, DELTA_F(J,II)*
    F(J,II)**RHO_F(J))**(-1)*DELTA_F(J,I)*F(J,I)**(RHO_F(J)-1);
```

The left hand sides of FDEMAND(J,I) and FSUPPLY(J,I) are the same, so together these two equations generate the first-order condition from above.

The completed program is available for download if you have trouble making the required adjustments. Some suggested exercises using the model can be found in the next section.[10]

21.5 Exercises

(1) Using the model we developed in the previous chapter, simulate a series of increasingly large wage differentials. How does the index of economic welfare change?

(2) See if you can construct a wage differential model with the differential defined in currency units rather than as a proportion.

---

[10]See in particular exercises 12 through 14.

(3) Using the short-run model with an economy-wide sticky wage that is binding, an increase in the price of either good will lower the level of unemployment. For a given proportional increment in price, a rise in which price lowers unemployment by more? Can you give an economic rationale for your result.

(4) Using the long-run model with an economy-wide sticky wage that is binding, what happens to the level of unemployment as the price of the capital-intensive good rises?

(5) Using the long-run model with an economy-wide sticky wage that is binding, will growth of the capital stock tend to increase or decrease unemployment? How about growth of the labor stock?

(6) Using the long-run model with an economy-wide sticky wage that is binding, Brecher (1974a) writes: (a) "Free trade may be inferior to no trade for the home country." (b) An increase in foreign demand for home exports may be detrimental to the home country." (c) "If the home country lacks (possesses) monopoly power in trade, this country's optimum trade policy is not necessarily free (taxed) trade." (d) "Removing the wage floor to restore full employment may decrease welfare or reverse the direction of trade." Do you understand why these propositions are true? Can you build GAMS models to illustrate these propositions?

(7) In Section 21.3 we built a long-run version of the model with sector-specific sticky wages and rural-urban migration. See if you can build a short-run version based on the specific factors model.

(8) Once you have completed the previous exercise, shock the model in various ways to evaluate the equilibrium responses. We showed in section 21.3 that imposing a binding minimum wage may raise or lower the wage in the rural sector relative to no intervention. Can you parameterize the model to illustrate both outcomes?

(9) Compare the long and short-run responses of the sector-specific sticky wage model to various shocks. In the short run, what will an increase in the price of the capital-intensive good do to the rate of employment? What about in the long run?

(10) In the long-run model with sector-specific sticky wages, with goods prices fixed the rate of employment is fixed also. Hence, an increase in an endowment should not alter the rate of employment. But what about the level?

(11) Corden and Findlay (1975) show that when a minimum wage is imposed in the long-run model with sector-specific sticky wages, it is possible

that output of the urban sector, which must pay the higher wage, could rise. See if you can replicate their result. (Hint: Corden and Findlay develop the paradox in the context of Leontief production technology).

(12) Using the model of imperfect factor mobility, can you set values for the RHO_F parameters such that the model approximates the HOS model? Verify by comparing the response of the model to various shocks with the same shocks applied to the HOS version of the model from Chapter 12.

(13) Using the model of imperfect factor mobility, can you set values for the RHO_F parameters such that the model approximates the specific factors model? Verify by comparing the response of the model to various shocks with the same shocks applied to the specific factors version of the model from Chapter 12.

(14) Using the model of imperfect factor mobility, what happens if the values for both RHO_F parameters are set at a very large number (say, 10). Explain the result of a price shock. What does the production possibility frontier look like in this case?

(15) The models that we have built in this chapter have all been calibrated to an initial undistorted equilibrium. Can you adjust the calibrations to replicate an initially distorted equilibrium?

(16) In this chapter we have concentrated on the small economy case. See if you can modify the large economy model from Chapter 14 to accommodate factor market distortions of various kinds.

(17) By modifying the model of Chapter 13, explore the implications of factor market distortions in the presence of non-traded goods.

(18) By modifying the models of Chapters 19 and 20, evaluate the consequences of other interventions (tariffs, subsidies, etc.) when the economy also has distorted factor markets. What interesting results can you find?

21.6   Further Reading

On proportional wage differentials see Bhagwati and Srinivasan (1971). Schweinberger (1979) discusses the case of constant absolute differentials. On the effect of downward inflexible wages see Brecher (1974a) and (1974b). The classic paper on sector-specific sticky wages is Harris and Todaro (1970). Bhagwati and Srinivasan (1974) and Srinivasan and Bhagwati (1975) consider the extensions to the open economy, while Corden and

Findlay (1975) extend to the case with mobile capital. The classic reference on imperfect labor mobility is Casas (1984). Gilbert and Tower (2002) have considered imperfect labor mobility in the context of sector-specific sticky wages.

PART 3
Computable General Equilibrium

Chapter 22

Multiple Households and Other Sources of Demand

The problems that we have been working on so far are small scale "toy" models that are closely tied to the literature on trade theory and policy. In the final part of this volume, we turn to some of the issues involved with extending those basic models to handle the more complex architecture of the computable general equilibrium, or CGE, models that are commonly used in trade policy analysis of real-world economies and policies. While the basic structure of these models is not very different from those that we have been examining, there are some important features of CGE models that are ignored for convenience in toy models.

We begin the process by explicitly introducing multiple households into the models. Our toy models have all featured a single "representative" consumer, but in many applications we are interested in how a policy affects different types of households, each of which may face different constraints. This may be because we want the system to better represent a real economy, or because we are particularly interested in income distribution issues. In large scale models we may also want to explicitly introduce other sources of final demand, such as investment and government consumption. We do so in a rudimentary way in this chapter, and consider some further details later.

22.1 Exchange Model

To simplify matters, let's start with the case of a simple exchange economy. We'll introduce production and international trade in the next section. Suppose that there are two household groups in the economy, each of which is modeled by a representative consumer, the preferences of whom satisfy the standard axioms discussed in Chapter 3. Let households be denoted by a superscript 1 or 2, while subscripts indicate goods. Since we are dealing only with the problem of exchange, the total supply of each good is fixed at the sum of each household's endowments of the goods. Hence, the total endowment of good 1 is $\bar{q}_1^1 + \bar{q}_1^2$. Similarly, the total endowment of good 2 is $\bar{q}_1^1 + \bar{q}_1^2$.

In a competitive equilibrium, each of the households takes market prices as given. Household 1 therefore maximizes:

$$\mathscr{L}_1 = U^1(c_1^1, c_2^1) + \lambda_1[p_1\bar{q}_1^1 + p_2\bar{q}_2^1 - p_1c_1^1 - p_2c_2^1]. \tag{22.1}$$

This is the standard consumer utility maximization problem. The term $p_1\bar{q}_1^1 + p_2\bar{q}_2^1$ is simply the money income of household 1. If you like, you can think of the household as selling its endowment at market prices, and buying back its preferred bundle at those same prices. The first-order conditions for a maximum are familiar:

$$\partial\mathscr{L}_1/\partial c_1^1 = \partial U^1/\partial c_1^1 - \lambda_1 p_1 = 0 \tag{22.2}$$

$$\partial\mathscr{L}_1/\partial c_2^1 = \partial U^2/\partial c_2^1 - \lambda_1 p_2 = 0 \tag{22.3}$$

$$\partial\mathscr{L}_1/\partial\lambda_1 = p_1\bar{q}_1^1 + p_2\bar{q}_2^1 - p_1c_1^1 - p_2c_2^1 = 0. \tag{22.4}$$

The optimization problem for household 2, and the associated first order conditions, are the same, with the superscripts appropriately adjusted. The solutions are the Marshallian demand curves for each household.

We can complete the exchange model by adding in market clearing conditions, which equate total household demands to the exogenously given total supplies, that is:

$$\bar{q}_1^1 + \bar{q}_1^2 = c_1^1 + c_1^2 \tag{22.5}$$

$$\bar{q}_2^1 + \bar{q}_2^2 = c_2^1 + c_2^2. \tag{22.6}$$

The market clearing conditions are not independent by Walras' law, as usual. Given the demand from each household, and the fixed supply of the desired goods, we can (in principle) determine a relative price (i.e., we must set the price of one good as the numéraire) that clears the markets. The solution is characterized by the condition:

$$\frac{\partial U^1/\partial c_1^1}{\partial U^1/\partial c_2^1} = \frac{\partial U^2/\partial c_1^2}{\partial U^2/\partial c_2^2} = \frac{p_1}{p_2}. \tag{22.7}$$

That is, both households have the same marginal rate of substitution (and, of course, are on their individual budget constraints).[1]

---

[1] It is also possible to set the problem up as a constrained optimization problem as usual if we introduce a social welfare function following Negishi (1960).

The significance of this outcome can be seen by considering the following problem. Suppose that we want to maximize the utility index of household 1, subject to maintaining a target level of utility for household 2, which we denote $\bar{U}^2$, and given the endowments of each good. The associated Lagrangian would be:

$$\mathscr{L} = U^1(c_1^1, c_2^1) + \lambda[\bar{U}^2 - U^2(c_1^2, c_2^2)]$$
$$+ \mu[\bar{q}_1^1 + \bar{q}_1^2 - c_1^1 - c_1^2] + \delta[\bar{q}_2^1 + \bar{q}_2^2 - c_2^1 - c_2^2]. \qquad (22.8)$$

Taking the first-order conditions and manipulating them we find that an optimal outcome requires that:

$$\frac{\partial U^1/\partial c_1^1}{\partial U^1/\partial c_2^1} = \frac{\partial U^2/\partial c_1^2}{\partial U^2/\partial c_2^2}.$$

But this is just the same condition as above. This result follows from what is called the first welfare theorem. It tells us that the competitive market solution is Pareto efficient — it is not possible to make one household better off by redistributing the available endowments without making the other worse off.

Figure 22.1 below illustrates the equilibrium. The construction is much like the production box that we have seen. The dimensions of the box are the total endowments of the goods. The lower left origin is the reference point for household 1, and the upper right is the reference point for household 2. The line connecting the origins is the locus of indifference curve tangencies, or the contract curve. It shows the Pareto efficient allocations of the two goods across the two households. The competitive equilibrium lies along the contract curve, with the slope of the indifference curves at that point being (minus) the relative price. The original endowment must lie somewhere along the illustrated price line.

Building a GAMS problem to replicate an exchange economy is not very difficult, but it is a useful exercise to illustrate how multiple households work in more complete models. The code is presented in Table 22.1, and has been adapted from the consumer choice model of Chapter 3.

Relative to the model from Chapter 3, we introduce a new set H to hold the households. Next we extend the parameter dimensions to accommodate. Hence, ALPHA, the shift parameter on the Cobb–Douglas utility function, become ALPHA(H). Similarly, BETA(I), the shares, become BETA(I,H), and so on. In this model we will be determining prices and incomes endogenously, so we also add parameters to hold the initial values, PO(I) and YO(H).

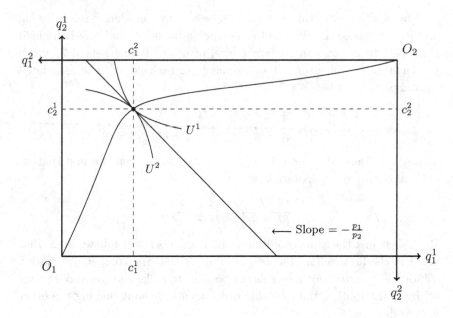

Fig. 22.1   Consumption Box.

The next section of the model is the calibration. This is the same as before, with the exception that we define initial income as the value of the initial endowments (which are also the initial consumption levels, following our usual approach of fitting the model to a solution).

Next we define the variables, and set the levels and lower bounds. Note that we have created a scalar called OBJ to act as the objective.

The equations of the model are the household utility functions UTILITY(H), and the associated demand functions DEMAND(I,H). With the exception of the extension to the household dimension, these equations are the same as Chapter 3. We introduce a function to define the market clearing conditions (total demands equal total supplies) and to endogenize household incomes:

```
CLEAR(I)..SUM(H, C(I,H))=E=SUM(H, CO(I,H));
INCOME(H)..Y(H)=E=SUM(I, P(I)*CO(I,H));
```

Note the use of CO(I,H) on the right-hand side of both expressions, representing the fixed goods supply (as opposed to C(I) which represents the variable goods demand.) We also add an objective function in the same way as Chapter 15. Once you have verified the benchmark, try some of the exercises at the end of the chapter.

Table 22.1   GAMS Program for Exchange Economy.

```
SET I Goods /1,2/;
SET H Households /A,B/;

PARAMETERS
ALPHA(H)                              Shift parameters in utility
BETA(I,H)                             Share parameters in utility
PO(I)                                 Initial prices
UO(H)                                 Initial utility levels
CO(I,H)                               Initial consumption levels
YO(H)                                 Initial household incomes ;


PO(I)=1;
CO('1','A')=75;
CO('2','A')=25;
CO(I,'B')=100-CO(I,'A');
YO(H)=SUM(I, PO(I)*CO(I,H));
UO(H)=YO(H);
BETA(I,H)=CO(I,H)*PO(I)/YO(H);
ALPHA(H)=UO(H)/PROD(I, CO(I,H)**BETA(I,H));

VARIABLES
U(H)                                  Utility indices
P(I)                                  Prices
C(I,H)                                Consumption levels
Y(H)                                  Household incomes
OBJ                                   Objective ;

U.L(H)=UO(H); C.L(I,H)=CO(I,H); Y.L(H)=YO(H); P.L(I)=PO(I);
U.LO(H)=0; C.LO(I,H)=0; Y.LO(H)=0; P.LO(I)=0;
P.FX('2')=1;


EQUATIONS
UTILITY(H)                            Utility function
DEMAND(I,H)                           Demand functions
CLEAR(I)                              Market clearing
INCOME(H)                             Household income
OBJECT                                Objective function ;

UTILITY(H)..U(H)=E=ALPHA(H)*PROD(I, C(I,H)**BETA(I,H));
DEMAND(I,H)..C(I,H)=E=BETA(I,H)*Y(H)/P(I);
CLEAR(I)..SUM(H, C(I,H))=E=SUM(H, CO(I,H));
INCOME(H)..Y(H)=E=SUM(I, P(I)*CO(I,H));
OBJECT..OBJ=E=0;

MODEL EXCHANGE /ALL/;
SOLVE EXCHANGE USING NLP MAXIMIZING OBJ;
```

22.2   Production and Trade

While the above model abstracted from production and trade, the model with these activities is not much more difficult. Consider the small, open economy problem that we developed in Chapter 12. As we have seen, the production decision under competition is independent of the consumption decision. We can represent the production side of the economy by the GDP maximization problem for given prices, just as in Chapters 5 and 6. Maximizing GDP ensures that the economy is on the production possibilities frontier.

With GDP determined, we can specify how the income is allocated across households. How is this done? We know from product exhaustion that GDP is equal to the sum of factor payments, hence if we specify the ownership of the primary factors of production across the households, along with any inter-household transfers, we can calculate household incomes.

Each representative household then maximizes its utility subject to their budget constraint. Because all households face the same relative prices, they have the same marginal rate of substitution, and the allocation of consumption across households lies on the contract curve. The model is completed by adding in the market clearing conditions requiring that net exports of each good equal the quantity of production less the sum of consumption over all households.

Figure 22.2 illustrates the solution. The production possibilities are given by the dotted line through point a. The slope of the tangent line through a is the relative world price of good 2. Hence, point a represents the optimal production solution. Given the world prices and the resources and technology that generated the production possibilities, we can determine factor prices, and the allocation of income across households. Total consumption is represented by point b. We can think of b as defined by the boundaries of a consumption box like Figure 22.1. The line connecting the origin and point b is the contract curve. Point c represents the household's position along the contract curve, the allocation of consumption across the households.

To implement the model in GAMS, we start with the basic small economy model that we developed in Chapter 12, and make amendments to the demand structure that are essentially the same as in the preceding section. Hence, we begin by adding a new set H for the households, and using it to index consumption, C(I,H) and household utility, U(H), and all related parameters, ALPHA(H), BETA(I,H), UO(H) and CO(I,H).

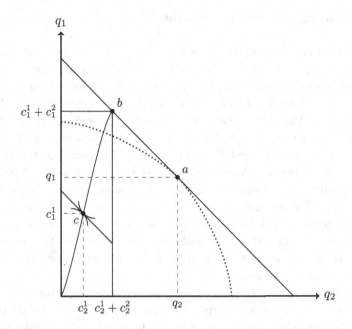

Fig. 22.2   Small, Open Economy With Two Households.

Next we add two new parameters. The first is initial household income
YO(H). The next is the factor ownership shares, which we denote FSHR(J,H).
These hold the proportions of each factor J that are owned by household
H. We can use these to calibrate the initial incomes as:

YO(H)=SUM(J, RO(J)*FBAR(J)*FSHR(J,H));

Of course, we have to be careful to ensure that the value of household
consumption is equal to the value of household income from factors.

Next we extend the equations characterizing the demand side of the
economy to accommodate multiple households. This is essentially the same
as in the preceding model, except that household income is defined as the
sum of the factor incomes accruing to each household. The market clearing
condition becomes:

X(I)=E=Q(I)-SUM(H, C(I,H));

This states that net exports are equal to production less the sum of consumption over all households. Once the adjustments are made, we run
a benchmark to check the calibration as usual. The completed model is
available for download, and some exercises are discussed below.

22.3   Government and Investment

While we did have an implicit government sector in the models of Chapters 19 through 21, its role was limited to taxing/subsidizing various activities and transferring resources to and from the households. Given this very limited role, there was no real need to introduce the government explicitly.

In most models of real economies, of course, the government is not only engaged in imposing taxes/subsidies, but is also a source of final demand that needs to be accounted for in the model. Moreover, in the analysis of real-world policy problems, we often need a more realistic description of the constraints that involve the relevant economic agents, including the government. For example, an export subsidy is unlikely to be financed through lump-sum transfers from the households in most cases as standard theory assumes, but rather by introducing other taxes into the system. To accurately assess the economic impact of the subsidy we need to account for this additional distortion.

In most trade-oriented CGE models the methods used for introducing a government are relatively simple. Consider the model that we developed in Chapter 20, which incorporated a variety of tax/subsidy instruments. To introduce the government explicitly into that model, we first need to split national income into a component that accrues to the household, and a component that accrues to the government, in much the same way as we split income across different households in the preceding section.

If we assume that all primary factors of production are owned by a single household, then we can add to the model an equation, HOUSE, defining household income, YH, as follows:

HOUSE..YH=E=SUM(J, FBAR(J)*R(J))-TRANS;

This states that household income is equal to factor payments, less any direct transfers (TRANS) to the government. We then need to modify the demand functions so that they are based on only the household income:

DEMAND(I)..C(I)=E=BETA(I)*YH/(P(I)*(1+TC(I)));

Government income, YG, can be defined in the equation GOVT as the sum of all tax revenues, less all subsidy expenditures, and plus any transfers from the household:

GOVT..YG=E=SUM(I, TC(I)*P(I)*C(I))
   -SUM(I, T(I)*PW(I)*X(I))-SUM(I, TP(I)*P(I)*Q(I))

```
-SUM((J,I), TF(J,I)*(R(J)/(1+TF(J,I)))*F(J,I))+TRANS;
```

The terms are, in order, net consumption tax revenue, net trade tax revenue, net output tax revenue, net factor tax revenue, and transfers.[2]

Next we introduce government consumption. For now, we will treat government consumption as fixed in quantity terms. Hence, we define `G(I)` as a parameter or as a fixed variable. We then alter the market clearing conditions to:

```
MAT_BAL(I)..X(I)=E=Q(I)-C(I)-G(I);
```

Finally, we add a government budget constraint that links government spending to government income as follows:

```
GBUDGET..SUM(I, G(I)*P(I))=E=YG;
```

The necessary adjustments to the model parameters, calibration and initialization section should be clear, and we leave them as an exercise.

Notice that, as we have specified the model, government spending is equal to government income. Since tax revenue is endogenous, as are government expenditures (the quantities are fixed), this implies that transfers adjust to maintain the constraint. We can think of `TRANS` as being the government deficit, which is financed through transfers (borrowing) from the household. In fact, this is the same story that we used in Chapters 19 and 20. We have just made it explicit.[3]

This is, of course, not the only story we could tell. We could, for example, fix the government deficit, and endogenize something else. Government spending could be scaled to ensure the budget equation holds, or a source of tax revenue could be endogenized. We discuss some of the choices further in Chapter 26 (which deals with the issue of closure).

Investment demands can be handled in a similar way. We can define a new parameter `INV(I)` to hold the exogenous investment values. We then need to adjust the market clearing conditions:

```
MAT_BAL(I)..X(I)=E=Q(I)-C(I)-G(I)-INV(I);
```

We also adjust the household income equation:

```
HOUSE..YH=E=SUM(J, FBAR(J)*R(J))-TRANS-SUM(I, P(I)*INV(I));
```

---

[2]Verify that the sum of household income and government income is GDP.

[3]If government consumption of all goods is zero, the model is the same.

Consider the implications. Investment quantities are given, but prices can vary. The current account is fixed at zero, hence total savings (private savings by the household less the government deficit) must equal investment, and must be varying to ensure balance. Again, this is not the only story that we could tell, and we discuss alternatives further in Chapter 26.

22.4   Exercises

(1) The exchange model illustrates the idea that competitive markets result in a Pareto efficient allocation of goods across households. But, there are many Pareto efficient outcomes. How can one of the alternatives be achieved? (Hint: Think about the second welfare theorem).

(2) Given that the consumers have Cobb–Douglas preferences, what is the shape of the contract curve? Can you use the GAMS program to help you find out?

(3) In the exchange economy, what happens to the welfare of the households as the size of the Edgeworth box is expanded? Does it matter how the increase in the endowments is divided among the households?

(4) Consider a production model of a small economy with multiple households. The free trade equilibrium is Pareto efficient. Is it necessarily a Pareto improvement relative to the autarkic equilibrium? Can you set up different outcomes? (Hint: Think about Stolper–Samuelson).

(5) Using the model with government and investment incorporated, verify that if investment spending and government spending are both zero, the model with explicit transfers to and from the households replicates the results you obtained when simulating interventions in Chapters 19 and 20.

(6) Can you alter the model to show how the effect of an export subsidy would change if it had to be financed via a consumption tax?

(7) Can you construct a model in which there are multiple households and imperfect labor mobility as discussed in Chapter 21? (Hint: Gilbert and Oladi (2010) discuss some of the issues involved.)

(8) Can you set up a model with multiple households and an explicit government? Can you set up the model so that the burden of financing a government deficit differs across the households?

Chapter 23

Armington Preferences

In the competitive models of international trade that we have been examining it makes no economic sense to engage in trade in both directions in the same product. Nonetheless, a characteristic of real world trading patterns is that countries often simultaneously import and export goods in the same product category, even when the category is quite narrowly defined. The theoretical literature has generally modeled intra-industry trade patterns as arising from imperfectly competitive market structures, as in Chapters 17 and 18. In the applied literature an alternative accommodation is generally made that is consistent with perfect competition, called the Armington assumption. This specification is almost universal in CGE models, so much so that they are often referred to as "Armington type" models. In this approach, consumers are assumed to have a "love of variety" that generates demand for both domestic and foreign produced products within a product category. In essence then, the Armington approach is a special case of the horizontal product differentiation that we saw in Chapter 18. In this chapter we modify our basic trade model to illustrate the concepts involved.

23.1 Formal Problem

The Armington assumption at its core amounts to making a specific set of assumptions on the structure of preferences. In Chapter 3, we defined the utility function of a consumer across consumption goods, e.g., $U = U(c_1, c_2)$, and, invoking a representative consumer, we have used this approach throughout our models.

In the Armington approach, consumers are assumed to differentiate between goods based on origin. If we denote consumption of domestically produced goods d_i and imported versions of the same good m_i, the utility function (in the two good case) becomes $U = U(d_1, d_2, m_1, m_2)$. Since goods are defined by how the consumer perceives them, there is really nothing new here provided the utility function continues to satisfy the basic axioms — we just have a problem of consumer choice with twice as many arguments as before.

In specifying the form of the preferences, Armington models make use of a nested consumption structure much like the nested production structure we considered in Chapter 10 in the context of intermediate goods. Figure 23.1 illustrates. Final household demand is represented by a standard utility function of the type we have been using, defined across consumption of composite goods. The composites are in turn defined across imported and domestically produced products.

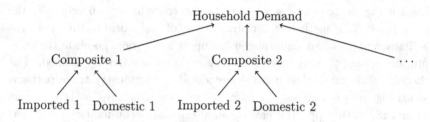

Fig. 23.1   Nested (Armington) Consumption Structure.

We can write the representative consumer's utility function as $U = U(c_1(d_1, m_1), c_2(d_2, m_2))$. The functions c_i are the Armington composite or aggregator functions. They are assumed to be continuous, increasing in both arguments, concave, and homogeneous of degree one.[1]

Now let's reconsider the consumer's maximization problem in the context of a utility function of this form. Let Y denote income as usual, and the prices of domestic goods are p_i^d and imported goods p_i^m. The Lagrangian for the problem is then:

$$\mathscr{L} = U(c_1(d_1, m_1), c_2(d_2, m_2)) + \lambda[Y - p_1^d d_1 - p_1^m m_1 - p_2^d d_2 - p_2^m m_2]. \quad (23.1)$$

The first-order conditions for a maximum are:

$$\partial \mathscr{L}/\partial d_1 = (\partial U/\partial c_1)(\partial c_1/\partial d_1) - \lambda p_1^d = 0 \quad (23.2)$$

$$\partial \mathscr{L}/\partial d_2 = (\partial U/\partial c_2)(\partial c_2/\partial d_2) - \lambda p_2^d = 0 \quad (23.3)$$

$$\partial \mathscr{L}/\partial m_1 = (\partial U/\partial c_1)(\partial c_1/\partial m_1) - \lambda p_1^m = 0 \quad (23.4)$$

$$\partial \mathscr{L}/\partial m_2 = (\partial U/\partial c_2)(\partial c_2/\partial m_2) - \lambda p_2^m = 0 \quad (23.5)$$

[1]In practice the aggregator functions are almost always of the now familiar CES form.

and that the consumer must spend all of their income. These conditions should look familiar — the consumer equates the marginal utility per dollar spent on each good to the marginal utility of income. We apply the chain rule to convert the units of domestic/importable consumption into units of composite consumption, and then into "utility" units. At an optimal solution it must be the case that the marginal rate of substitution between any pair of commodities is equal to (minus) the relative price.

The above approach emphasizes the fact that the Armington assumption is really nothing more than the choice of a particular form for the utility function. The assumption is more frequently presented, however, as a two-stage optimization problem. In first stage, the consumer minimizes the expenditure required to generate a unit of the composite good. Using good 1 as an example, the Lagrangian is:

$$\mathscr{L} = p_1^d a_{d1} + p_1^m a_{m1} + \mu_1[1 - c_1(a_{d1}, a_{m1})] \qquad (23.6)$$

where a_{d1} is the unit demand for the domestic version of good 1 and a_{m1} is the unit demand for the imported version. The first-order conditions for a minimum are:

$$\partial \mathscr{L} / \partial a_{d1} = p_1^d - \mu_1(\partial c_1 / \partial a_{d1}) = 0 \qquad (23.7)$$

$$\partial \mathscr{L} / \partial a_{m1} = p_1^m - \mu_1(\partial c_1 / \partial a_{m1}) = 0 \qquad (23.8)$$

$$\partial \mathscr{L} / \partial \mu_1 = 1 - c_1(a_{d1}, a_{m1}) = 0. \qquad (23.9)$$

From these, we can solve for the optimal per unit consumption of the domestic and imported versions of the good, as functions of the relative prices, and the multiplier, μ_1. The latter represents the change in the optimal level of expenditure for an increment in the quantity of the aggregate. In other words, it is the price of the good 1 composite.[2] We solve the same problem for good 2.

With the prices of the composites in hand, we can solve the consumer utility maximization in terms of the composites. That is, we maximize:

$$\mathscr{L} = u(c_1, c_2) + \lambda[Y - p_1 c_1 - p_2 c_2]. \qquad (23.10)$$

From here we can solve for the total consumption levels of the composite in terms of the composite prices as usual (i.e., the Marshallian demands). The composite prices are in turn functions of the (given) prices of domestic

---

[2]To see this, rearrange (23.7) to see that $\mu_1 = p_1^d/(\partial c_1/\partial d_1)$. Now, from (23.2) we have $p_1^d/(\partial c_1/\partial d_1) = (\partial U/\partial c_1)/\lambda$. The latter is the money value of the utility generated by the last unit of the composite consumed, which as we saw in Chapter 3, is equal to the price at an optimal choice.

and imported goods. Since the aggregator functions are homogeneous of degree one, $d_1 = a_{d1}c_1$ and $m_1 = a_{m1}c_1$.

The main benefit of approaching the Armington assumption from the two-stage angle is that it leaves the upper level utility maximization problem, and its solution, intact. Therefore, the lower level Armington aggregation functions, along with the first-order conditions to the lower level problem, can simply be appended to the models that we have already developed.

Finally, let's consider how the Armington preferences are incorporated into a complete model of the economy. We use the small country case as an example. As usual, the problem is to maximize the social welfare index subject to the limitations of technology and resources, and the ability to exchange goods on world markets. Assuming free trade, the prices of both exports and imports are determined by world markets. The Lagrangian for the maximization problem is:

$$\mathscr{L} = \theta U(c_1(d_1, m_1), c_2(d_2, m_2)) + \lambda_1[q_1 - d_1 - x_1] + \lambda_2[q_2 - d_2 - x_2]$$
$$+ \delta[S - \psi(q_1, q_2)] + \gamma[p_1^d x_1 + p_2^d x_2 - p_1^m m_1 - p_2^m m_2]. \qquad (23.11)$$

In addition to introducing the new utility function as the objective, there are changes in the market clearing and trade balance conditions. In the market clearing equations, consumption is replaced with consumption of the domestic good. Exports are now interpreted as being the difference between domestic production and domestic consumption, and are non-negative. The imported versions of the goods are available only through trade, and appear in the trade balance condition. Again, imports are defined as non-negative.

23.2   Example

The CES function is generally used as an aggregator, taking the form $c_i = \gamma_i^A[\delta_i^A d_i^{\rho_i^A} + (1 - \delta_i^A)m_i^{\rho_i^A}]^{1/\rho_i^A}$, for all goods i. As we have seen in other contexts, this function has one free parameter, which reflects the elasticity of substitution between domestic and imported versions of a good (in this context the elasticity is usually called, for obvious reasons, the Armington elasticity). The Lagrangian for the minimization problem is then written:

$$\mathscr{L} = p_i^d d_i + p_i^m m_i + p_i\{c_i - \gamma_i^A[\delta_i^A d_i^{\rho_i^A} + (1 - \delta_i^A)m_i^{\rho_i^A}]^{1/\rho_i^A}\}. \qquad (23.12)$$

Notice that we have given the multiplier on the constraint the symbol p_i (the composite price) for convenience. Notice also that we have expressed the problem in terms of the level of aggregate consumption rather than the on a per unit basis. Since the Armington function is linearly homogeneous this is valid and somewhat more convenient in the context of amending our numerical model. Differentiating the Lagrangian with respect to d_i, m_i and p_i yields the first-order conditions for a minimum:

$$\partial \mathscr{L}/\partial d_i = p_i^d - p_i c_i [\delta_i^A d_i^{\rho_i^A} + (1 - \delta_i^A) m_i^{\rho_i^A}]^{-1} \delta d_i^{\rho_i^A - 1} = 0 \qquad (23.13)$$

$$\partial \mathscr{L}/\partial m_i = p_i^m - p_i c_i [\delta_i^A d_i^{\rho_i^A} + (1 - \delta_i^A) m_i^{\rho_i^A}]^{-1} (1 - \delta_i^A) m_i^{\rho_i^A - 1} = 0 \qquad (23.14)$$

$$\partial \mathscr{L}/\partial p_i = c_i - \gamma_i^A [\delta_i^A d_i^{\rho_i^A} + (1 - \delta_i^A) m_i^{\rho_i^A}]^{1/\rho_i^A} = 0. \qquad (23.15)$$

These three equations determine the three new unknowns (for each industry) that we are introducing to the model, and can be incorporated directly into the model as we show in the next section.

Before turning to the GAMS model, we should note that the use of CES functions for Armington aggregation has an important implication beyond providing a mechanism by which intra-industry trade can be introduced into the model. Assuming that a good is initially consumed in both its domestic and imported versions, it will continue to be consumed in both versions even when the economic system is shocked. In other words, Armington preferences ensure that goods that are imported in the initial equilibrium always continue to be imported (although the volume may of course change). This is probably a good thing. In practice we do not observe the large swings in trade and production that tend to be associated with standard textbook general equilibrium models. However, the feature cuts in both directions. Suppose that in the initial equilibrium the level of consumption of the imported version of a good is zero, so that consumption of the composite is equivalent to consumption of the domestically produced good. Even if the price of the imported version of goods falls in a simulation, imports will remain at zero. This is something to be aware of when using an Armington model, especially if there are some goods that are not imported in the initial equilibrium.

23.3   GAMS Implementation

We begin with the small economy model that we developed in Chapter 12. First, we add in the new parameters. We use RHO_A(I) for the substitution parameter, DELTA_A(I) for the shares of domestic goods in the composites, and GAMMA_A(I) for the shift parameters. Next we assign new parameters for the prices of domestically produced and imported goods, PD(I) and PM(I). We also add parameters to hold the initial values of our new variables, DO(I) and MO(I), and since the price of the composite is a variable too, initial composite prices PO(I). We continue to use XO(I), but now we interpret it as exports rather than net exports.

The next step is to calibrate the model by assigning values to the parameters. First we normalize prices, for imported goods, domestically produced goods, and the composites, at unity. Next we set the base equilibrium values, using the equilibrium conditions to ensure that the model balances. In particular, note that (with prices all normalized at unity) exports XO(I) must equal production QO(I) less consumption of domestic goods DO(I), composite consumption CO(I) must equal consumption of domestic goods DO(I) plus consumption of imported goods MO(I), and the total value of production (GDP, viewed from the both output and input sides) must equal the total value of consumption.

With base data specified, next we have to calibrate the behavioral parameters. For the utility and production functions nothing has changed from our previous models, so we only need concern ourselves with the parameters of the Armington aggregator functions. We begin by setting values for RHO_A(I), which are free. Because the functions should be concave, these values should be less than one.[3]

Given the values of RHO_A(I), we can now determine the values of the DELTA_A(I) parameters by using the first order conditions to the first stage optimization problem:

```
DELTA_A(I)=(PD(I)/DO(I)**(RHO_A(I)-1))/(PD(I)/DO(I)**
    (RHO_A(I)-1)+PM(I)/MO(I)**(RHO_A(I)-1));
```

Then we can determine the GAMMA_A(I) parameters by using the Armington aggregator function directly:

```
GAMMA_A(I)=CO(I)/((DELTA_A(I)*DO(I)**RHO_A(I)+(1-DELTA_A(I))*
    MO(I)**RHO_A(I))**(1/RHO_A(I)));
```

As you can see, the process is essentially the same as the one we used to calibrate the parameters of the production functions in Chapter 4. This should not be too surprising, the first stage of the Armington problem is essentially cost minimization for a given target level of composite consumption.

---

[3]In practice, typical values for the elasticities are in the range of 2 to 5, implying values for the RHO_A parameters of between 0.5 and 0.8.

In the variables section of the model we introduce three new endogenous variables D(I), M(I), and P(I), which represent the domestic consumption of domestically produced goods, consumption of imported goods, and the price of the composite, respectively. We then set the lower bounds of all of these variables at zero and the initial levels of the variables at their calibrated values. Since X(I) now represents exports and not net exports, we also set the lower bound on this variable at zero.

Next we define names for the new equations of the model. ARM(I) generates the composites, DOM_D(I) is the demand for domestically produced goods and IMP_D(I) for imported goods. These are then assigned:

```
ARM(I)..C(I)=E=GAMMA_A(I)*(DELTA_A(I)*D(I)**RHO_A(I)+
   (1-DELTA_A(I))*M(I)**RHO_A(I))**(1/RHO_A(I));
DOM_D(I)..PD(I)=E=P(I)*C(I)*(DELTA_A(I)*D(I)**RHO_A(I)+
   (1-DELTA_A(I))*M(I)**RHO_A(I))**(-1)*DELTA_A(I)*D(I)**
   (RHO_A(I)-1);
IMP_D(I)..PM(I)=E=P(I)*C(I)*(DELTA_A(I)*D(I)**RHO_A(I)+
   (1-DELTA_A(I))*M(I)**RHO_A(I))**(-1)*(1-DELTA_A(I))*
   M(I)**(RHO_A(I)-1);
```

Finally, we adjust the material balance equations to set exports equal to domestic production less domestic consumption of domestically produced goods:

```
MAT_BAL(I)..X(I)=E=Q(I)-D(I);
```

All of the equations are then assigned to a model with a MODEL statement as usual, and we are ready to go. As usual, the completed model is available for download.

23.4   Exercises

(1) Try changing the price of one of the imports by 10 percent. What happens? What if you change the price of both exportable and both importable goods by the same proportion? What is the numéraire of the model?

(2) Can you build a large country model with Armington preferences? (Hint: The usual convention is to fix the price of imports, but allow the world price of exports to vary.)

(3) How would you go about adding taxes on trade and other activities to this model? Are import and export taxes still symmetric? In what sense?

(4) In models with multiple sources of demand (intermediates, government, etc.), separate Armington aggregator functions are sometimes specified for each source of demand. This may make sense if, for example, intermediate production tends to use imported and domestic goods in different proportions than household consumption.[4] Using the model from Chapter 22 as a base, see if you can build a model where government and investment demands use a different Armington aggregator from the household.

23.5 Further Reading

The original reference is Armington (1969). Lloyd and Zhang (2006) provide a detailed comparison of the Armington approach with the standard trade model. For further discussion of how Armington preferences are incorporated into modern CGE models like GTAP, see Hertel (1997), while the review of Kehoe (2003) is useful to better understand the consequences of the specification. Recent empirical estimates of the size of the Armington elasticities can be found in Hertel *et al.* (2007).

---

[4]This is called the SALTER specification, after the SALTER model (a precursor to GTAP, which uses the same specification). See Jomini *et al.* (1994).

Chapter 24

Joint Production

Joint production refers to a situation where firms produce more than one output at the same time. For example, in the chemical industry joint production can occur by the very nature of chemical transformations. In the dairy industry, the basic raw input gives rise to a number of different outputs, and it may make economic sense for a single firm to process and sell many of them. Generally, a given commodity may be produced by a number of different industries, perhaps in different proportions, and indeed, in many national accounts the input-output table is defined on an industry× commodity basis rather than an industry × industry basis as is common in trade-oriented CGE models.

In many trade-oriented CGE models joint production occurs because firms are assumed to produce differentiated products for sale in domestic and foreign markets. This may arise from, for example, different regulations or standards that must be met in different countries, or different language requirements in labeling, and so on. In this chapter we consider how this type of joint production problem can be formally modeled and programmed in GAMS.

24.1 Formal Problem

The problem of joint production is similar in many respects to the Armington preferences we considered in the previous chapter, except that it deals with differentiation on the producer rather than consumer side. Figure 24.1 illustrates the structure of production under consideration. Firms produce what we will consider to be a composite output using primary factors of production as usual, and possibly intermediate goods as introduced in Chapter 10. The composite output is then split, or transformed, into two differentiated products, one of which is to be sold in the international market (i.e., exported) the other being destined for the domestic market.

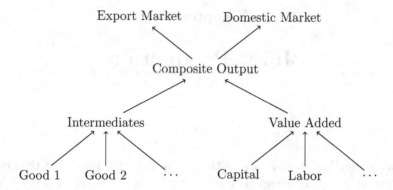

Fig. 24.1   Joint Production Structure.

For expositional purposes we will consider the case where the firm uses only primary factors of production as inputs. As with Armington preferences, we can consider the firm's problem under joint production as a two-stage optimization. Suppose that firm 1 faces prices p_1^x in the export market and p_1^d in the domestic market. The firm's ultimate objective is of course to maximize profit, but first it solves the problem of how to maximize the value of sales of one unit of the composite output. The Lagrangian for the problem is:

$$\mathscr{L} = p_1^d a_{d1} + p_1^x a_{x1} + \mu_1[1 - t_1(a_{d1}, a_{x1})]. \qquad (24.1)$$

The terms a_{d1} and a_{x1} represent the supply of the production of firm 1 that is destined for domestic and international markets respectively, per unit of aggregate output. The function t_1 is the aggregator or transformation function, which is assumed to be continuous, increasing in both arguments, convex, and homogeneous of degree one. The function governs how the composite output can be transformed into either the export good or the domestic good.[1] The first-order conditions for a maximum are:

$$\partial\mathscr{L}/\partial a_{d1} = p_1^d - \mu_1(\partial t_1/\partial a_{d1}) = 0 \qquad (24.2)$$
$$\partial\mathscr{L}/\partial a_{x1} = p_1^x - \mu_1(\partial t_1/\partial a_{x1}) = 0 \qquad (24.3)$$
$$\partial\mathscr{L}/\partial\mu_1 = 1 - t_1(a_{d1}, a_{x1}) = 0. \qquad (24.4)$$

---

[1] In practice the transformation functions are almost always of the constant elasticity of transformation, or CET, form.

From these, we can solve for the optimal per unit production of the domestic and exported versions of the good and the multiplier, μ_1, as functions of the relative prices of exportable and domestic goods. The multiplier represents the change in the optimal revenue generated by an increment in the quantity of the aggregate produced. In other words, it is the value to the firm of a unit of the composite, or the composite producer price.

With the price of the composite known, we can consider the second stage of the optimization. Here the firm maximizes profit, defined as the value of composite production less the cost of inputs, as usual, i.e:

$$\pi_1 = p_1^T q_1(K_1, L_1) - rK_1 - wL_1. \tag{24.5}$$

The derivatives yield the familiar conditions that the value of the marginal product of each input must equal its market price, and can be solved for the optimal input levels, and thereby the production level of the composite, all in terms of the composite producer price. Given the linear homogeneity of the transformation function, we can then determine the total levels of export and domestic production as $x_1 = a_{x1}q_1$ and $d_1 = a_{d1}q_1$, respectively. The problem for other representative firms is of the same form.

The advantage of the two-stage optimization is that it makes clear the fact that we can essentially append the joint production decision onto our basic trade models, without having to alter the primary production model that we have already developed, just as we could add Armington preferences to our models without altering the underlying demand specification.

24.2 Example

The constant elasticity of transformation function that we introduced in Chapter 21 is usually used as an aggregator function, so we have $t_i = \gamma_i^T [\delta_i^T d_i^{\rho_i^T} + (1 - \delta_i^T) x_i^{\rho_i^T}]^{1/\rho_i^T}$, for all goods i, where $1 < \rho^T < \infty$. The Lagrangian for the maximization problem is then written:

$$\mathscr{L} = p_i^d d_i + p_i^x x_i + p_i^T [q_i - \gamma_i^T [\delta_i^T d_i^{\rho_i^T} + (1 - \delta_i^T) x_i^{\rho_i^T}]^{1/\rho_i^T}]. \tag{24.6}$$

Notice that we have given the multiplier on the constraint the symbol p_i^T (the composite producer price) for convenience. Notice also that we have expressed the problem in terms of the level of aggregate production rather than on a per unit basis (recall the transformation function is linearly homogeneous). Differentiating the Lagrangian with respect to d_i, x_i and p_i^T yields the first-order conditions for a maximum:

$$\partial \mathscr{L}/\partial d_i = p_i^d - p_i^T q_i [\delta_i^T d_i^{\rho_i^T} + (1 - \delta_i^T) x_i^{\rho_i^T}]^{-1} \delta d_i^{\rho_i^T - 1} = 0 \tag{24.7}$$

$$\partial \mathscr{L}/\partial x_i = p_i^x - p_i^T q_i [\delta_i^T d_i^{\rho_i^T} + (1 - \delta_i^T) x_i^{\rho_i^T}]^{-1} (1 - \delta_i^T) x_i^{\rho_i^T - 1} = 0 \quad (24.8)$$

$$\partial \mathscr{L}/\partial p_i^T = q_i - \gamma_i^T [\delta_i^T d_i^{\rho_i^T} + (1 - \delta_i^T) x_i^{\rho_i^T}]^{1/\rho_i^T} = 0. \quad (24.9)$$

These three equations determine the three new unknowns (for each industry) that we are introducing to the model (d_i, x_i, and p_i^T), and can be incorporated directly into any of our models of an open economy, as we demonstrate in the next section.[2]

Just as with Armington preferences, joint production of this form, while having some advantages, has some serious limitations. Assuming that a good is initially produced in both its domestic and exported versions, it will continue to be produced in both versions even when the economic system is shocked. In other words, goods that are exported in the initial equilibrium always continue to be exported (although the volume may change). Moreover, goods that are not exported in the initial equilibrium will never become exported — so trade changes only occur along the intensive margin not the extensive margin in this type of model.

24.3 GAMS Implementation

The GAMS implementation is much the same as for Armington preferences as covered in the previous chapter. For demonstration purposes, we begin with the small economy model that we developed in Chapter 12, and add in the new parameters RHO_T(I) for the transformability parameters, DELTA_T(I) for the shares of domestic goods in the production composites, and GAMMA_T(I) for the shift parameters. Next we assign new parameters for the prices of exported goods, PX(I). The price of imported and domestically produced goods remains P(I). We also add parameters to hold the initial values of our new variables, DO(I) and MO(I), the latter being imports, which are now distinguished from exports. Since the price of the producer composite is a variable too, initial composite producer prices are also added, PTO(I). We continue to use the symbol XO(I), but we will now consider this to be exports, not net exports.

---

[2]Notice that we have used the same symbol, d_i, to represent production for the domestic market as we used in the previous chapter to represent consumption of the domestic good. In a model with both joint production and Armington preferences, this is effectively substituting in the market clearing condition for domestic goods, which determines the domestic price.

The next step is to calibrate the model by assigning values to the parameters. First we normalize prices, for imported goods and domestically produced goods, exported goods, and the producer composites, at unity. Next we set the base equilibrium values, using the equilibrium conditions to ensure that the model balances. In particular, note that (with prices all normalized at unity) imports MO(I) must equal total consumption CO(I) less production for domestic consumption DO(I), composite production QO(I) must equal production of domestic goods DO(I) plus exports XO(I), and the total value of production (GDP, viewed from the both output and input sides) must equal the total value of consumption.

With base data specified, next we have to calibrate the behavioral parameters. For the utility and production functions nothing has changed from our previous models, so we only need concern ourselves with the parameters of the transformation functions. We begin by setting values for RHO_T(I), which are free. Because the functions should be convex, these values should be greater than one. Numbers close to one indicate relatively small degrees of product differentiation, which probably make sense in most applications. Given the values of RHO_T(I), we can determine the values of the DELTA_T(I) parameters by using the first order conditions of the first stage optimization problem:

```
DELTA_T(I)=(P(I)/DO(I)**(RHO_T(I)-1))/(P(I)/DO(I)**
   (RHO_T(I)-1)+PX(I)/XO(I)**(RHO_T(I)-1));
```

Then we can determine the GAMMA_T(I) parameters by using the transformation function directly:

```
GAMMA_T(I)=QO(I)/(((DELTA_T(I)*DO(I)**RHO_T(I)+(1-DELTA_T(I))*
   XO(I)**RHO_T(I))**(1/RHO_T(I))));
```

As you can see, the process is essentially the same as the one we used to calibrate the parameters of the Armington functions.

In the variables section of the model we introduce three new endogenous variables D(I), M(I) and PT(I), which represent the domestic consumption of domestically produced goods, consumption of imported goods, and the price of the composite, respectively. We then set the lower bounds of all of these variables at zero and the initial levels of the variables at their calibrated values. Since X(I) now represents exports and not net exports, we also set the lower bound on this variable at zero.

Next we define names for the new equations of the model. TRANS(I) generates the composites, DOM_S(I) is the supply of domestically produced goods and EXP_S(I) is the supply of exported goods. These are then assigned:

```
TRANS(I)..Q(I)=E=GAMMA_T(I)*(DELTA_T(I)*D(I)**RHO_T(I)+
   (1-DELTA_T(I))*X(I)**RHO_T(I))**(1/RHO_T(I));
DOM_S(I)..P(I)=E=PT(I)*Q(I)*(DELTA_T(I)*D(I)**RHO_T(I)+
   (1-DELTA_T(I))*X(I)**RHO_T(I))**(-1)*DELTA_T(I)*D(I)**
   (RHO_T(I)-1);
EXP_S(I)..PX(I)=E=PT(I)*Q(I)*(DELTA_T(I)*D(I)**RHO_T(I)+
   (1-DELTA_T(I))*X(I)**RHO_T(I))**(-1)*(1-DELTA_T(I))*
   X(I)**(RHO_T(I)-1);
```

Finally, we adjust the material balance equations to set imports equal to total domestic consumption less domestic consumption of domestically produced goods:

```
MAT_BAL(I)..M(I)=E=C(I)-D(I);
```

All of the equations are then assigned to a model with a MODEL statement as usual. The completed model is available for download. Once you have verified that the initial equilibrium has been correctly calibrated, you can start exploring the model properties.

24.4   Exercises

(1) Try changing the price of one of the exports by 10 percent. What happens? Do the basic results remain consistent with the Stolper-Samuelson theorem?
(2) Can you build a large country model with joint production?
(3) Can you build a model in which intermediate goods are used in a joint production process?

24.5   Further Reading

A good exposition of the joint production model that we have examined here can be found in Gunning and Keyzer (1995). A recent example of the application of the theory of joint production to trade policy analysis is Charteris and Winchester (2010), who consider trade liberalization in the dairy industry.

Chapter 25

Social Accounting Matrices

A CGE model of any real economy will (obviously) have to be based on actual data representing said economy. In this chapter we discuss how we can conceptualize and organize the equilibrium data representing the economy of interest into a "social accounting matrix" or SAM. We also discuss how we can use GAMS to help us in the process of constructing a consistent SAM.

25.1 SAM Structure

All of the general equilibrium models that we have been working with describe transactions between various agents in an economic system. Those transactions involve movements of goods and factors of production, and corresponding flows of payments. A social accounting matrix is just a systematic method of representing those flows. It is conceptually very much like an input-output table (and in fact much of the data for a SAM comes from the input-output table).[1]

Any social accounting matrix is constructed as a square matrix, with the same column and row headings. The rows represent flows of goods/factors, while the columns represent the corresponding flows of payments. The order of the row/column entries is arbitrary, although we usually keep related entries grouped together.

Every entry in the SAM is in value terms. Because every payment by an agent in the economic system represents a receipt to some other agent in the system, the row and column sums of the SAM must be equal at an

---

[1] Social accounting matrices are also used for multiplier analysis, although our concern is primarily with how they organize the data necessary to build a CGE model.

equilibrium. In other words, the SAM must balance. Once we have a balanced SAM, we can calibrate a CGE model to it.[2]

25.1.1   *Closed Economy SAM*

Perhaps the easiest way to understand how a SAM organizes the data for a general equilibrium model is to examine some examples. We will illustrate the ideas with a series of cases of increasing complexity. Let's begin with the 2×2 model of an autarkic (closed) economy that we introduced in Chapter 11. The SAM for this model, using the same data that we used in the chapter, is presented in Table 25.1.

First, note how we break the economic system down into three broad groups of agents. The first, labeled "Activities" corresponds to the industries in the model (1 and 2). The second, labeled "Factors" corresponds to the factors of production (K and L), and the third, labeled "Final Demands" lists the agents that consume the product of the economy, in this case only the household (H).[3]

Table 25.1   SAM for the Closed 2×2 Economy.

		Activities		Factors		Final Demands	
		1	2	K	L	H	Total
Activities	1					100	100
	2					100	100
Factors	K	80	20				100
	L	20	80				100
Final Demands	H			100	100		200
Total		100	100	100	100	200	

Now let's think about how the various values are entered. First look at the factors-activities section (we will reference entries by row label-column label). The value 80 in the K-1 entry, for example, indicates that industry 1 makes a payment of 80 currency units to capital (and capital receives 80 from industry 1). The other entries in this block are interpreted similarly.

---

[2]In fact, we have been doing just that all along, but as the models we want to build become more complex we need to be more systematic about the process.

[3]The "agent" terminology is standard when talking about the representative firms and households, but may seem peculiar when discussing factors of production. It is really a definition of convenience. We can think of these rows/columns as an artificial "agent" that sells the factors of production to the firms of behalf of the household, collects the corresponding factor payments, and returns the payments to the household.

The H-K entry is 100, as is the H-L entry. These are the payments from the artificial factor agent to the owner of the factors, the household. The payments are equal to the total payments by firms to each factor agent.

Finally, the entries in the activities-H section correspond to the values of final consumption by the household. Hence, for example, the 1-H entry of 100 indicates that industry 1 supplies a quantity of good 1 of value 100 to the household, and the household makes a corresponding payment of 100 to industry 1 for the product. Since this is an autarkic economy, the value of household consumption is equal to the value of production for each good, which is also equal to the value of factor payments, and the SAM balances. We can see this by observing that the column/row for each agent has the same sum.

25.1.2   *Open Economy SAM*

Now consider an open economy, as in Chapter 12 or 14.[4] An example is presented in Table 25.2. The main difference is that we add a new "agent" under the final demand section to represent transactions with the rest of the world (X, for external).

Table 25.2   SAM for the Open 2 × 2 Economy.

		Activities		Factors		Final Demands		
		1	2	K	L	H	X	Total
Activities	1					50	50	100
	2					150		150
Factors	K	80	20					100
	L	20	80					100
Final Demands	H			100	100			200
	X		50					50
Total		100	150	100	100	200	50	

The external section of the SAM accounts for the economy's international transactions. Hence, the 1-X entry (50) represents supply of good 1 worth 50 currency units to the rest of the world, and a corresponding payment, i.e., exports. Similarly, the entry X-2 represents supply from the rest of the

---

[4]Note that the SAM can be consistent with the theoretical representation of Chapter 12 (small country) or Chapter 14 (large country). The SAM tells us about the flows at a point in time, but we still need to use other information to determine some aspects of the model structure.

world of a quantity of good 2 worth 50 currency units, and the corresponding payment, i.e., imports.

In the model presented in Chapter 12, the only international transactions are trade in goods. However, we can incorporate other transactions as necessary. For example, an X–K entry would represent repatriated profits, an X–L entry would represent worker remittances, and an L–X entry would represent inward remittances, and so on.

Moreover, the model of Chapter 12 did not allow for product differentiation, so a good must either be exported or imported, but not both. Hence, we have (in the 2 × 2 case) only one entry in both the X column and the X row. This will not usually be true if we have Armington-type preferences as discussed in Chapter 23. In that case we may have both a row and a column entry in X for the same activity. Non-traded goods, as discussed in Chapter 13, are simply represented in the SAM as activities with no entry in X rows or columns.

25.1.3 *Intermediates, Government and Investment*

In Chapter 10 we considered a model of production with intermediate inputs, while in Chapter 22 we considered government and investment consumption. These flows can easily be introduced into a SAM as shown in Table 25.3 below.

Table 25.3   SAM With Intermediates, Government and Investment.

		Activities		Factors		Final Demands				
		1	2	K	L	H	G	I	X	Total
Activities	1	40	10			30	10	10	50	150
	2	10	40			130	10	10		200
Factors	K	80	20							100
	L	20	80							100
Final Demands	H			100	100					200
	G					20				20
	I					20				20
	X		50							50
Total		150	200	100	100	200	20	20	50	

Intermediate input demands appear in the activities-activities section of the SAM. Hence, the 1-1 entry of 40 indicates that a quantity of good 1 worth 40 currency units is used in producing good 1, and so on.

Government spending and investment are introduced as two new agents (G and I) under the final demand heading, with the corresponding column entries representing payments by the agents, and row entries payments to the agents.

As illustrated in Table 25.3, the government purchases 10 currency units worth of each good. It finances its spending in this case through a transfer from the household (the entry of 20 in G–H).[5] Of course, the spending may also be financed in part through external borrowing, which would be reflected by an entry in G–X, or through other taxes, which we deal with in the next example. Payments from the government to the households would appear in the H–G entry.

We can think of the investment column/row as representing an artificial investment agent. The agent takes saving from other agents and uses it to acquire goods for domestic investment. As illustrated in Table 25.3, the agent purchases 10 currency units of each good for investment purposes. The entry of 20 in I–H indicates that investment is financed through household savings in this SAM. More generally, we could have entries in I–G and/or I–X, representing government and foreign savings, respectively.

25.1.4 *Indirect Taxes*

In the previous example, government spending was financed through transfers from the household. In most economies, the government also collects taxes from other sources (taxes on production, trade, etc.) We introduced these types of taxes into our models in Chapters 19 and 20. They are incorporated into a SAM by specifying a set of new artificial "tax" agents, much like the artificial factor agents. For example, in the case of tariffs, we can think of there being a customs agent that collects tariff revenue and passes it to the government. Other types of taxes are treated in the same way.

In Table 25.4, we introduce a new section heading to the SAM called taxes (you will sometimes see this section headed "indirect taxes" to distinguish it from direct (i.e., income) taxes). Under this heading we add rows/columns for each of the taxes that appear in the model. To illustrate, in this case we have allowed for tariffs (T), production or output taxes (TP), and consumption taxes (TC). We might also see factor use taxes, and taxes on intermediate use.

---

[5] In a static (one period) CGE model we can think of this as borrowing from the household, or income taxes, or some combination thereof.

Table 25.4   SAM for the 2 × 2 Economy With Taxes.

		Activities		Factors		Taxes			Final Demands				Total
		1	2	K	L	T	TP	TC	H	G	I	X	
Activities	1	40	10						35	20	10	50	165
	2	10	40						135	20	10		215
Factors	K	80	20										100
	L	20	80										100
Taxes	T	0	5										5
	TP	10	10										20
	TC	5											5
Final Demands	H			100	100					10			210
	G					5	20	5	20				50
	I								20				20
	X		50										50
Total		165	215	100	100	5	20	5	210	50	20	50	

Consider the tariff row/column. The entry of 5 under T-2 indicates that the customs agent collects revenue of 5 currency units on imports of good 2. This revenue is then returned to the government, as indicated by the entry of 5 in the G–T cell. Similarly, the entries of 10 in cells TP-1 and TP-2 represent production tax revenues, which are returned to the government (the entry of 20 in cell G-TP).

Now, total government revenue in this SAM is 50 currency units (the sum of direct and indirect taxes). Government spending in this example is 20 currency units on each good, a total of 40 currency units. Hence the government runs a surplus of 10 currency units. This must go somewhere. In the example in Table 25.4 it is returned to the households (the entry of 10 in H-G) in the form of transfer payments. Households spend the transfer on the two goods, ensuring that the row/column sums balance. Of course, in a real SAM the revenue might be put to another use.

We have now covered the basics of the SAM. In general, further rows and columns can be added as necessary to cover more activities. Hence, for example, the household section can be expanded if we have multiple households as in Chapter 22, and we can of course add more rows/columns for models with more factors and/or goods. Further rows/columns can also be added for different types of taxes that may appear in the model.

25.2   Sources of SAMs

In general a new SAM is constructed from national statistics, with most of the data coming from the input-output table and the balance of payments statistics.

In some cases it is possible to obtain a complete or near complete (depending on the model for which the data is required) SAM from other sources. In particular, the Global Trade Analysis project (GTAP, www.gtap.org) provides GAMS codes for constructing social accounting matrices from the GTAP database.[6] The current version of the data, version 8, covers 129 regions and 57 commodities with dual base years of 2004 and 2007.

Another useful source is the International Food Policy Research Institute (IFPRI, www.ifpri.org). It makes available a series of fully documented social accunting matrices, often at a quite detailed sectoral level and with information for multiple households. Coverage is not as wide as GTAP, and the available SAMs are for developing economies.

---

[6]McDonald and Thierfelder (2004) provide further details.

25.3   Balancing a SAM

As we have seen, the columns and rows of a balanced SAM must have the same sums. Because in practice the elements of a SAM come from a variety of statistical sources, however, it is unlikely that a newly constructed SAM will in fact balance. This can be because of statistical discrepancies or because of variations in definitions across sources. It can also be because variations in the availability of data necessitate combining information from different time periods. For example, the input–output table is generally only constructed once every five to ten years in most countries, while trade data and production data is available much more frequently. Hence, once a SAM has been constructed, it must be further manipulated to ensure that it in fact balances.

There are a variety of methods that can be used. For very small discrepancies, it is obviously possible to force the SAM to balance by making adjustments to a single row and/or column such that the desired totals are obtained. However, this places all of the burden of adjustment onto a single row/column when in reality the errors are likely to be throughout the matrix. Hence, we usually use this method only at the final stage of balancing (when we are essentially dealing with tiny rounding errors only).

A widely used alternative is called bi-proportional matrix scaling, which is also known as the "RAS" procedure. In this method we scale the row and column entries by a factor that ensures target row and column sums are reached.

The GAMS code for the procedure is quite simple. Suppose that the SAM data is contained in the parameter AO(I,J), where I and J are the same set, and that the target row/column sums are contained in the parameter TOTAL(I).[7] The following code will scale the matrix:

```
PARAMETERS
HSCALE(I)
CSCALE(J) ;
SCALAR K ;
FOR (K=1 TO 100,
HSCALE(I)=TOTAL(I)/SUM(J, AO(I,J));
AO(I,J)=AO(I,J)*HSCALE(I);
CSCALE(J)=TOTAL(J)/SUM(I, AO(I,J));
```

---

[7]The same procedure can also be used for matrices that are not square and where the target row and column sums are different.

```
AO(I,J)=AO(I,J)*CSCALE(J);
);
```

We begin by defining parameters HSCALE(I) and CSCALE(J) to hold the row and column scale factors, respectively, and a scalar K to control the iterations. Next we set up a FOR loop, with 100 iterations. The HSCALE factor is set as the ratio of the desired row total to the current row total. Next we multiply each element by HSCALE. The rows sums are now correct, but the column sums are not (in general). We repeat the procedure for the columns. This will disturb the row sums, so we repeat until the process converges.

The above procedure in effect finds a set of "optimal" weights for each row and column, and in fact the RAS procedure can also be set up directly as an optimization problem.[8] The following code illustrates:

```
VARIABLES
A(I,J) R(I) S(J)
OBJECT ;
A.L(I,J)=AO(I,J);
R.L(I)=1;
S.L(J)=1;
A.LO(I,J)=EPS;
A.FX(I,J)$(AO(I,J)=0)=0;
EQUATIONS
HCON(I)
CCON(J)
RAS(I,J) OBJ ;
HCON(I)..SUM(J, A(I,J))=E=TOTAL(I);
CCON(J)..SUM(I, A(I,J))=E=TOTAL(J);
RAS(I,J)..A(I,J)=E=R(I)*AO(I,J)*S(J);
OBJ..OBJECT=E=SUM(I, R(I)**2+(1/R(I))**2)
   +SUM(J, S(J)**2+(1/S(J))**2);
MODEL RAS /ALL/;
SOLVE RAS USING NLP MINIMIZING OBJECT;
```

We begin by setting up four variables: A(I,J) to hold the new matrix values, R(I) to hold the row weights, S(J) to hold the column weights and OBJECT to hold the objective function. The levels of A(I,J) are set at

---

[8]Technically, RAS is a type of entropy optimization method. See McDougall (1999) for further details.

the initial values A0(I,J), and any zero values are fixed. We then define four equations, the row sum constraint HCON(J), the column sum constraint CCON(J), the new matrix RAS(I,J), and an objective function OBJ. Finding the row and column weights that minimize this particular objective generates the same outcome as the iterative procedure above (we will leave it to you to verify).

While the RAS procedure is popular, the second implementation method makes clear that it corresponds to one of many possible constrained optimization problems. While a complete discussion of the possibilities is beyond the scope of this volume, we can set up such an optimization problem in a number of different ways. For example, we can take a least squares approach, minimizing the sum of the squared deviations (usually in percentage form) of the adjusted matrix elements from the original elements, subject to the adding up constraints. The following code illustrates:

```
VARIABLES
A(I,J)
OBJECT ;
A.L(I,J)=A0(I,J);
A.LO(I,J)=EPS;
A.FX(I,J)$(A0(I,J)=0)=0;
EQUATIONS
HCON(I)
CCON(J)
OBJ ;
HCON(I)..SUM(J, A(I,J))=E=TOTAL(I);
CCON(J)..SUM(I, A(I,J))=E=TOTAL(J);
OBJ..OBJECT=E=SUM((I,J)$A0(I,J),
    SQR((A(I,J)-A0(I,J))/A0(I,J)));
MODEL BALANCE /ALL/;
SOLVE BALANCE USING NLP MINIMIZING OBJECT;
```

The main difference relative to RAS is in how we set up the objective function, defining the problem as minimizing as the sum of the squared percentage deviations (note the exception handling for division by zero in the objective).[9] GAMS can solve the minimization problem and thereby determine the adjusted matrix.

---

[9]Another widely used alternative objective function takes the form SUM((I,J), A(I,J)*LOG(A(I,J)/A0(I,J))). In this case the problem is called cross entropy.

Different methods will not generally result in the same SAM (try them and see); so which should be used? Unfortunately this issue has not been definitively settled, so you have to use your own judgment to a degree.

One advantage of using an explicit optimization rather than the basic RAS procedure is that we can incorporate further information into the problem. Suppose, for example, that we know that in the target SAM trade is to be balanced, we can add that as a constraint. Or, suppose that we have more confidence in the trade data than in the consumption data, we could weight the deviations accordingly (i.e., impose a higher penalty for deviations in the trade data than in the consumption data). In that sense, the optimization approach is slightly more flexible than basic RAS.[10]

25.4 Exercises

(1) Try and adjust the calibration of the model from Chapter 12 so that it replicates the SAM from Table 25.2.
(2) Using model elements from Chapters 10, 12 and 22, see if you can build a model that fits the SAM illustrated in Table 25.3.
(3) Build a SAM consistent with the Armington model presented in Chapter 23.
(4) Enter the SAM from Table 25.2 into a GAMS matrix A0(I,J). Make one or two adjustments to the interior values such that it no longer balances, then try out some of the methods for re-balancing. Which method gets you a matrix that looks most like the original?

25.5 Further Reading

Classic papers on social accounting matrices include Pyatt and Round (1977) and (1979). A more recent overview is Reinert and Roland-Holst (1997). Hosoe *et al.* (2010) give a simple step-by-step example of constructing a SAM using data from the Japanese economy. On the various data manipulations, Bacharach (1970) gives a comprehensive overview of the RAS procedure, while Robinson *et al.* (2001) is a detailed account of using "cross entropy" methods as an alternative.

---

[10]If the new SAM is an updated version of an older SAM, Hosoe *et al.* (2010) suggest a third method, scale the old SAM (which is presumably balanced) by GDP. While this is simple and does result in a balanced SAM, it has the disadvantage of ignoring other available information on the changes in the SAM structure.

Chapter 26

Closure

In any economic model we must make a choice as to what is to be determined within the model (the endogenous variables) and what is to be considered external to the model (the exogenous variables). A model, numerical or otherwise, is just a way of explaining the endogenous variables in terms of the exogenous. Where we choose to draw the line between endogenous and exogenous and exactly which variables we choose to be exogenous depends on a number of factors, including model tractability, and of course the purpose for which the model simulations are to be used. The choice that we make is called the model closure.

Mathematically, ensuring that a model is "closed" amounts to ensuring that we have enough independent equations to explain the endogenous variables. Hence, for all of the models presented in this volume we have chosen a closure, even if we have not explicitly stated it as such. Moreover, many of the different model specifications that we have examined in previous chapters can be thought of as alternative closures of the same basic model. If a model is closed and we want to explain another exogenous variable, we must either add a new equation to the model to explain it, or switch it for a currently endogenous variable. Because the choice of a closure defines the direction of causality in a model, our choices can have significant implications. In this chapter we discuss some alternative closures that are used in CGE models, and consider some common issues that arise.

26.1 Microeconomic Closure

Much of the CGE literature on closure is concerned with the macroeconomic aspects of closing a general equilibrium model. We discuss that topic in the next section. First though, we consider some issues relating to microeconomic aspects of the closure, most of which concern the choice of how to model factor markets.[1]

Consider the specific factors and HOS models of production. We have covered these two models extensively in earlier chapters. The key difference between the two is that in the former the stock of capital in each industry is exogenous, and the price of capital in each sector is endogenous (and may differ from sector to sector). We can think of this as a closure choice — the specific factors model does not attempt to explain the allocation of capital. By contrast, the HOS model does, and to do so it must introduce two new conditions (one for capital in each industry). These are full employment of capital and capital price arbitrage. Which of these closure options we choose will depend on the adjustment time-frame that we want the results to represent, with the specific factors case being thought of as "short run" and the HOS case as "long run."

Another alternative is sometimes called a "steady-state" closure. In this case, the price of capital is assumed to be at a long-run equilibrium rate and the capital stock is at its optimal level given that return. Increases in the return to capital caused by a shock to the economic system would induce an increase in investment, thereby driving the marginal product of capital down to its original level. Hence, to implement the closure we "swap" the exogenous/endogenous status of the capital stock and the return to capital. The expansion of the capital stock generates an endowment effect that can be thought of as capturing the dynamic effects of the shock.[2]

When it comes to the labor market, we have similar choices. Most of the models that we have examined have been neoclassical. That is, the wage rate is assumed to vary to ensure full employment of labor. However, as we saw in Chapter 21, we can instead fix the wage rate (in terms of the numéraire) and endogenize the level of employment.[3] Which approach we use depends on the economic problem at hand. Although the neoclassical approach certainly dominates in applications, a fixed wage (with endogenous unemployment) might make sense in an economy with significant involuntary unemployment. It might also make sense (with an endogenous labor stock) in an economy where immigration is relatively free.[4]

---

[1]The tariff/quota equivalence argument we considered in Chapter 19 is another example.

[2]Since the foregone consumption necessary to obtain the larger capital stock is not accounted for, welfare effects would represent an upper bound. See Harrison *et al.* (1997) for further discussion of this closure rule.

[3]As we saw in Chapter 21, this can result in corner solutions in some cases. This is unlikely in a model with an Armington demand structure, as with most CGE models.

[4]What if we want to allow both the price of labor and the quantity of labor supplied to

26.2 Macroeconomic Closure

In Chapter 22 we introduced government spending and investment to our basic model. In CGE models of real economies this is necessary because government spending and investment are significant sources of final demand. Nonetheless, their introduction to the model sits somewhat awkwardly within the static economic framework that we have developed. This is because the models represent a single period, but investment and saving (by the household or the government) represent activities directed to future periods which are not explicitly modeled. Similarly, government expenditure presumably reflects, at least in part, investment in public goods, but the optimization process behind spending choices is not explicitly modeled. This necessitates that a closure choice be made for key macroeconomic variables.[5] In particular, we need to specify the workings of the savings-investment balance, the government balance, and the trade balance.

26.2.1 *Closed Economy*

To keep things simple, let's begin by considering a closed economy in which there is no government. From the income identity we know that $Y = C + I$. By definition, consumption is equal to income less savings, i.e., $C = Y - S$, but that of course means that $S = I$. This is the most simple form of the balance identity for a closed economy. While the equation does not usually appear within our models directly, it is nonetheless implicit.

In the absence of a complete theory of savings/investment, we have only this identity to determine both savings and investment. This cannot be done, so we need to find a way to close the model. Suppose that we choose to treat total investment as exogenous, or determine it by some rule (as in Chapter 22, where we treated investment in each sector as fixed, with total investment the sum of the value of investment across all sectors). In that case, total savings must be endogenously determined by the balance identity. This is called an investment-driven, or "Johansen" (from Johansen, 1974) closure; investment determines how much savings will be.

---

vary? This amounts to drawing the line for what is inside the model in a different place. We would need to provide another equation to describe the labor supply. This could be accomplished by allowing for the consumption of leisure by the household and adding a time constraint, or by specifying an immigration function.

[5]The other option is to build a dynamic model, which is possible but beyond the scope of this volume.

Alternatively, we could fix savings or add an equation to determine its value. We might assume that the household saves a fixed proportion of its disposable income, for example. In this case we would have to endogenize total investment. This is called a savings-driven, or neoclassical, closure; savings determines the level of investment. If we try and apply a savings rule without endogenizing total investment, the model is overdetermined. We can calibrate to an initial point, but the model will fail to solve when we introduce a shock to the system.

So which approach should we use? That depends again on what our objectives are. The investment driven approach is quite common, and we can interpret the results of policy simulations (including welfare changes) as the effect for a given level of investment in future consumption. On the other hand, if we want to determine how a policy impacts the economy through its effect on savings, the savings-driven closure may be preferred.

Now let's suppose that we have a government. The basic problem does not change, although we have more options for dealing with it. In particular, we will now have to specify the determination of government savings (the government deficit/surplus).

To make things concrete, suppose that the government collects tax revenue R, makes transfers to the household (social security and so on) of T, and spends on consumption G. The income identity is now $Y = C + I + G$. The government deficit is $D = R - G - T$, while household consumption is $C = Y - R + T - S$. This implies that $S + D = I$. In other words, the sum of household savings and government savings must equal investment.

Now we have only one equation with which to determine three values. We have to find some way of determining two of them. Suppose that we treat investment as exogenous. If tax policy instruments are fixed, we have an equation to determine government revenues. If we also fix government spending (both G and T) then D is determined. Private savings must be left free to properly close the model. We can interpret the results of simulations with a model closed this way as representing the effect of a shock for given levels of investment, provision of public services, and taxes.

This is not the only story we could tell. Suppose we believe the government faces a binding budget constraint. In that case we fix D. If T is also fixed (say the government is committed to those programs) and R is determined by fixed tax rates, then G must vary to maintain the government deficit level. Fixing either S or I then closes the model.

Instead of changing expenditures to maintain the government budget, perhaps the government changes revenues. Suppose we believe the government will adjust a sales tax to achieve its spending aims. Then we can fix both D and G, but must allow the tax rate to be endogenous so that R can adjust to maintain the balance. None of these closures is the "right" closure, it just depends on which you believe characterizes the the economy of interest most accurately. Whatever closure you choose for your own modeling work, however, it is good practice to be very clear about it so that readers can properly evaluate the results of your study.

26.2.2 *Open Economy*

Now let's briefly consider the open case. Again, we will use an economy in which there is no government to simplify. From the open economy income identity we know $Y = C + I + X - M$. Using the definition of private savings, this implies that $S - I = CA$. This is the basic balance identity for an open economy. It states that the difference between domestic savings and investment must equal the current account balance. The latter reflects savings/borrowing from the rest of the world.

To close the open economy model we need to determine two of S, I and CA. If we try and determine all three, the model will again be overidentified. We can fix the current account balance and investment and let private savings adjust to maintain balance, or we can fix savings and the current account and let investment adjust, or we can fix savings and investment and let the current account adjust.

In practice, for almost all CGE models the current account is fixed, and then either a savings-driven or investment-driven closure is chosen.[6] There are several reasons. First, many CGE models are of developing economies, and foreign credit may in fact be limited, so a fixed current account may simply reflect economic reality. Second, we can legitimately interpret the results of simulations with such a closure as representing the economic effect of a policy for a given level of foreign borrowing and investment. Third, measures of economic welfare based on household consumption become invalid if the current account is free (since borrowing foreign funds increases consumption in the current period, and the model does not account for paying the debt back). So if we want to measure the welfare effect of a

---

[6]If the exchange rate is used as the numéraire we can fix the current account directly, or we could let the money supply and hence spending vary in accordance with the Hume mechanism. Otherwise we may set another numéraire (perhaps a CPI index) and allow the exchange rate to vary to maintain current account balance. Robinson and Lofgren (2005) provide further details.

policy, we need to fix the current account.[7] Fourth, as Hosoe *et al.* (2010) note, with the foreign exchange rate fixed as the numéraire, if the current account is endogenous, the model is no longer homogeneous of degree one in prices (i.e., it is no longer the case that only relative prices matter).

If we have a government as well then $S + D - I = X - M$, i.e., the sum of private and government savings and borrowing from the rest of the world must equal investment. The same issues that arise with respect to the government in the closed economy case then arise in the open case also.

26.3   Money, Wealth, Taxes and Quotas in the Open Economy

Instructive stories can be told by choosing the closure appropriately. Scitovsky (1969) closes his model of an open economy by allowing wealth to flow from a deficit economy to a surplus one, until consumption is reduced in the former and expanded in the latter by enough to balance trade. This is a variant of the Hume mechanism. Tsiang (1961) analyzes devaluation in a two country world when money stocks are held constant, or as a second alternative adjusted to hold the interest rates constant, or as a third alternative, adjusted to maintain full employment. He could have allowed money flows to occur via the Hume mechanism to balance trade, as those who have written on the monetary approach to the balance of payments have done. Krueger (1978) considers devaluation in developing countries as a mechanism that permits trade-distorting quotas to be liberalized without damaging the balance of trade. One of the most important points in Corden's (2002) analysis of exchange rates is that flexible exchange rates can restore employment if the problem is that nominal wages are inflexible downward, but not if the economy is tormented by real wage inflexibility.

Han and Tower (1999) show that the foreign aid allows the recipient to lower taxes, and the beneficial impact of foreign aid on the recipient will be larger the more distorting are the taxes that are reduced.

Loo and Tower (1989) show that reduced agricultural protectionism by the developed world would allow the less developed world, which exported agricultural goods and imported industrial goods, to collect higher export taxes on their now more highly priced and expanded agricultural exports and more import tariff revenue on the new imports financed by these big-

---

[7]The GTAP model gets around this problem by specifying a welfare function that includes savings as an argument in addition to consumption.

ger export earnings. Hence less developed countries could reduce distorting taxes without shrinking their tax revenue, augmenting the gain from developed country agricultural liberalization. In an alternative closure, Loo and Tower show that agricultural liberalization by the developed world could enable it to reduce its foreign aid, since the higher agricultural prices would raise the welfare of developing countries. In the process the developed world could cut the distorting taxes of their own used to finance foreign aid, for a further welfare gain.

The moral of this discussion is that picking the appropriate closure allows the modeler to tell stories that weave different markets together, enable one to think creatively about the opportunity cost of distorting policies, and relate seemingly disparate issues.

26.4 Exercises

(1) Using the model that we developed in Chapter 22, try out some of the different closure options that we have discussed to develop a feel for how they work.

26.5 Further Reading

A classic reading on closure rules in computable general equilibrium models is Dewatripont and Michel (1987). Robinson and Lofgren (2005) give a nice overview of the macroeconomic stories that underlie common closure rules.

Chapter 27

Single Country Competitive CGE

We have now learned enough about the basic building blocks of computable general equilibrium models to be in a position to build a "standard" CGE model. In this penultimate chapter we pull all of the pieces together, demonstrating how to construct a typical competitive model for a single, open economy.

27.1 Model Structure

Before turning to programming details, we begin by setting out the basic characteristics of the model, and relating them back to the simple models that we have developed in the preceding chapters.

Demand: The model features four distinct sources of final demand. There is a single representative household, which has an objective function of the Cobb–Douglas form. The household optimization problem was covered in Chapter 3. Government and investment are also sources of final demand, both in fixed quantities, as in the model of Chapter 22. Finally, the rest of world (the external sector) is a source of demand for exports. Foreign demand is modeled using the constant elasticity of demand function that we introduced in Chapter 14.

Supply: We will consider two industries, operating under competitive conditions. The underlying production technology is as described in Chapter 10. Firms use two primary factors (capital and labor) in variable proportions (modeled via CES), combined with intermediate goods used in fixed proportions. Each industry produces a good aimed at foreign markets and a good aimed at the domestic market (i.e., the joint produc-

251

tion model introduced in Chapter 24). The transformation function takes the CET form.

Trade: International trade is modeled via the Armington assumption that we introduced in Chapter 23.[1] We use a single Armington composite for household, intermediate, government and investment demands. The Armington aggregator function is of the CES form. The economy is assumed to be small with respect to import markets.

Distortions: For simplicity the only policy-based distortions in the model are tariffs, which are applied to imports of all goods. Tariffs were discussed extensively in Chapter 19. Of course, adding other distortions would be possible (see exercise 2).

Closure: The factor market closure is neoclassical. We assume that all factors of production are available in fixed supply, are fully employed, and are fully mobile across sectors (as in the model covered in Chapter 5). On the macroeconomic side, we use a Johansen-style savings-investment closure. Investment at the commodity level (i.e., investment final demand for each composite) is fixed, as are government purchases. Government revenues are determined endogenously, with all tax rates exogenous. Government saving is endogenous, financed by (implicit) transfers from the household. Household savings vary to match the value of total investment. The current account balance is fixed, and the foreign exchange rate is the numéraire.

27.2   Model Data

Social Accounting Matrix: The data to which we will fit the model are described in the social accounting matrix presented in Table 27.1. The structure is much the same as the examples given in Chapter 25. There are only two new elements. First, we have allowed for simultaneous imports and exports in the same industrial category (since this is an Armington-

---

[1]Note that use of the Armington specification along with joint production eliminates the need to separately consider non-traded goods in the manner of Chapter 13. Any goods that have zero coefficients in the joint production transformation function and the Armington aggregator are effectively non-traded by the usual definition. The specification is more general, however. A good may be exported but not imported, imported but not exported, neither exported nor imported, or both exported and imported with this specification.

type model). Second, we have an entry in the I–X cell of the SAM. This represents foreign savings, i.e., it is the current account deficit.

Table 27.1   SAM for the Standard CGE Model

		Activities		Factors		Taxes	Final Demands				Total
		1	2	K	L	T	H	G	I	X	Total
Activities	1	40	10			-	50	12	15	45	172
	2	10	40				110	15	15	15	205
Factors	K	80	20								100
	L	20	80								100
Taxes	T	2	5								7
	H			100	100						200
Final Demands	G					7	20				27
	I						20			10	30
	X	20	50								70
Total		172	205	100	100	7	200	27	30	70	

Parameters: We have used the CES form for value-added, and the Armington functions. We have also used CED functions to represent foreign demand, and CET functions to model the transformation between production for domestic markets and production for export markets. We need to specify elasticities for each of these. To keep things simple, we will use an elasticity of substitution of 0.99 for value-added (approximately Cobb–Douglas), 2.0 for the elasticity of substitution in the Armington functions, -10 for the elasticity of foreign demand (approximating a relatively small country) and -20 for the elasticity of transformation in the CET (making domestic and export production highly substitutable).

27.3   GAMS Implementation

To implement the model in GAMS, we follow much the same procedure as we have outlined in previous chapters. We will present the basic outline. The complete model is available for download, but it is an excellent exercise to see if you can build it yourself by combining the relevant model attributes from your earlier work.

The first task is to set up the model sets. These will be the goods (`SET I Goods /1,2/;`) and the factors (`SET J Factors /K,L/;`). Next we set out the parameter names. These are given in Table 27.2. We have used the same labels as in previous chapters. Notice that we have broken the parameters into three blocks. The first is the set of behavioral parameters

Table 27.2   Parameters of the Standard CGE Model.

PARAMETERS

ALPHA	Shift parameters in utility
BETA(I)	Share parameters in utility
GAMMA(I)	Shift parameters in production
DELTA(J,I)	Share parameters in production
RHO(I)	Elasticity parameters in production
GAMMA_A(I)	Shift parameters in Armington
DELTA_A(I)	Share parameters in Armington
RHO_A(I)	Elasticity parameters in Armington
GAMMA_T(I)	Shift parameters in transformation
DELTA_T(I)	Share parameters in transformation
RHO_T(I)	Elasticity parameters in transformation
EPSILON(I)	Export demand elasticities
XI(I)	Shifts on foreign demands
PW(I)	World importable prices
XR	Exchange rate
A(II,I)	Input-output coefficients
FBAR(J)	Endowments
G(I)	Government consumption
INV(I)	Investment
CA	Current account
TM(I)	Import tariffs
UO	Initial utility level
CO(I)	Initial consumption levels
XO(I)	Initial export levels
QO(I)	Initial output levels
RO(J)	Initial factor prices
FO(J,I)	Initial factor use levels
DO(I)	Initial domestic consumption
MO(I)	Initial imported consumption
INTO(II,I)	Initial intermediate use levels
GDPO	Initial gross domestic product
YHO	Initial household income
YGO	Initial government income
TRANSO	Initial transfers from household to government
PDO(I)	Initial domestic good prices
PMO(I)	Initial imported good prices
PNO(I)	Initial net prices
PTO(I)	Initial composite producer prices
PXO(I)	Initial exported good prices
PAO(I)	Initial aggregate consumption prices ;

associated with the various functions describing production, consumption and trade. These will either be provided or calibrated. Next we have the exogenous variables of the model. Notice that we have explicitly included an exchange rate XR which will act as the numéraire, and a current account deficit CA. The others should be familiar. Lastly, we have the initial values of the endogenous variables, which will be taken from the SAM.

Table 27.3 lists the variables and equations of the model. Both should be familiar be familiar from previous chapters. Note that we have used TRANSFORM for the transformation functions rather than TRANS as with did in Chapter 24. The reason is simply that we have already used TRANS as a variable that represents household-government transfers, and each label for a GAMS model element must be unique.

The next major task is to define the equations of the model. The code is presented in Table 27.4. Again, each equation should look quite familiar from earlier programs. There are only a few points of note. First, all domestic demand in the model is assumed to be for the Armington composite. Hence, it is the price of the composite, PA, which appears in the DEMAND functions, the NET_PRICE functions, the government budget GBUDGET and investment spending (embedded within HOUSE). Similarly, in the equations of the Armington system (ARM, DOM_D and IMP_D) we must specify total domestic absorption as C(I)+SUM(II, A(I,II)*Q(II))+G(I)+INV(I), which is the sum of household, intermediate, government and investment demands.

Second, note the introduction of the exchange rate XR and the current account balance CA. The world prices are defined in foreign currency units, and are converted into domestic currency units in the FOREIGN_DEM and FOREIGN_SUP equations, and in the tariff revenue terms appearing in INCOME and GOVT.[2] The current account balance, the difference between the value of exports and imports at world prices, is converted into domestic currency units and subtracted from household income (i.e., a deficit grants the household increased ability to consume in the current period).

The next task is to calibrate the model. The process is presented in Table 27.5. As in previous chapters, the objective of the calibration is to ensure that the model replicates the benchmark equilibrium. The first step we have taken is to define a new set S with the dimensions of our SAM. Next we use the TABLE command to enter the SAM from Table 27.1.

---

[2]Also note that we have inverted the foreign demand function, which we did not do in Chapter 14. This is just for convenience.

Table 27.3   Variables and Equations of the Standard CGE Model.

VARIABLES

U	Utility level
C(I)	Consumption levels
X(I)	Export levels
Q(I)	Output levels
R(J)	Factor prices
F(J,I)	Factor use levels
D(I)	Domestic consumption
M(I)	Imported consumption
GDP	Gross domestic product
YH	Household income
YG	Government income
TRANS	Transfers from household to government
PD(I)	Domestic good prices
PM(I)	Imported good prices
PN(I)	Net prices
PT(I)	Composite producer prices
PX(I)	Exported good prices
PA(I)	Aggregate consumption prices ;

EQUATIONS

UTILITY	Utility function
DEMAND(I)	Demand functions
PRODUCTION(I)	Production functions
RESOURCE(J)	Resource constraints
FDEMAND(J,I)	Factor demand functions
INCOME	Gross domestic product
ARM(I)	Armington composites
DOM_D(I)	Demand for domestic goods
IMP_D(I)	Demand for imported goods
NET_PRICE(I)	Net price functions
TRANSFORM(I)	Transformation functions
DOM_S(I)	Domestic supplies
EXP_S(I)	Export supplies
FOREIGN_DEM(I)	Foreign demand functions
FOREIGN_SUP(I)	Foreign supply functions
HOUSE	Household income
GOVT	Government income
GBUDGET	Goverment budget ;

Table 27.4   Equation Definitions of the Standard CGE Model.

```
UTILITY..U=E=ALPHA*PROD(I, C(I)**BETA(I));
DEMAND(I)..C(I)=E=BETA(I)*YH/PA(I);
PRODUCTION(I)..Q(I)=E=(GAMMA(I)/(1-SUM(II,A(II,I))))*SUM(J$FO(J,I),
   DELTA(J,I)*F(J,I)**RHO(I))**(1/RHO(I));
RESOURCE(J)..FBAR(J)=E=SUM(I, F(J,I));
FDEMAND(J,I)..R(J)=E=PN(I)*Q(I)*SUM(JJ$FO(JJ,I), DELTA(JJ,I)*F(JJ,I)**
   RHO(I))**(-1)*DELTA(J,I)*F(J,I)**(RHO(I)-1);
INCOME..GDP=E=SUM(I, PN(I)*Q(I))+SUM(I, TM(I)*XR*PW(I)*M(I));
ARM(I)..C(I)+SUM(II, A(I,II)*Q(II))+G(I)+INV(I)=E=GAMMA_A(I)*(DELTA_A(I)*
   D(I)**RHO_A(I)+(1-DELTA_A(I))*M(I)**RHO_A(I))**(1/RHO_A(I));
DOM_D(I)..PD(I)=E=PA(I)*(C(I)+SUM(II, A(I,II)*Q(II))+G(I)+INV(I))*
   (DELTA_A(I)*D(I)**RHO_A(I)+(1-DELTA_A(I))*M(I)**RHO_A(I))**(-1)*DELTA_A(I)*
   (D(I)**(RHO_A(I)-1);
IMP_D(I)..PM(I)=E=PA(I)*(C(I)+SUM(II, A(I,II)*Q(II))+G(I)+INV(I))*
   (DELTA_A(I)*D(I)**RHO_A(I)+(1-DELTA_A(I))*M(I)**RHO_A(I))**(-1)*
   ((1-DELTA_A(I))*M(I)**(RHO_A(I)-1);
NET_PRICE(I)..PN(I)=E=PT(I)-SUM(II, PA(II)*A(II,I));
TRANSFORM(I)..Q(I)=E=GAMMA_T(I)*(DELTA_T(I)*D(I)**RHO_T(I)+(1-DELTA_T(I))*
   X(I)**RHO_T(I))**(1/RHO_T(I));
DOM_S(I)..PD(I)=E=PT(I)*Q(I)*(DELTA_T(I)*D(I)**RHO_T(I)+(1-DELTA_T(I))*
   X(I)**RHO_T(I))**(-1)*DELTA_T(I)*D(I)**(RHO_T(I)-1);
EXP_S(I)..PX(I)=E=PT(I)*Q(I)*(DELTA_T(I)*D(I)**RHO_T(I)+(1-DELTA_T(I))*
   X(I)**RHO_T(I))**(-1)*(1-DELTA_T(I))*X(I)**(RHO_T(I)-1);
FOREIGN_DEM(I)..PX(I)=E=XR*XI(I)*X(I)**(1/EPSILON(I));
FOREIGN_SUP(I)..PM(I)=E=XR*PW(I)*(1+TM(I));
HOUSE..YH=E=SUM(J, FBAR(J)*R(J))-TRANS-SUM(I, PA(I)*INV(I))-XR*CA;
GOVT..YG=E=SUM(I, TM(I)*PW(I)*XR*M(I))+TRANS;
GBUDGET..SUM(I, G(I)*PA(I))=E=YG;
```

The next step is to assign the correct values to each of the parameters that hold the initial equilibrium. As usual, we start by normalizing all prices to unity including the exchange rate (an exception is the world prices of imports, because we have tariffs in the initial equilibrium). Next we assign the values from the SAM to the appropriate model elements, and use the basic adding up conditions to determine the remaining initial values and exogenous variable values.

We then assign values for the free parameters (the elasticities). Notice that we have omitted the elasticities themselves for the Armington functions, the transformation functions, and the production functions, and have defined the values of the corresponding RHO parameters directly. Finally, we calculate the various shift and share parameters, just as in previous chapters.

Table 27.5   Calibration of the Standard CGE Model.

```
SET S Social /S1*S9/;
ALIAS (S, SS);

TABLE SAM Social Accounting Matrix
        S1    S2    S3    S4    S5    S6    S7    S8    S9
S1      40    10                      50    12    15    45
S2      10    40                     110    15    15    15
S3      80    20
S4      20    80
S5       2     5
S6                 100   100
S7                             7    20
S8                                  20                10
S9      20    50                                        ;

PAO(I)=1;
PDO(I)=1;
PTO(I)=1;
PMO(I)=1;
PXO(I)=1;
RO(J)=1;
XR=1;

INTO('1','1')=SAM('S1','S1');
INTO('2','1')=SAM('S2','S1');
INTO('1','2')=SAM('S1','S2');
INTO('2','2')=SAM('S2','S2');
CO('1')=SAM('S1','S6');
CO('2')=SAM('S2','S6');
XO('1')=SAM('S1','S9');
XO('2')=SAM('S2','S9');
MO('1')=SAM('S9','S1')+SAM('S5','S1');
MO('2')=SAM('S9','S2')+SAM('S5','S2');
QO('1')=SAM('S1','S1')+SAM('S2','S1')+SAM('S3','S1')+SAM('S4','S1');
QO('2')=SAM('S1','S2')+SAM('S2','S2')+SAM('S3','S2')+SAM('S4','S2');
FO('L','1')=SAM('S4','S1');
FO('L','2')=SAM('S4','S2');
FO('K','1')=SAM('S3','S1');
FO('K','2')=SAM('S3','S2');
G('1')=SAM('S1','S7');
G('2')=SAM('S2','S7');
INV('1')=SAM('S1','S8');
INV('2')=SAM('S2','S8');
TRANSO=SAM('S7','S6');
TM('1')=SAM('S5','S1')/SAM('S9','S1');
TM('2')=SAM('S5','S2')/SAM('S9','S2');
```

continued on next page

continued from previous page

```
DO(I)=QO(I)-XO(I);
A(II,I)=INTO(II,I)/QO(I);
PNO(I)=PAO(I)-SUM(II, PAO(II)*A(II,I));
PW(I)=PMO(I)/(1+TM(I));
FBAR(J)=SUM(I, FO(J,I));
GDPO=SUM(I, PNO(I)*QO(I))+SUM(I, TM(I)*PW(I)*MO(I));
CA=SUM(I, PXO(I)*XO(I))-SUM(I, PW(I)*XR*MO(I));
YHO=SUM(J, FBAR(J)*RO(J))-XR*CA-TRANSO-SUM(I, PAO(I)*INV(I));
YGO=TRANSO+SUM(I, TM(I)*PW(I)*XR*MO(I));
UO=YHO;

RHO(I)=0.01;
RHO_A(I)=0.5;
RHO_T(I)=1.05;
EPSILON(I)=-10;

BETA(I)=CO(I)*PAO(I)/YHO;
ALPHA=UO/PROD(I, CO(I)**BETA(I));
DELTA(J,I)$FO(J,I)=(RO(J)/FO(J,I)**(RHO(I)-1))/(SUM(JJ$FO(JJ,I), RO(JJ)/
   FO(JJ,I)**(RHO(I)-1)));
GAMMA(I)=(QO(I)/(SUM(J$FO(J,I), DELTA(J,I)*FO(J,I)**RHO(I)))**(1/RHO(I)))*
   (1-SUM(II,A(II,I)));
DELTA_A(I)=(PDO(I)/DO(I)**(RHO_A(I)-1))/(PDO(I)/DO(I)**(RHO_A(I)-1)+PMO(I)/
   MO(I)**(RHO_A(I)-1));
GAMMA_A(I)=(CO(I)+SUM(II, A(I,II)*QO(II))+G(I)+INV(I))/((DELTA_A(I)*DO(I)**
   RHO_A(I)+(1-DELTA_A(I))*MO(I)**RHO_A(I))**(1/RHO_A(I)));
DELTA_T(I)=(PDO(I)/DO(I)**(RHO_T(I)-1))/(PDO(I)/DO(I)**(RHO_T(I)-1)+PXO(I)/
   XO(I)**(RHO_T(I)-1));
GAMMA_T(I)=QO(I)/((DELTA_T(I)*DO(I)**RHO_T(I)+(1-DELTA_T(I))*XO(I)**
   RHO_T(I))**(1/RHO_T(I)));
XI(I)=PXO(I)/(XO(I)**(1/EPSILON(I)));
```

The model is now essentially complete. To finish, we install the initial values as the levels of the corresponding variables, and set the lower bounds, as usual (we omit the details for brevity). We can then set up the model and run a benchmark test with the commands:

```
MODEL STANDARD /ALL/;
SOLVE STANDARD USING NLP MAXIMIZING U;
```

This completes the "standard" CGE model. Models very much like this one are commonplace in the CGE literature. As you can see, once each of the component parts has been mastered, the model structure is relatively straightforward. Once you have the model working and have verified the initial equilibrium, try some of the exercises below to get a feel for how the model works and how you can adapt it to address your own research questions.

27.4   Exercises

(1) Try simulating the removal of tariffs. What is the effect? How does the effect vary as you alter the parameters of the model. You might want to consider the Armington elasticities and the elasticities of foreign demand in particular.
(2) See if you can add other policy distortions to the model, such as production, consumption and factor taxes (Chapter 20).
(3) Experiment with various model closures (Chapter 26). How do the effects of simulations with the model vary with different closure rules?
(4) Try incorporating other features into the basic model, such as variable proportions production technology (Chapter 10) or specific factors (Chapter 6) or a more general form of imperfect factor mobility (as in Chapter 21).
(5) Rather than using the utility index directly, see if you can modify the code to report alternative welfare measures, as discussed in Chapter 3.

27.5   Further Reading

An excellent overview of the basic model structure used in this chapter is Devaragan *et al.* (1990). Other useful readings on constructing a CGE model include the classic work of Shoven and Whalley (1992), and Gunning and Keyzer (1995). For a detailed exposition of welfare measures in CGE models see Francois and Martin (2010).

Chapter 28

Concluding Comments

Numerical simulation of international trade and trade policy issues using computable general equilibrium models is a dynamic and constantly evolving field, and one that can be intimidating to the uninitiated. By working through this book, we hope that you have developed a better understanding of how to build and program a basic general equilibrium model, how such models work, how they can be used to address interesting policy questions, and in particular how their fundamental structure is closely tied to the theoretical literature on international trade and trade policy, which we can use to frame our modeling efforts. In short, we hope that what is often called the "black box" of computable general equilibrium has been pried open.

So where to now? While we have covered the foundations, there are, of course, a large number of important topics in computable general equilibrium modeling for trade and trade policy that cannot be adequately dealt with in an introductory treatment such as this. Hence, we conclude the volume with a few recommended readings.

To learn more about the structure of basic computable general equilibrium models, Hosoe *et al.* (2010) and/or Burfisher (2011) provide accessible introductions to the "standard" computable general equilibrium model and applications. Both are written with the beginner in mind. These volumes focus somewhat less on the "pure" theory of international trade than ours, and correspondingly more on the intricacies of the modern CGE model. Whalley (2012) is a more advanced treatment that describes applications of general equilibrium computational methods to a range of policy and other issues involving the global economy and international trade.

One of the most widely used CGE models at present is the GTAP model, which we have mentioned at various stages throughout this volume. The GTAP model is a global trade model, but the basic structure of each

261

region within the model is essentially the same as the one that we have outlined. You will undoubtedly come across studies using the GTAP model, and, having worked through this book, you should have a pretty good understanding of how the model works.

If you are interested learning more details about the GTAP model, you will probably want to start with Hertel (1997), which documents the basic model structure and notation, and presents some interesting applications.[1] Many of these applications can be replicated using the resources available on the GTAP website (www.gtap.org). Ianchovichina and Walmsley (2012) detail the structure of a recursive dynamic version of the model, along with applications. Even if you are not planning on using the GTAP model itself, you will find the website to be a rich resource for data and advice on various modeling issues.

An excellent way to get a feel for the different types of problems that computable general equilibrium models have been used to address, and the ways in which they have been used to address them, is simply to read a lot of published studies. There are far too many to list, but survey articles are a good place to start. Recent overviews of computable general equilibrium analyses (with a focus on trade policy issues) include Scollay and Gilbert (2000), Gilbert and Wahl (2002), Robinson and Thierfelder (2002), Lloyd and MacLaren (2004), and Gilbert (2008).[2]

Finally, while we have focused on a relatively standard set of model structures, we should note that computable general equilibrium techniques are quite adaptable. Many extensions to the basic models that we have presented can be made either by incorporating alternative economic theories into the models (e.g., to address the implications of imperfect competition or firm heterogeneity), or by integrating computable general equilibrium models with other modeling paradigms (e.g., to address issues such as poverty or climate change). Gilbert (2010) contains a number of interesting applications at the frontiers of computable general equilibrium analysis along these lines, including work on firm heterogeneity, trade and poverty, and trade and the environment. Used with care, CGE techniques can help us to assess the economic implications of a wide range of important issues.

---

[1] GTAP is built using the GEMPACK software package rather than GAMS, so some investment in learning about that package is also required.

[2] Scollay and Gilbert (2000) consider studies of trade reform in the Asia-Pacific, Gilbert and Wahl (2002) Chinese trade reforms, and Robinson and Thierfelder (2002) and Lloyd and MacLaren (2004) regional trade agreements. Gilbert (2008) surveys applications addressing the effect of trade policy changes on poverty.

Appendix A

Lagrangian Multipliers, Shadow Prices and Marginal Social Values

Here is a simple derivation of the method of Lagrangian multipliers and their use to obtain shadow prices and marginal social values. We take the simple problem of utility maximization subject to a budget constraint, assuming only two goods. Once you understand this approach, you can generalize it to more goods and more constraints.

A.1 The Lagrangian Multiplier

The consumer's problem is to maximize $U(c_1, c_2)$ where U is utility and c_1 and c_2 are consumptions of the two goods. Their constraint is that $Y = p_1 c_1 + p_2 c_2$, where Y is money income and the p's are prices. Thus they face the following constrained maximization problem:

$$\text{Maximize} \quad U(c_1, c_2) \tag{A.1}$$

$$\text{Subject to} \quad Y - p_1 c_1 - p_2 c_2 = 0. \tag{A.2}$$

Suppose that instead they decide to solve the Lagrangian problem:

$$\text{Maximize} \quad \mathcal{L} = U(c_1, c_2) + \lambda[Y - p_1 c_1 - p_2 c_2]. \tag{A.3}$$

Are the two problems the same? They solve the first problem by recognizing that at an optimum small changes in consumption that keep the consumer adhering to their budget constraint will not change utility. Thus at the optimum we have:

$$dU = \frac{\partial U}{\partial c_1} dc_1 + \frac{\partial U}{\partial c_1} dc_2 = 0 \tag{A.4}$$

where the consumption changes are constrained by:

$$p_1 dc_1 + p_2 dc_2 = 0. \tag{A.5}$$

Substituting (A.5) into (A.4) yields:

$$\frac{\partial U/\partial c_1}{\partial U/\partial c_1} = \frac{p_1}{p_2}. \tag{A.6}$$

Equations (A.2) and (A.6) enable us to solve for c_1 and c_2.

To solve the Lagrangian problem we take partial derivatives of the Lagrangian function $\mathscr{L}$ with respect to the choice variables c_1, c_2 and λ and set them all equal to zero. This gives us:

$$\frac{\partial U}{\partial c_1} - \lambda p_1 = 0 \tag{A.7}$$

$$\frac{\partial U}{\partial c_2} - \lambda p_2 = 0 \tag{A.8}$$

and equation (A.2). Solving (A.7) and (A.8) to eliminate λ gives us equation (A.6). Thus the two approaches give us the same equations. This shows that Lagrangian maximization yields exactly the same solution as constrained maximization does.

If we had had 3 consumer goods, we would have imagined that the consumer perturbs the consumption of goods 1 and 2 to get equation (A.6). Then they perturb the consumption of goods 1 and 3 to get the sister of equation (A.6) except with subscripts 1 and 3. This is combined with the three good variant of equation (A.2).

A.2   Shadow Prices and Marginal Social Values

Now let's figure out what the increment to utility is of an increment to money income and changes in prices, assuming that consumption of goods 1 and 2 continue to be adjusted to be optimum.

We take the total differential of $\mathscr{L}$ in equation (A.3), allowing changes in money income, prices and consumption levels.

$$d\mathscr{L} = dU + \frac{\partial \mathscr{L}}{\partial \lambda} d\lambda + \lambda d[Y - p_1 c_1 - p_2 c_2]. \tag{A.9}$$

The second two terms drop out, so, $d\mathscr{L} = dU$. Thus, starting from the optimum, any increment to the Lagrangian is the same increment to utility. Now we take the differential of the Lagrangian in equation (A.3) to obtain:

$$dU = \frac{\partial \mathscr{L}}{\partial c_1} dc_1 + \frac{\partial \mathscr{L}}{\partial c_2} dc_2 + \frac{\partial \mathscr{L}}{\partial \lambda} d\lambda + \lambda [dY - c_1 dp_1 - c_2 dp_2]. \tag{A.10}$$

Since consumption is initially at an optimum, the partial derivatives of $\mathscr{L}$ with respect to c_1, c_2, and λ are all zero. Thus, the first three terms on the right hand side drop out. That leaves only the fourth term. Consequently, the change in utility is:

$$dU = \lambda[dY - c_1 dp_1 - c_2 dp_2].$$ (A.11)

We conclude that λ is the increment to utility made possible by an increment to income. The Lagrangian multiplier, λ, is the shadow price of income, or more simply the marginal utility of income. The increment to utility made possible by an increment to the price of good i is $-\lambda c_i$. This is called "the marginal social value of the price." Thus we have evaluated the effects of changes in the consumer's environment on their welfare.

Appendix B

GAMS Tips and Tricks

If you have worked through the problems in this volume, you should have a pretty good understanding of the process of building a basic GAMS model for evaluating international trade and trade policy. In this appendix we provide some parting advice on a number of different aspects of constructing models in GAMS that may be helpful as you move on to building your own models. We consider how to better organize a large model by structuring it into several files, how to efficiently evaluate the sensitivity of a model to parameter choices, and various options for efficiently reporting the results of your simulations. We conclude with some notes on the process of debugging a model.

B.1   Structuring a Large Program

The programs we have been using are all quite small, and we have presented them all in single GAMS program files. For more complex models, or those with high dimensions, this may become impractical, and it may make sense to try and organize the program in a modular fashion. This makes for models that are easier to read, modify and maintain.

For example, when building a CGE model, you may want separate out the data used by the model from the model itself. It may even make sense in very large models to separate data files by type (e.g., a file for the equilibrium flow data, and another for parameters). This has the advantage of making it easier to work with the model, and also facilitates adapting the same model code to different datasets.

You may also want to create different modules for the various components of a model. For example, suppose that you have several alternative demand structures. One might be Cobb–Douglas, another CES, and a third

Stone–Geary, and you want to be able to easily swap which structure you use. One way to do that would be to have all of the elements associated with each demand structure (PARAMETERS, VARIABLES and EQUATIONS, both definitions and assignments) in different files, from which you choose the one that fits your current task.

GAMS offers the $INCLUDE facility for the purpose of creating and using such modules. The command is very simple. It takes the form $INCLUDE <filename>, where <filename> is the name of the file to be included.[3] For example, if your data is contained in a file labeled DATA.GMS, it can be called with the command $INCLUDE DATA. The file to be included should be an ordinary text file containing the desired GAMS commands, and should be located in the same working directory as the main program file (or alternatively a full path can be provided.)

When you run the main program containing the $INCLUDE command, GAMS will insert the contents of the referenced file at the point where the $INCLUDE statement is encountered. As far as GAMS is concerned, it is as if the contents of the file were part of the main file at that point, so the usual rules regarding the order of assignments and so on must be followed.

B.2   Sensitivity Analysis

In numerical simulation models the results of a simulation are ultimately a function of the parameters of the model. Some parameter values may be known with reasonable certainty, but in most cases the true values of parameters are not known. Hence, while the values of parameters are fixed (by definition) within a simulation, the parameters are really random variables, and therefore so are the results of the simulations.

For example, in CGE models the values of the Armington elasticities, which govern the degree of substitutability between domestic and foreign varieties in consumption, as we saw in Chapter 23, have an important effect on the size of changes in trade associated with growth or trade policy reforms, and therefore on other variables such as the estimated welfare effect. While some estimates of these parameters exist (see Hertel *et al.*, 2007), the values are not known with certainty. Ideally, we want to take this uncertainty into account when evaluating the simulation results. This

---

[3]Two related commands are $BATINCLUDE and $LIBINCLUDE. These function in much the same way, but optionally allow the passing of arguments to the included file. For details see the GAMS manual.

is called sensitivity analysis.

At the most basic level, sensitivity analysis might involve simply setting high/medium/low values for a key parameter, running the desired simulation for each parameter value and reporting all three sets of results. This approach is fairly common, and is called "conditional" sensitivity analysis.

Using the FOR command that we introduced in Chapter 8, we can quickly set up a slightly more sophisticated version. Suppose that our model is MOD, which requires maximizing the objective OBJ, and a critical parameter RHO. Consider the following code:

```
FOR(S = -10 to -1 BY 1,
RHO=S;
SOLVE MOD USING NLP MAXIMIZING OBJ;
);
```

This will solve the model repeatedly for values of RHO between -10 and -1, in increments of 1. We can then observe how key variables respond to different RHO values.

Perhaps, however, some values of RHO are much more likely than others. Suppose for example we know from econometric estimation that RHO has a mean value of -5 and a standard deviation of 1. In that case, we would be roughly 95 percent confident that RHO lies between -7 and -3. How can we use this information? One way would be to use Monte-Carlo techniques. While a detailed discussion of this approach is beyond the scope of this volume, the basic idea is simple. We could repeatedly draw parameter values at random from the distribution of RHO, solve the model many times with these parameter values, and thereby derive an approximate distribution for results of interest.

To facilitate this type of analysis, we can use the GAMS command NORMAL (assuming the parameter in question is normally distributed), which generates a random number drawn from the normal distribution.[4] The code might look like:

```
OPTION SEED=123;
SCALAR XSUM, X2SUM;
FOR(S = 1 to 10000 BY 1,
RHO=NORMAL(-5,1);
SOLVE MOD USING NLP MAXIMIZING OBJ;
XSUM=XSUM+X.L;
```

---

[4]GAMS has similar commands for drawing values from a wide variety of distributions.

```
X2SUM=X2SUM+POWER(X.L,2);
);
SCALAR XMEAN, XSD;
XMEAN=XSUM/10000;
XSD=SQRT(X2SUM/(10000*2)-POWER(XMEAN,2));
```

The first line sets the GAMS SEED, which determines which pseudo-random numbers are generated. The number can be set to anything (for example, the time when you run the program), but it is important to set a seed if you want to be able to replicate the analysis exactly. Suppose that we are interested in how the variable X responds to different values of RHO. We begin by specifying two new scalars, XSUM and X2SUM, which will hold the sum of X and the sum of X squared, respectively. We then use the FOR command to set up a large number of model solves (in this case 10,000). For each iteration we begin by drawing a random value for RHO from its distribution, we then solve the model, and add the generated values for X and its square to the appropriate running totals.[5] After we have run the model 10 thousand times, we compute the mean value of X, which we have labeled XMEAN, and the standard deviation, XSD, using standard formulae.

When reporting the results, we can describe both a mean estimate and a measure of its variability. This is more useful than a point estimate for two reasons. First, because the models we are dealing with are usually nonlinear, the mean value of a simulated result is not generally the same as the value generated by simulating at the mean values of the random parameter. That is, in the above example, the value for X we obtain by running the model at the mean value of RHO, -5, is not the same as XMEAN, and may therefore be misleading as a measure of central tendency. Second, in a real policy analysis, if the variables truly are random, it is misleading to present the results as if they are not.

The extensions to analyzing the variability of more than one simulated outcome should be clear. We can also allow all random parameters to vary at the same time, drawing each from their respective distributions (assuming they are independent). This is called "unconditional" sensitivity analysis. For an example see Gilbert and Wahl (2003).

How many iterations are used will depend on how expensive (i.e., time-consuming) each model run is, and the desired level of accuracy of the estimates. The standard error is defined as the standard deviation divided

---

[5]We have used the POWER command rather than ** to allow for negative values of X. This command is discussed further in Section B.4.2.

by the square root of the number of iterations. It provides a measure of confidence in the estimate of the mean. This does not depend on the number of parameters that are varying. So, running the model 10,000 times ensures that we are roughly 95 percent confident that the true mean lies within 2 times one percent of the standard deviation. To double the precision, we need to quadruple the number of iterations.

B.3   Reporting Results

So far we have been reading results directly from the GAMS list file. This is fine for relatively small models, but inconvenient when the models are larger, or when we want to compare the results of a large number of simulations (e.g., with sensitivity analysis). Fortunately GAMS offers a number of more powerful and useful options.

B.3.1   *Display*

The DISPLAY statement continues to place results in the list file, but offers some further flexibility and a more easily readable format. The basic command takes the form keyword DISPLAY, followed by list of parameters, or variable attributes (e.g., levels or marginals), and a semicolon. Hence, to display the current values of a parameter RHO we would use DISPLAY RHO; and for the levels of a variable Q we would use DISPLAY Q.L;. Items to be displayed can be listed with one DISPLAY statement, each separated with a comma.

There are a limited number of controls on the format. To alter the number of decimals displayed we can use OPTION DECIMALS = 1;, where the number is the number of decimals. This will change the display depth for all subsequent display statements. For further details see Chapter 14 of the GAMS manual.

B.3.2   *Put*

The GAMS "put" facility is designed for creating output files distinct from the listing, and is much more flexible than the DISPLAY command. The trade-off for the increased flexibility and control over the output is that it is more difficult to use. We will discuss only a few basic details; for further information see the GAMS manual.

The basic format consists of three commands. First, a file (or several files) is created into which information will be written, next GAMS is told to write to the file, and then a series of commands do the actual writing, one element at a time. Because one element is written at a time, we have a lot of control over exactly which data is written and how it is written. To facilitate the writing, we need to use loops, however.

If the file to which we want to write data is to be called RESULTS, the first statement we need is:

```
FILE RESULTS /RESULTS.TXT/;
```

The creates a file RESULTS.TXT, and assigns to it the name RESULTS.[6] Next we tell GAMS that this is where we want the results to go with the command:

```
PUT RESULTS;
```

Finally, we write the data. Suppose that we want to write a simple table of output results for the HOS model. The code, which we place after the SOLVE statement, would be:

```
PUT 'Output Levels'//;
LOOP(I,
PUT I.TL, @10, Q.L(I)/;
);
```

The first line writes a title, with the required text quoted. The forward slashes represent carriage returns. Next we start a LOOP over the elements of the set I. The next line will place the element name, move across 10 spaces, and place the output level, then move to the next line. To create tables with more dimensions, it is necessary to loop over all of the dimensions.

B.3.3 *Lists and Tables*

Thomas Rutherford has created some very useful files that simplify the process of using the put facility for converting GAMS data into other formats. These include GAMS2TXT (Rutherford, 1999) for writing data files and GAMS2TBL (Rutherford, 1998) for writing tables.

---

[6]To control the formatting, GAMS allows various options to be specified globally. For example, to change the number of decimal places displayed to two we can specify RESULTS.ND=2;. For full details of the controls available see the GAMS manual.

To use the utilities, you first need to install the libraries. The instructions are available at http://www.mpsge.org/inclib/gams2txt.htm. Once you have followed the instructions you can call the files using the $LIBINCLUDE command. As an example, to create a simple table of results (the factor demands) from the HOS model we can use:

```
FILE RESULTS /RESULTS.TXT/;
$LIBINCLUDE GAMS2TBL
PUT RESULTS;
$SETGLOBAL TITLE "Factor Demands"
$SETGLOBAL ROW_SET J
$LIBINCLUDE GAMS2TBL FD.L
```

The first line creates the file in which the table/s will be created. Next we have a blank $LIBINCLUDE call to the GAMS2TBL routine, which is necessary if you want to create multiple tables within a loop. We then issue a PUT command to tell GAMS to write data to the file we created. The next two lines set a title for the table, and tell GAMS to put the factors into the rows. Finally, we call GAMS2TBL to write the factor demands. GAMS2TBL offers a number of convenient options, including the ability to generate LATEX tables directly.

GAMS2TXT has a very similar syntax, just replace the GAM2TBL with GAMS2TXT, and eliminate the two $SETGLOBAL lines. The routines will write a data file in the format introduced in Chapter 13 (i.e., K.1 80, K.2 20, etc.) For further details on the utilities see Rutherford (1998) and (1999).

B.3.4 *Spreadsheets*

It is also possible to have GAMS write data directly to Excel spreadsheets. This is particularly useful if simulation results or model datasets are to be distributed, or if you would like to use Excel's graphical capabilities to analyze simulation results. The process works through the use of GAMS Data Exchange or GDX files, which can store the values associated with **SETS**, **PARAMETERS**, and **VARIABLES**. The GDX file can be processed into an Excel file.[7]

To see how this works, suppose that you have solved the HOS model of production from Chapter 5 and want to place the solution values for factor use into an Excel sheet for further analysis. Following the SOLVE statement,

---

[7]This can work the other way too, allowing you to store data in an Excel file, and read it directly into GAMS.

we put the command:

```
execute_unload "RESULTS.GDX" FD.L
```

This will create the GDX file RESULTS.GDX, containing the levels of the variable FD (the factor demands). We can list more variables, variable characteristics (e.g., marginals) or parameters if we wish.

Next we need to convert the GDX file into an Excel file. The command that we need is:

```
execute 'gdxxrw.exe RESULTS.GDX var=FD.L'
```

This will generate an Excel file called RESULTS.XLS with the data written starting in the first cell of the first worksheet.[8] For parameters var is replaced with par.

Another example might involve the tariff model from Chapter 19. Suppose we want to graph how the welfare index U varies with the size of a tariff on good 2 ranging from 1 to 50 percent. The following code will do the trick:

```
SET ITER /1*50/;
PARAMETER USAVE(ITER);
LOOP(ITER,
SOLVE SMALL USING NLP MAXIMIZING U;
USAVE(ITER)=U.L;
T('2')=T('2')+0.01;
);
execute_unload "RESULTS.GDX" USAVE
execute 'gdxxrw.exe RESULTS.GDX par=USAVE'
```

The first line creates a set ITER with the elements 1 though 50. Then we create a new parameter USAVE, which will hold the values of the welfare index for each tariff. Next we start a LOOP over the elements of the set, solve the model for each element of ITER and store the value of the welfare index in USAVE. The first solve will be with a zero tariff. With each subsequent SOLVE, we increase the value of the tariff by 1 percent. When we are done, we write the Excel file. Try copying the above code to the end of the GAMS program from Chapter 19 to see the process in action.[9]

---

[8]The position can be controlled. See the GAMS manual for further details.

[9]You could also try replacing the last two lines of the code above with DISPLAY USAVE; to display the results into the list file. Another alternative is to use GAMS2TBL.

B.4 Debugging

All of the programs included in this volume have been verified to run correctly, but as you begin to modify the programs to suit your own needs, and to develop your own programs, you will inevitably find that the process of writing a GAMS program involves a considerable amount of time spent on debugging or removing errors. Unfortunately, it is difficult to know how to fix a model without knowing exactly what is going wrong with it, and there are many things that can potentially go wrong. Nonetheless, we offer a few tips drawn from our experience. With practice and experience, the process of identifying and eliminating model bugs becomes easier and faster, even if it sometimes remains a little frustrating.

Problems with GAMS programs can arise in multiple different ways, some of which are much easier to deal with than others. The main possibilities are:

(1) *Compilation errors.* Also called pre-processing errors, these are problems that arise within the GAMS compiler, before the model has been sent to the solver. They are generally syntax errors of some kind, and usually the easiest to eliminate.

(2) *Execution or solution errors.* If there are no errors in the pre-processing stage, GAMS will attempt to build the model and pass it to the solver. Errors may arise here if there are mistakes in the assignments or if the model equations are not well behaved at the initial point. Usually this is a problem with the calibration, but it may be an error in the model itself.

(3) *Infeasibilities.* In this case there are no problems with the initialization, but the model does not replicate the calibrated solution, or the model fails to reach a solution at all. This may mean that the starting points are poor (calibration problems), that the model is poorly scaled, or that there is an error in the model logic.

(4) *Simulation errors.* It may be that GAMS finds a solution to the model, but the solution is not what is expected, or when the parameters of the model are changed in some way, the model does not behave in the manner that economic logic suggests that it will.

We consider each of these possibilities in turn.

B.4.1   Compilation Errors

When you run a GAMS program, the GAMS compiler will begin by checking through the entire program and identifying any basic errors in syntax or logic. If any are found, the program will stop and the model will not be submitted to the solution algorithm. In the list file, GAMS will mark each error that it has found with the mark ***, and will place a numeric code at the point of the error (e.g., $8). At the end of the list file GAMS will provide a list of all of the error codes that have been found, along with some explanatory text on the nature of the problem.

Which error codes appear will, of course, depend on what kind of errors you make. The GAMS manual contains a complete list of the possible error codes, but here are some of the ones that we see frequently:

- 140. This indicates an unknown symbol. There is a mismatch between a defined name for a VARIABLE, PARAMETER or EQUATION and the expression used in an assignment. Most likely a typo. Check the declarations and assignments carefully.
- 141. This occurs when you try and use a parameter that has not been assigned a value in previous assignment as part of a calculation. In other words, your calibration is out of order — you must provide values in the order in which are used in an assignment expression.
- 8 and 408. These errors relate to brackets. In any expression there must be an equal number of left (opening) and right (closing) brackets. The message 8 indicates that you have fewer closing brackets than opening, and 408 that you have more. The solution is to check the expression carefully to match bracketed terms correctly. One way to do this is to paste the expression into Excel, which color codes bracket pairs, making it them easier to see.
- 171. This error indicates that you have assigned an expression using a set that is different from the set over which the object was defined. For example, if you define C(I), then an expression involving C(J) will generate this error unless J is a subset or an ALIAS of I. The solution is to correctly define the sets/subsets before attempting any assignments.
- 125. GAMS will report that the set is under control already. This means that you are trying to make an assignment to an object for all values of a set, but the assignment involves a summation or a product across the elements of the same set. The solution is to use an ALIAS for the summation/product. For example, in Chapter 4 we calibrated DELTA using DELTA(J)=(R(J)/FO(J)**(RHO-1))/(SUM(JJ,

R(JJ)/FO(JJ)**(RHO-1))). If we instead use DELTA(J)=(R(J)/FO(J)**(RHO-1))/(SUM(J, R(J)/FO(J)**(RHO-1))), GAMS will report the error.

- 149.   GAMS reports an uncontrolled set entered as a constant. This means that you have an expression on the right hand side of an assignment that does not match the left, and is not part of a summation or a product. Using the same example as above, this happens if we use DELTA(J)=(R(JJ)/FO(JJ)**(RHO-1))/(SUM(JJ, R(JJ)/FO(JJ)**(RHO-1))).

- 409. This usually means that you have a missing semi-colon in the preceding line of code, error **96** may appear in similar circumstances (depending on where the semicolon is missing.)

- 257. You will see this after the SOLVE statement if there were errors previously. It should disappear once all preceding errors are eliminated.

When running a program for the first time, GAMS will often find a fairly intimidating number of errors, but these types of error are generally easy to find and correct. Begin by opening the list file and searching for the first occurrence of ***. Identify the first error code, and then repair the corresponding section of the program file. Next, save the program file and run it again. Repeat the process until all of the error messages are eliminated.

The reason for only looking for the first error, and fixing them one at a time, is that in many cases a single mistake can lead to many subsequent errors, so it is usually more efficient to fix them sequentially. Once you have them all cleared, GAMS will proceed to generating the model.

B.4.2   *Execution Errors*

Once the program has passed the pre-processor, we may see what is called execution or solve errors as GAMS attempts to build the model for solution. Typically these are a consequence of attempts to undertake mathematically undefined operations in either the calibration of the model (i.e., in parameter assignments) or in the model equations themselves when evaluated at the initial point, or at a subsequent point in an attempt to find a solution. The problem is usually one of:

- Division by zero.
- Taking the logarithm of a negative number.

- An illegal operation in a power (e.g., bringing a negative number to a power of less than one).
- A power operation that leads to a number that is too large for GAMS to handle.

How to deal with these types of problems will depend on what exactly is causing them. There are a number of possibilities. First, check that you have made assignments to all the initial levels of variables, and that the assigned values make sense. If you do not assign an initial level, GAMS will default to zero, which may lead to an error (e.g., division by zero).

Second, impose bounds. If, for example, a negative value for a variable makes no economic sense, you should be imposing a lower bound of zero. This will also prevent problems if an expression would become illegal at negative values of the variable (e.g. taking a logarithm).

Third, check that you have used exception handling when necessary. For example, a problem may arise when GAMS evaluates a factor demand function for a factor that is not used in an industry. Proper exception handling would prevent this from occurring.

Fourth, if you are getting power errors and the number that you are raising to a power is negative (and it is is economically meaningful for it to be negative), use the POWER function rather than the ** operator, provided that the exponent is a positive integer. The reason is that GAMS calculates X**Y as EXP(Y*LOG(X)), and the log of a negative number is not defined.

If you are getting problems with very large or small numbers, you can try scaling the problematic variables. This can be done manually, but GAMS has a facility to simplify the process. Each variable can be assigned a scale parameter, in much the same way as it is assigned a level or a bound. The format is <variable name>.SCALE(INDEX)=<scale factor>. For example, to scale consumption data in millions to billions we use C.SCALE(I)=1000;. After defining the model, we enable scaling by using the option <model name>.SCALEOPT=1; before the solve statement. GAMS will scale the values before passing them to the solver, and rescale the results to the initial units before presenting them to the user.[10]

Finally, in some circumstances it may be useful to rewrite your model in such a way that potentially problematic operations are avoided altogether, if this is possible. Hence, suppose a model involves the expression $y = x/z$,

---

[10] A question arises as to what a "good" scale parameter will be. GAMS solver algorithms tend to perform best when initial values are close to 1. This suggests one possibility in a calibrated model is to scale every (non-zero) variable by its own initial value.

and it is possible that z could either at a solution or in the search for one hit zero, causing the expression to become undefined.[11] The problem could easily be avoided by rewriting the relationship as $zy = x$.

B.4.3 *Infeasibilities*

Infeasibility simply means that one or more of a model's constraints is not satisfied for a particular set of values of the endogenous variables. In a calibrated model, all of the model constraints should hold at the initial point. Hence, if there are significant infeasibilities on an initial model run, but GAMS does eventually find a solution, that indicates a problem with the calibration. The listing will tell you which equations are infeasible (do a search for INFES). Check that the associated variables have had a level set correctly, and if they have, go back and check the calibration of the parameters in those equations.[12]

It may be the case that GAMS is not able to find any set of values for the variables that satisfy the constraints. In this case GAMS will report that the model is infeasible. This could again be a problem with the calibration, or something more fundamental. Again, you will be able to tell from the listing exactly which equations are infeasible, and you will want to narrow down your search for the problem to that part of the system. If you are convinced that there is no problem with the model itself but rather that the problem is numerical you can try the following:

- Check the bounds, and impose logical bounds if you have not done so. This usually makes it easier for GAMS to find a solution.[13] Look for obvious bounding errors (e.g., have you specified a lower bound of zero for a variable that can logically be negative?)
- Try scaling the model.
- Allow the model to run for longer. If your model calibrates correctly and the infeasibility arises when you consider a very large shock, it may be that GAMS gives up before it finds a solution, reporting it as infeasible

---

[11] This often happens with corner solutions. See the small, open economy problem with more goods than factors in Chapter 9, and long run minimum wage problem from Chapter 21 for some ways of dealing with these cases.

[12] If you have a lot of trouble, you might try getting GAMS to calibrate for you. You can do this by reversing the role of the parameters and variables, and getting GAMS to solve for the correct parameter values. This approach can also be used if a functional form is not easily amenable to calibration.

[13] In some cases, however, the opposite can be true, so relaxing bounds can sometimes help.

when really the solution is just too far away from the initial point.[14] You can deal with this by either breaking the shock down into smaller pieces, or by setting the ITERLIM option. If your model is named HOS, for example, then specifying HOS.ITERLIM=10000; before the SOLVE statement will cause GAMS to search 10 times longer than the default value of 1000 for a solution.

- Guide the solution. For example if you ask GAMS to solve for the optimum tariff and it is very large, ask GAMS to initially solve for the best tariff under 500 percent, and then use that solution as the start for the next stage in which the tariff is unconstrained.

- Try a different solver. Different solver algorithms work in different ways, and it is possible that one algorithm may solve a model where another fails. However, if your model is well specified, we have found most of GAMS solvers to be quite robust, so an error in specification is more likely.

B.4.4   *Simulation Errors*

Even when you have a model running, it is vitally important to run lots of trial simulations and check the results against your intuition. A final type of problem is where the program does run and GAMS is able to find a solution, but the solution is incorrect or does not match with theoretical predictions. This type of error can be hard to track down and solve, so it is difficult to offer general advice. Some general strategies are:

- Reduce the dimensions of the model. It is generally easier to see if the core economic relationships in a model are working correctly in a toy model than in a large-scale model.

- See if you can parameterize the model in such a way that the results should be theoretically clear (for example, fixed proportions technology, or Cobb–Douglas preferences).

- Try blocking off the model components to see if you can identify in which part of the model the error is occurring. For example, check the demand system by exogenizing income and prices and determining if demand responds correctly to shocks to those variables. Once you are sure that component of the model is working correctly, you can shift to another until you identify the problem.

---

[14]Of course, it may also be that the model truly is infeasible in a range far away from your initial solution, e.g., perhaps if you hit a bound.

- Verify the first order conditions. First order conditions can be messy and difficult to deal with. One way to check them is to solve the model (or a component of the model) as an NLP rather than as a system of equations. If you get a different answer, it is likely that the first order conditions have been incorrectly derived or entered into GAMS.

B.5 Further Reading

Hosoe *et al.* (2010) also offer some basic tips on debugging a GAMS model. The other main resources are the GAMS manual itself, and the McCarl GAMS User Guide, by Bruce McCarl. Both of the latter are available on the GAMS website. Rutherford's website of GAMS utilities provides details on various utilities.

Bibliography

Armington, P.S. (1969) "A Theory of Demand for Products Distinguished by Place of Production" International Monetary Fund Staff Papers 16: 159–76.

Bacharach, M. (1970) Biproportional Matrices and Input-Output Change (Cambridge University Press, Cambridge).

Batra, R. (1973) "Non-traded Goods, Factor Market Distortions, and Gains From Trade" American Economic Review 63: 706–13.

Bhagwati, J. (1958) "Immiserizing Growth: A Geometrical Note" Review of Economic Studies 25: 201–5.

Bhagwati, J.N. (1965) "On the Equivalence of Tariffs and Quotas" in Caves et al., eds., Trade, Growth and the Balance of Payments (Rand-McNally, Chicago).

Bhagwati, J.N. (1971) "The Generalised Theory of Distortions and Welfare" in Bhagwati et al., eds., Trade, Balance of Payments, and Growth (North-Holland, Amsterdam).

Bhagwati, J.N. and T.N. Srinivasan (1969) "Optimal Intervention to Achieve Non-economic Objectives" Review of Economic Studies 36: 27–38.

Bhagwati, J.N. and T.N. Srinivasan (1971) "The Theory of Wage Differentials: Production Response and Factor Price Equalisation" Journal of International Economics 1: 19–35.

Bhagwati, J.N. and T.N. Srinivasan (1974) "On Reanalyzing the Harris–Todaro Model: Policy Ranking in the Case of Sector-Specific Sticky Wages" American Economic Review 64: 502–8.

Bhagwati, J., R.A. Brecher and T. Hatta (1983) "The Generalized Theory of Transfers and Welfare: Bilateral Transfers in a Multilateral World" American Economic Review 73: 606–18.

Bhagwati, J., T.N. Srinivasan and A. Panagariya (1998) Lectures on International Trade, 2nd Edition, (MIT Press, Cambridge).

Brander, J. (1981) "Intra-Industry Trade in Identical Commodities" Journal of International Economics 11: 1–14.

Brander, J. and P. Krugman (1983) "A 'Reciprocal Dumping' Model of International Trade" Journal of International Economics 15: 313–21.

Brecher, R. (1974a) "Minimum Wage Rates and the Pure Theory of International Trade" *Quarterly Journal of Economics* 88: 98–116.

Brecher, R. (1974b) "Optimal Commercial Policy for a Minimum Wage Economy" *Journal of International Economics* 4: 139–49.

Brecher, R.A. and C.F. Diaz-Alejandro (1977) "Tariffs, Foreign Capital and Immiserizing Growth" *Journal of International Economics* 7: 317–22.

Burfisher, M.E. (2011) *Introduction to Computable General Equilibrium Models* (Cambridge University Press, Cambridge).

Casas, F.R. (1972) "Pure Intermediate Products, Factor Intensities and Technical Progress in the Theory of International Trade" *Southern Economic Journal* 39: 72–8.

Casas, F.R. (1984) "Imperfect Factor Mobility: A Generalization and Synthesis of Two-sector Models of International Trade" *Canadian Journal of Economics* 17: 747–61.

Charteris, A. and N. Winchester (2010) "Dairy Disaggregation and Joint Production in an Economy-Wide Model" *Australian Journal of Agricultural and Resource Economics* 54: 491–507.

Chiang, A.C. and K. Wainwright (2005) *Fundamental Methods of Mathematical Economics*, 4th Edition, (McGraw Hill, New York).

Copeland, B., E. Tower and M. Webb (1989) "On Negotiated Quotas, Tariffs, and Transfers" *Oxford Economics Papers* 41: 774–88.

Corden, W.M. (1997) *Trade Policy and Economic Welfare* (Clarendon, Oxford).

Corden, W.M. (2002) *Too Sensational: On the Choice of Exchange Rate Regimes* (MIT Press, Cambridge).

Corden, W.M. and R. Findlay (1975) "Urban Unemployment, Intersectoral Capital Mobility and Development Policy" *Economica* 42: 59–78.

Deardorff, A.V. (2010) *Glossary of International Economics*, available at: `http://www-personal.umich.edu/~alandear/glossary/`.

Deardorff, A.V. and R.M. Stern (1986) *The Michigan Model of World Production and Trade: Theory and Applications* (MIT Press, Cambridge).

Deardorff, A.V. and R.M. Stern (1990) *Computational Analysis of Global Trading Arrangements* (University of Michigan Press, Ann Arbor).

Devaragan, S., J.D. Lewis and S. Robinson (1990) "Policy Lessons From Trade-Focused, Two-Sector Models" *Journal of Policy Modeling* 12: 625–57.

Dewatripont, M. and G. Michel (1987) "On Closure Rules, Homogeneity and Dynamics in Applied General Equilibrium Models" *Journal of Development Economics* 26: 65–76.

Dixit, A.K. (1990) *Optimization in Economic Theory*, 2nd Edition, (Oxford University Press, Oxford).

Dixit, A. and V. Norman (1980) *Theory of International Trade: A Dual General Equilibrium Approach* (Cambridge University Press, Cambridge).

Dixit, A. and J. Stiglitz (1977) "Monopolistic Competition and Optimum Product Diversity" *American Economic Review* 67: 297–308.

Dixon, P.B., B.R. Parmenter, J. Sutton and D.P. Vincent (1982) *ORANI: A Multisectoral Model of the Australian Economy* (North-Holland, Amsterdam).

Ethier, W.J. (1974) "Some of the Theorems of International Trade With Many Goods and Factors" *Journal of International Economics* 4: 199–206.

Ethier, W.J. (1979) "Internationally Decreasing Costs and World Trade" *Journal of International Economics* 9: 1–24.

Francois, J. and W. Martin (2010) "Ex Ante Assessment of the Welfare Impacts of Trade Reforms With Numerical Models" in J. Gilbert, ed., *New Developments in Computable General Equilibrium Analysis of Trade Policy*; Volume 7 of Frontiers of Economics and Globalization (Emerald, Bingley).

Gilbert, J. (2008) "Agricultural Trade Reform and Poverty in the Asia-Pacific: A Survey and Some New Results" *Asia-Pacific Development Journal* 15: 1–34.

Gilbert, J., ed., (2010) *New Developments in Computable General Equilibrium Analysis of Trade Policy*; Volume 7 of Frontiers of Economics and Globalization (Emerald, Bingley).

Gilbert, J. and R. Oladi (2008) "A Geometric Comparison of the Transformation Loci With Specific and Mobile Capital" *Journal of Economic Education* 39: 145–52.

Gilbert, J. and R. Oladi (2010) "Regional Trade Reform Under SAFTA and Income Distribution in South Asia" in J. Gilbert, ed., *New Developments in Computable General Equilibrium Analysis of Trade Policy* Volume 7 of Frontiers of Economics and Globalization (Emerald, Bingley).

Gilbert, J. and R. Oladi (2011) "Excel Models for International Trade Theory and Policy" *Journal of Economic Education* 42: 95.

Gilbert, J. and E. Tower (2002) "Protectionism, Labor Mobility, and Immiserizing Growth in Developing Economies" *Economics Letters* 75: 135–40.

Gilbert, J. and T. Wahl (2002) "Applied General Equilibrium Assessments of Trade Liberalization in China" *World Economy* 25: 697–731.

Graaff, J. (1949) "On Optimum Tariff Structures" *Review of Economic Studies* 17: 47–59.

Gunning J.W. and M. Keyzer (1995) "Applied General Equilibrium Models for Policy Analysis" in J. Behrman and T.S. Srinivasan, eds. *Handbook of Development Economics* Volume III (North-Holland, Amsterdam).

Han, K. and E. Tower (1999) "Cost Benefit Analysis of Foreign Aid for a Highly Distorted Economy: The Case of Sudan" in K. Gupta, ed., *Foreign Aid: New Perspectives* (Kluwer, AH Dordrecht).

Harris, J.R. and M.P. Todaro (1970) "Migration, Unemployment and Development: A Two-Sector Analysis" *American Economic Review* 60: 126–42.

Harrison, G.W., T.F. Rutherford and D.G. Tarr (1997) "Quantifying the Uruguay Round" *Economic Journal* 107: 1405–30.

Helpman, E. and P.R. Krugman (1985) *Market Structure and Foreign Trade: Increasing Returns, Imperfect Competition, and the International Economy* (MIT Press, Cambridge).

Hertel T.W., ed., (1997) *Global Trade Analysis: Modeling and Applications* (Cambridge University Press, Cambridge).

Hertel, T., D. Hummels, M. Ivanic and R. Keeney (2007) "How Confident Can We Be of CGE Based Assessments of Free Trade Agreements?" *Economic Modeling* 24: 611–35.

Hosoe, N., K. Gasawa and H. Hashimoto (2010) *Textbook of General Equilibrium Modelling: Programming and Simulations* (Palgrave, New York).

Ianchovichina, E. and T. Walmsley, eds., (2012) *Dynamic Modeling and Applications for Global Economic Analysis* (Cambridge University Press, Cambridge).

Jansson, T. and T. Heckelei (2010) "Estimation of Parameters of Constrained Optimization Models" in J. Gilbert, ed., *New Developments in Computable General Equilibrium Analysis of Trade Policy* Volume 7 of Frontiers of Economics and Globalization (Emerald, Bingley).

Johansen, L. (1974) *A Multi-Sectoral Study of Economic Growth* (North-Holland, Amsterdam).

Johnson, H.G. (1953) "Optimum Tariffs and Retaliation" *Review of Economic Studies* 21: 142–53.

Johnson, H.G. (1955a) "Economic Expansion and International Trade" *Manchester School* 23: 95–112.

Johnson, H.G. (1955b) "The Transfer Problem: A Note on Criteria for Changes in the Terms of Trade" *Economica* 23: 113–21.

Johnson, H.G. (1960) "The Cost of Protection and the Scientific Tariff" *Journal of Political Economy* 68: 142–53.

Johnson, H.G. (1967) "The Possibility of Income Losses From Increased Efficiency or Factor Accumulation in the Presence of Tariffs" *Economic Journal* 77: 151–4.

Jomini, P., R. McDougall, G. Watts and P.S. Dee (1994) "The SALTER Model of the World Economy: Model Structure, Database and Parameters" SALTER Working Paper No. 24, (Industry Commission, Canberra).

Jones, R.W. (1956) "Factor Proportions and the Heckscher–Ohlin Theorem" *Review of Economic Studies* 24: 1–10.

Jones, R.W. (1965) "The Structure of Simple General Equilibrium Models" *Journal of Political Economy* 73: 557–72.

Jones, R.W. (1971) "A Three Factor Model in Theory, Trade, and History" in J.N. Bhagwati, R.W. Jones, R.A. Mundell and J. Vanek, eds., *Trade, Balance of Payments and Growth* (North-Holland, Amsterdam).

Jones, R.W. and J. Scheinkman (1977) "The Relevance of the Two-Sector Production Model in Trade Theory" *Journal of Political Economy* 85: 909–35.

Kaempfer, H. and E. Tower (1982) "The Balance of Payments Approach to Trade Tax Symmetry Theorems" *Weltwirtschaftliches Archiv* 118: 148–65.

Kehoe, T.J. (2003) "An Evaluation of the Performance of Applied General Equilibrium Models of the Impact of NAFTA" Federal Reserve Bank of Minneapolis Research Department Staff Report 320.

Komiya, R. (1967) "Non-Traded Goods and the Pure Theory of International Trade" *International Economic Review* 8: 132–52.

Krueger, A.O. (1978) *Foreign Trade Regimes and Economic Development, Vol X: Liberalization Attempts and Consequences* (Ballinger, Cambridge).

Krugman, P.R. (1979) "Increasing Returns, Monopolistic Competition, and International Trade" *Journal of International Economics* 9: 469–80.

Krugman, P.R. (1980) "Scale Economies, Product Differentiation, and the Pattern of Trade" *American Economic Review* 70: 950–9.

Krugman, P.R. (1993) "What Do Undergrads Need to Know About Trade?" *American Economic Review* 83: 23–6.

Lerner, A.P. (1936) "The Symmetry Between Import and Export Taxes" *Economica* 3: 306–13.

Lloyd, P.J. and D. MacLaren (2004) "Gains and Losses From Regional Trading Agreements: A Survey" *Economic Record* 80: 445–97.

Lloyd, P.J. and X-G. Zhang (2006) "The Armington Model" Productivity Commission Staff Working Paper, Melbourne, January.

Loo, T. and E. Tower (1989) "Agricultural Protectionism and the Less Developed Countries: The Relationship Between Agricultural Prices, Debt Servicing Capacities and the Need for Development Aid" in A.B. Stoeckel, D. Vincent and S. Cuthbertson, eds., *Macroeconomic Consequences of Farm Support Policies* (Duke University Press, Durham). (Summarized as "Protection Through a Wide-Angle Lens" constituting the "Economics Focus" section of *The Economist*, June 4, 1988.)

Mayer, W. (1974) "Short-Run and Long-Run Equilibrium for a Small Open Economy" *Journal of Political Economy* 82: 955–67.

McDonald, S. and K. Thierfelder (2004) "Deriving a Global Social Accounting Matrix from GTAP Versions 5 and 6 Data" GTAP Technical Paper Number 22.

Melvin, J.R. (1969a) "Intermediate Goods, the Production Possibility Curve, and Gains From Trade" *Quarterly Journal of Economics* 83: 141–51.

Melvin, J.R. (1969b) "Intermediate Goods and Technological Change" *Economica* 36: 400–8.

Metzler, L. (1949) "Tariffs, the Terms of Trade and the Distribution of National Income" *Journal of Political Economy* 57: 1–29.

Mikic, M. and J. Gilbert (2009) *Trade Statistics in Policymaking: A Handbook of Commonly Used Trade Indices and Indicators* (United Nations ESCAP, Bangkok).

Mussa, M. (1979) "The Two-Sector Model in Terms of Its Dual: A Geometric Exposition" *Journal of International Economics* 9: 513–26.

Neary, J.P. (1978) "Short-Run Capital Specificity and the Pure Theory of International Trade" *Economic Journal* 88: 488–510.

Negishi, T. (1960) "Welfare Economics and Existence of an Equilibrium for a Competitive Economy" *Metroeconomica* 12: 92–7.

Perloff, J.M. (2011) *Microeconomics: Theory and Applications With Calculus* (Addison Wesley Longman, Reading).

Pyatt, G. and J. Round (1977) "Social Accounting Matrices for Development Planning" *Review of Income and Wealth* 23: 339–64.

Pyatt, G. and J. Round (1979) "Accounting and Fixed Price Multipliers in a Social Accounting Matrix Framework" *Economic Journal* 89: 850–73.

Reinert, K.A. and D.W. Roland-Holst (1997) "Social Accounting Matrices" in J.F. Francois and K.A. Reinert, eds., *Applied Methods for Trade Policy Analysis: A Handbook* (Cambridge University Press, Cambridge).

Robinson, S., A. Cattaneo and M. El-Said (2001) "Updating and Estimating a Social Accounting Matrix Using Cross Entropy Methods" Economic Systems Research 13: 47–64.

Robinson. S. and H. Lofgren (2005) "Macro Models and Poverty Analysis: Theoretical Tensions and Empirical Practice" Development Policy Review 23: 267–83.

Robinson, S. and K. Thierfelder (2002) "Trade Liberalisation and Regional Integration: The Search for Large Numbers" Australian Journal of Agricultural and Resource Economics 46: 585–604.

Rutherford, T.F. (1998) "GAMS2TBL: A GAMS LIBINCLUDE Program for Producing Formatted Tables" available at:
http://www.mpsge.org/inclib/gams2tbl.htm.

Rutherford, T.F. (1999) "LIBINCLUDE Tools for Writing GAMS-Readable Data Files" available at: http://www.mpsge.org/inclib/gams2txt.htm.

Rybczynski, T.M. (1955) "Factor Endowments and Relative Commodity Prices" Economica 22: 336–41.

Samuelson, P.A. (1949) "International Factor Price Equalisation Once Again" Economic Journal 59: 181–97.

Samuelson, P.A. (1951) "Abstract of a Theorem Concerning Substitutability in Open Leontief Models" in T.C. Koopmans, ed., Activity Analysis of Production and Allocation (Wiley, New York).

Samuelson, P.A. (1952) "The Transfer Problem and Transport Costs: The Terms of Trade When Impediments Are Absent" Economic Journal 62: 278–304.

Samuelson, P.A. (1953) "Prices of Factors and Goods in General Equilibrium" Review of Economic Studies 21: 1–20.

Schweinberger, A.G. (1979) "The Theory of Factor Price Equalization: The Case of Constant Absolute Differentials" Journal of International Economics 9: 95–115.

Scitovsky, T. (1969) Money and the Balance of Payments (Rand-McNally, Chicago).

Scollay, R. and J. Gilbert (2000) "Measuring the Gains From APEC Trade Liberalisation: An Overview of CGE Assessments" World Economy 23: 175–93.

Shoven, J.B. and J. Whalley (1992) Applying General Equilibrium (Cambridge University Press, Cambridge).

Srinivasan, T.N. and J.N. Bhagwati (1975) "Alternative Policy Rankings in a Large, Open Economy With Sector-Specific Minimum Wages" Journal of Economic Theory 11: 356–71.

Stolper, W.E. and P.A. Samuelson (1941) "Protection and Real Wages" Review of Economic Studies 9: 58–73.

Sweeney, R.J., E. Tower and T.D. Willett (1977) "The Ranking of Alternative Tariff and Quota Policies in the Presence of Domestic Monopoly" Journal of International Economics 7: 349–62.

Tower, E. (1977) "Ranking the Optimum Tariff and the Maximum Revenue Tariff" Journal of International Economics 7: 73–9.

Tower, E. (1979) "The Geometry of Community Indifference Curves" Weltwirtschaftliches Archiv 114: 680–700.

Tower, E. and G. Pursell (1987) "On Shadow Pricing Labor and Foreign Exchange" *Oxford Economic Papers* 39: 318–32.

Tsiang, S.C. (1961) "The Role of Money in Trade-Balance Stability: Synthesis of the Elasticity and Absorption Approaches" *American Economic Review* 51: 912–36.

Varian, H.R. (1992) *Microeconomic Analysis*, 3rd Edition, (W.W. Norton & Company, New York).

Varian, H.R. (2009) *Intermediate Microeconomics: A Modern Approach*, 8th Edition, (W.W. Norton & Company, New York).

Vanek, J. (1963) "Variable Factor Proportions and Interindustry Flows in the Theory of International Trade" *Quarterly Journal of Economics* 77: 129–42.

Vandendorpe, A.L. (1974) "On the Theory of Non-economic Objectives in Open Economies" *Journal of International Economics* 4: 15–24.

van de Mensbrugghe, D. (2005) *LINKAGE Technical Reference Document*, Development Prospects Group (DECPG), The World Bank.

Warne, R.D. (1971) "Intermediate Goods in International Trade With Variable Proportions and Two Primary Inputs" *Quarterly Journal of Economics* 85: 225–36.

Whalley, J., ed., (2012) *General Equilibrium Global Trade Models* (World Scientific, Singapore).

Woodland, A.D. (1982) *International Trade and Resource Allocation* (North-Holland, Amsterdam).

Zenios, S.A. (1996) "Modeling Languages in Computational Economics: GAMS" in H. Amman and D.A. Kendrick, eds., *Handbook of Computational Economics I* (North-Holland, Amsterdam).

Index